From War to Pea

From War to Peace

A Guide to the Next Hundred Years

KENT D. SHIFFERD

McFarland & Company, Inc., Publishers
Jefferson, North Carolina, and London

LIBRARY OF CONGRESS CATALOGUING-IN-PUBLICATION DATA

Shifferd, Kent D., 1940–
    From war to peace : a guide to the next hundred years /
Kent D. Shifferd.
        p.   cm.
    Includes bibliographical references and index.

    ISBN 978-0-7864-6144-8
    softcover : 50# alkaline paper ∞

    1. Peace movements.   2. Sociology, Military.   3. War and society.
    I. Title.
    JZ5574.S54 2011
    303.6'6 — dc22   2011000793

BRITISH LIBRARY CATALOGUING DATA ARE AVAILABLE

Front cover: Nuclear weapon detonated at Bikini Atoll (Prints &
Photographs Division, Library of Congress, LC-USW33-059244);
Dr. Wangari Maathai, environmental, peace and rights activist in
Kenya (UN Photo/Jackie Curtis)

Manufactured in the United States of America

*McFarland & Company, Inc., Publishers
    Box 611, Jefferson, North Carolina 28640
    www.mcfarlandpub.com*

To Mel Duncan and David Hartsough,
founders of the Nonviolent Peaceforce.
You took Gandhi's dream and made it a reality.

"For telling ourselves and others that evil is inevitable while good is impossible, may we stand corrected."
—*Harry Meserve*

Table of Contents

Preface

This is a book about the reality of war and the prospects for peace in the next hundred years. My own serious interest in war began in middle school when my grandmother gave me Churchill's *The Gathering Storm*, his initial volume in the World War II series. Majoring in history as an undergraduate and then getting a doctorate in European history gave me ample opportunity for much more serious study since, as I point out in the book, the teaching of history has a war-ist bias. It was also as an undergraduate that I became interested first in the anti-nuclear weapons movement and then in peace issues in general, thanks to a wonderful sociology professor, Dr. Ray Short. However, it was not until the nuclear crises of the early 1980s that I began a scholarly interest in peace, joining with many others in the academic world who were creating peace studies programs. In 1985 we created an interdisciplinary undergraduate major in peace studies at Northland College where I was teaching. As director of the program I taught Introduction to Peace Studies, the History of Peace, Conflict Resolution, and related courses. At the same time I was fortunate to join with a number of scholars from colleges and universities in Wisconsin who created the Wisconsin Institute for the Study of War, Peace and Global Cooperation. Now the Wisconsin Institute for Peace and Conflict Studies, a consortium of twenty-one campuses, it has functioned for over twenty-five years to promote teaching and scholarship in the field. I was privileged to serve two terms as associate director and then two more as executive director and was founding editor of its main publication, the *Journal for the Study of Conflict and Peace*. In conjunction with the Annenberg Corporation, the Corporation for Public Broadcasting and University Extension, we launched the *Dilemmas of War and Peace* project, under the general editorship of Dr. Dick Ringler, which resulted in some 1500 pages of print material and 13 half-hour audio tapes. It was distributed as a distance-learning course and used as a curriculum in university classrooms and remains the

1

most comprehensive single collection of material on these issues. In addition to an interest in issues of war and peace, I became very much involved in environmental studies after my college turned to that emphasis in the early 1970s under the leadership of President Malcolm McLean. For twenty-five years I taught courses in environmental history and environmental ethics and was one of the founders of the American Society for Environmental History, all of which is pertinent to the sections in this book on the environmental impacts of war. Since leaving full-time teaching in 1999 I have continued to test my ideas with students, teaching War, Peace and Ethics at United Theological Seminary (St. Paul, Minnesota) on two separate occasions, and continuing to do occasional lectures, most recently to law students at Hamline University and the Mitchell School of Law. This book is the result of these many years of study and reflection.

The thesis of this book is that we have a good chance to outlaw war in the next hundred years. I am well aware of the degree to which war has penetrated all aspects of our culture and I take pains to point this out at length in the first half of the book. The academic field of peace studies is like the study of medicine in that it recognizes the very real nature of disease and does not try to merely wish it away. We study it objectively and scientifically, but at the same time, like medicine, we have as our aim a normative function. Medicine has a presumption in favor of health. So, too, peace studies has a presumption in favor of peace. Therefore I have grounded the thesis not in wishful thinking but in a recognition of some very real, revolutionary historic trends that began in the early nineteenth century with the appearance of the world's first peace societies and then in the twentieth century with the development of international institutions aimed at controlling war, the evolution of nonviolence as a real-world power shifter, the rise of global civil society, the growing permeability of the old national boundaries, and a number of other trends.

The Introduction begins with a reflection on the great paradox that most people want peace but support the institutions that perpetuate war. Then, briefly, I explain the cultural systems approach in which positive feedback strengthens the war system and negative feedback strains it. The first chapter, "Describing and Analyzing War," begins Section I, "War," and opens with definitions of international war, civil war and terrorism, and moves on to a brief history of war, the necessity of war in our cultural system as illuminated by Schmookler's *Parable of the Tribes*, the development of conventional warfare, nuclear war, the timeless nature of battle, the modern battlefield and war wounds. War is an iron cage in which we have trapped ourselves, but it is not human nature; it is a social invention whose history we can trace from its beginning.

The second chapter, "The Psychology of Killing," explains how we get young men to take part in the slaughter of modern war by exposing them to various forms of psychological conditioning as illuminated by Army Lt. Col. (Ret.) David Grossman and the enduring psychological effects on them as a result of the experience of combat. In that chapter I also examine the disturbing thesis of Richard Koenigsberg and others who argue that we have war because we are engaged in a massive psychopathology, a set of motivations buried in the subconscious from which we go to war not to kill others but to kill our own children as proof that our existence as a nation is real, a viewpoint that draws on the nineteenth-century sociologist Durkheim, on Freud, and on the anthropologist René Girard. I take this thesis seriously, because we certainly seem in some ways to worship the state, but in the end I reject it simply because there are enough observable causes for the perpetuation of the war system. Their thesis is non-disconfirmable and, anyway, I remain a positivist on this issue. The following two chapters, "The War System, Part 1" and "The War System, Part 2," explain how some very observable and obvious feedback mechanisms result in the fact that the cause of war is war itself. War has created a social structure that is self-fueling and self-perpetuating.

Section II, "Peace," opens by suggesting that the question "What if we had not fought the Nazis?"—and its obvious answer "We had to fight them"—is the wrong question if we want to discover how to end war. Thinking in terms of "security" rather than "peace" leads inevitably to insecurity and war. Here, too, is a brief argument that empire is becoming impossible. I then distinguish between negative and positive peace, point out the relevance of John Paul Lederach's approach by way of "moral imagination," and suggest that there is already a great deal of peace in the world.

Chapters 6 and 7, "The History of Peace in Ancient and Medieval Times" and "The History of Peace, 1800 to the Present," demonstrate the fact that there is more peace than war in human history. Most people live at peace most of the time. We have a great deal of experience with it. What is more, in spite of the fact that the twentieth century was the bloodiest in history, the last 100 years has been a revolutionary time for the development of institutions of peace and changing attitudes about war and war preparation. A new story is being created on the ground. Chapter 8 is devoted to a major component of that story, the rise of nonviolent struggle as a real-world power shifter that, along with other trends, will allow us to eventually escape the iron cage of war into which we trapped ourselves some 6,000 years ago. Chapter 9, "Abolishing War and Building a Comprehensive Peace System," describes a set of social feedback mechanisms that will provide a robust, redundant peace system and which are being created on the ground in our time, including governance structures, nonviolence, peace education, the rise of global civil society, the emergence of a human rights regime, the international conference movement, the rise of the global environmental movement, United Nations reform, and others. I provide real-world examples. Enormous progress is being made toward a culture of peace in spite of the ongoing wars. The final chapter deals with "The Wellsprings of Peace," the cultural sources that inform and inspire those who are working for peace. It ends with the reflections of astronaut Russell Schweickart, who rode around and around Earth and realized that down below there were, as he put it, "no frames and no boundaries," and that we are riders together.

While many, many people stand behind every author, I would like to thank my good colleagues over many years at the Wisconsin Institute, especially Dick Ringler, who edited the *Dilemmas of War And Peace* project. Also, I received much-needed patient support from my wife, Dr. Patricia Shifferd, who not only read the final manuscript but also was always there when the struggle seemed so endless. As usual, whatever mistakes remain are mine.

There are many other books on peace studies. This one differs from most in that it adopts a cultural systems approach and makes this bold argument that we are on the way toward outlawing war, that there will be a phase change from a war to a peace system sometime in the next hundred years, and that, like slavery, war can be very nearly eliminated and the remains brought under control for the common good of humanity. The alternative is stark, but I believe that evil need not prevail, that we will prove to be *Homo sapiens* after all and that we are rational, if only in our own, collective self-interest. Time will tell.

Introduction:
The Tragedy of War and
the Expectation of Peace

And we are here as on a darkling plain
Swept with confused alarms of struggle and flight,
Where ignorant armies clash by night.
— Matthew Arnold, "Dover Beach," 1867[1]

We have suffered in the dark night of war for thousands of years, where the "ignorant armies clash by night" in fearful slaughter and destruction. The destructiveness of war has increased exponentially in the last hundred years — World War II saw at least 50 million deaths and some estimates are twice that. The largest proportion by far of those killed in war are now civilians. A nuclear war could easily take hundreds of millions of lives in the first week and, in the worst case scenario, bring on nuclear winter and the destruction of civilization itself.[2] Paul Hawken's terrible observation can hardly capture the reality: "The twentieth century ... was also the cruelest, harshest century in history. Eighty million were slaughtered from the beginning of the century through World War II: since then, more than 23 million people (mostly civilians) have been killed in more than 149 wars."[3] Former National Security Advisor Zbigniew Brzezinski has called it the "politics of organized insanity."[4]

There is a puzzling paradox about war. As awful as it is, good people support it. We will never understand and eliminate it unless we start from this premise. In war time, people who in their normal lives would never hurt anyone support both the preparation for and the carrying out of massive violence. Perfectly nice young men who grew up in small towns in mid–America; who went to church on Sundays and learned the Ten Commandments, includ-

5

PLOESTI RAID, 1943. A costly low-level attack by Liberators on the German-controlled Romanian oil refineries by 178 aircraft resulted in 53 planes lost, 300 crew killed and 140 captured and 440 wounded. Only one in six of the returning planes was able to fly again. Damage was repaired and the refineries were attacked again and again, resulting in total losses of 2900 men. In World War II, nothing was more dangerous than flying in a bomber. (U.S. Army Military History Institute)

ing "Thou shalt not kill"; who were taught decency, kindness and fair play by their parents back in the 1930s, found themselves flying over Germany in Liberator bombers in 1943, dropping white phosphorous fire bombs that burned alive the men, women and children hiding below. Good men who love their families nevertheless work in munitions factories making land mines and cluster bombs that blow the feet off children on the other side of the world. At this moment, a boy who would never think of hitting a dog or kicking a cat is being trained to shove a bayonet in the belly of another boy he does not know who is being trained to do the same thing to him. People who hate war and its maiming, killing, and destruction nevertheless fall in line when their leaders declare war. Almost no one of these people is evil,[5] but they acquiesce to, and some of them perform, evil deeds. Almost nobody wants war; almost everyone supports it. Why?

The following, rather curious poem was circulated anonymously over the Internet at Christmastime, 2006. While it is stylistically crude, it is

nonetheless poignant and helps us to understand a great deal about why good
people support war.

A Different Christmas Poem

The embers glowed softly, and in their dim light,
I gazed round the room and I cherished the sight.
My wife was asleep, her head on my chest,
My daughter beside me, angelic in rest.
Outside the snow fell, a blanket of white,
Transforming the yard to a winter delight.
The sparkling lights in the tree I believe,
Completed the magic that was Christmas Eve.
My eyelids were heavy, my breathing was deep,
Secure and surrounded by love I would sleep.
In perfect contentment, or so it would seem,
So I slumbered, perhaps I started to dream.

The sound wasn't loud, and it wasn't too near,
But I opened my eyes when it tickled my ear.
Perhaps just a cough, I didn't quite know,

Then the sure sound of footsteps outside in the snow.
My soul gave a tremble, I struggled to hear,
And I crept to the door just to see who was near.
Standing out in the cold and the dark of the night,
A lone figure stood, his face weary and tight.

A soldier, I puzzled, some twenty years old,
Perhaps a Marine, huddled here in the cold.
Alone in the dark, he looked up and smiled,
Standing watch over me, and my wife and my child.
"What are you doing?" I asked without fear,
"Come in this moment, it's freezing out here!
Put down your pack, brush the snow from your sleeve,
You should be at home on a cold Christmas Eve!"

For barely a moment I saw his eyes shift,
Away from the cold and the snow blown in drifts.
To the window that danced with a warm fire's light
Then he sighed and he said "It's really all right,
I'm out here by choice. I'm here every night."
"It's my duty to stand at the front of the line,
That separates you from the darkest of times.
No one had to ask or beg or implore me,
I'm proud to stand here like my fathers before me.
My Gramps died at "Pearl on a day in December,"
Then he sighed, "That's a Christmas 'Gram always remembers.
My dad stood his watch in the jungles of 'Nam,
And now it is my turn and so, here I am.

I've not seen my own son in more than a while,
But my wife sends me pictures, he's sure got her smile."

Then he bent and he carefully pulled from his bag,
The red, white, and blue ... an American flag.
"I can live through the cold and the being alone,
Away from my family, my house and my home.
I can stand at my post through the rain and the sleet,
I can sleep in a foxhole with little to eat.
I can carry the weight of killing another,
Or lay down my life with my sister and brother
Who stand at the front against any and all,
To ensure for all time that this flag will not fall."

"So go back inside," he said, "harbor no fright,
Your family is waiting and I'll be all right."
"But isn't there something I can do, at the least,
Give you money," I asked, "or prepare you a feast?
It seems all too little for all that you've done,
For being away from your wife and your son."
Then his eye welled a tear that held no regret,
"Just tell us you love us, and never forget.
To fight for our rights back at home while we're gone,
To stand your own watch, no matter how long.
For when we come home, either standing or dead,
To know you remember we fought and we bled.
Is payment enough, and with that we will trust,
That we mattered to you as you mattered to us."

Here we see powerful and important values: love of family, the desire to protect children, the willingness to sacrifice even one's life and appropriate gratitude for those who do, and love of freedom and of one's country. Of course, this can all be said of soldiers on both sides of any conflict; they all believe they are defending their homes and loved ones. What could be wrong with this? As far as it goes, nothing. Those of us who are working to abolish war share these same values. Those who support war are not the enemy. The enemy is war, and the beliefs, emotions, and cultural systems that make it appear to be, on certain occasions and under certain conditions, a good choice in spite of its horrors.

The poem contains laudable virtues. It says nothing that is untrue, but it does not say everything that is true. It masks the whole truth and is therefore, in the end, misleading. First, its unstated premise is that war is inevitable, a part of human nature, built into our genes and inseparable from the human psyche, an irremovable feature of human societies. What if none of these were true?

Second, it is based on a foundation of fear, and while there are fearsome people and even whole nations out there willing to do us harm, it does nothing to explain why there are those who feel justified in causing us harm. It does nothing to advance our understanding of the causes of war. And finally, since we must be honest with ourselves, our soldier does not in reality just stand outside the door to guard us. Sometimes he goes to the "neighbor's" house and blows them away — rips their bodies to shreds, for that is the nature of modern war, as we shall see shortly. Of course, some (at least) of these "neighbors" were indeed fixing to do the same to our Christmas Eve family. But it is useful to stop here and again ask "Why?" Why were they? And what we will uncover, if we go deep enough, is a basic truth. "They" are imitating "us" out of the same basic emotion — fear.

Let us consider two not so hypothetical families observing Christmas Eve in World War II, one in Bavaria and one in Nebraska, quite possibly both at a Lutheran church for midnight services. And the family in Germany looks up as they hear the drone of the bombers, and they are afraid. And the family in Nebraska knows that their son is in the sky over Bavaria and they hope he won't fall out of that sky as the wings are blown off his Liberator by explosions from the anti-aircraft guns. We fear each other, and with good reason. It is a self-fulfilling prophecy, a self-fueling process, a continuous feedback cycle, as we shall see when we examine war as a cultural system. And what if the cycle could be broken?

And so, while nearly all people would be delighted if war were abolished, they never think to ask the question "How do we abolish war?" because they believe it is inevitable and sometimes perfectly justified, and because they share a mutual fear of one another. And if they never ask the question, they will never get the answer. This book asks and answers that question.

For the last century there has been a trend away from war, in spite of the headlines that scream at us every day, in spite of the distorted histories in our textbooks. We will look first at the nature of war, then at the nature of peace and the way to spread and accelerate this trend.

In fact, this entire book is defined by its paradoxes. It begins by pointing out that everyone wants peace but supports war. It is at once realistic about how deeply rooted the present war system is and optimistic about the changeover to a peace system. It is prophetic in that it passes harsh judgment on present practices of nation states and foretells a future that is much changed from these, and it is practical in that it provides a realistic alternative to them. It argues that we know where we are going, but not what the exact outcome will look like. It argues that we need leaders who are both visionary and cautious, who see the big picture and can manage the details. The changeover from a war system to peace system will require both centralized and decentralized actions, planning and spontaneity, grassroots mobilization and hierarchical decision-making, individualism and cooperation.

"Endless research speculates about the exercise of war, but little is concerned with the maintenance of peace."[6] But over the last hundred years we have begun to move toward the dawning of a new age. It is not easy to see. Surely we are still in that very early moment before the sun clears the horizon, or even lights up the high clouds, but it is indisputably lighter on the horizon. My reasons for asserting such an optimistic view are multifold.

First, the old belief that war is honorable is beginning to fade in the terrible blood-letting of the modern battlefield, where bravery and courage count for little when the air is filled with the hail of flying metal and rent by concussive explosions. Not many men still believe that war is an honorable and romantic undertaking sanctioned by God. Such views sound peculiar today; for example, the German philosopher Georg Hegel (d. 1831) believed that war "saves the state from social petrifaction and stagnation," while in 1832 General von Clausewitz characterized it as nothing more than "the continuation of policy by other means," and the German General Helmut von Moltke believed that "perpetual peace is a dream" and that "war is an integral part of God's ordering of the universe.[7] Lest one think that only Germans looked on war in this way, Winston Churchill believed that life is "at its healthiest and its best " on the battlefield and William Ernest Henley called war the "giver of kingship, the famesmith, the song-master."[8] These ideas are now antiquated in all but a few quarters.

Second, while many still believe that war is, however nasty, nevertheless inevitable, many others are beginning to see that war is a social phenomenon, a social problem with clearly understood causes and conditions that can be changed. Two prominent students of war, John Keegan and John Mueller, have each written books arguing that the wars we see in the world now are "residual" and that war is becoming obsolete. Keegan, a well-respected military historian and professor at Sandhurst, the premier British military institute, writes:

> War, it seems to me, after a lifetime of reading about the subject, mingling with men of war, visiting the sights of war, and observing its effects, may well be ceasing to commend itself to human beings as a desirable or productive, let alone rational, means of reconciling their discontents.[9]

And Mueller, a professor of national security at Ohio State University, sums up his new book by writing,

> The central burden of this book is that war is merely an idea. Unlike breathing, eating or sex, war is not something that is somehow required by the human condition or by the forces of history. Accordingly, war can shrivel up and disappear, and it seems to be in the process of doing so.[10]

Many now believe that we will see the end of war in this century, just as we saw the end of legalized slavery in the nineteenth century. But it is more than just beliefs and attitudes that convince me that war is on its way out, even as it rages in the Middle East. It is the development of new institutions and techniques of dealing with conflict that have arisen since the World Court came into being in 1899. These include international political institutions associated with the United Nations and with regional organizations such as the European Union, thousands of non-government agencies working for peace, justice and international cooperation, and, too, the development of peace research and education. Finally, the existence of real peace in many parts of the world where war used to be the dominant mode, such as Scandinavia, North America, and now Western Europe, confirms Kenneth Boulding's maxim "Anything that exists, is possible." Peace is just as real as war.

Most of what needed to be invented to end war has been invented. Now what we need to do is to spread the knowledge of these developments and inspire even more people to join the ongoing work of changing the behavior of individuals and governments. That's what this book is intended to do. I have discovered nothing not already discovered by others before me. My task is just to collect it into one place and to pass it on.

A Systems Analysis Approach to War and Peace

The most useful approach to peace and war is drawn from systems analysis. Systems thinking is the opposite of our more familiar linear thinking in which we perceive that A causes B, which in turn causes C, which in turn causes D (in this case, an outbreak of war), in a linear sequence. Linear analysis is not necessarily wrong, but it is not very helpful when trying to comprehend the workings of complicated social systems.

A systems analysis diagram would look more like a spider web with feedbacks running in both directions along all the lines. In a social system, each of the elements, is continually influencing the others and is influenced by them in a complicated interplay of feedbacks over time. A single element can have influences on several of the other elements either at the same time or over time. And it will in its turn be influenced by them. The feedback is considered to be either positive or negative. Positive and negative are not moral terms but rather indicate only that they stabilize and perpetuate the system (positive feedback), or they destabilize it (negative feedback). Another way of thinking about this is in terms of strain and strength. Negative feedback imposes strain on a system. If the strain outweighs the positive feedback, the system will change phase, or disintegrate, and a new equilibrium may take its place.

Experts in chaos theory say that long-stable systems can and do undergo rapidly cascading changes, or bifurcations, and can shift into another phase in a very short time. A system that has been stable for a very long time can change into something else in a very short time. A good case in point is the sudden collapse of the Soviet system in 1989 to 2001. They also point out that it is very difficult to tell when a system has destabilized and is headed for cascading bifurcations or sudden, dramatic and far-reaching changes. The CIA, for example, with all of its intelligence-gathering activity, failed completely to predict the coming collapse of the Soviet empire.

Thus, in a system, there are the elements that make up its structure, and there are the ways in which the elements behave, which are themselves governed by certain rules. In a traffic system, for instance, there are the vehicles, roadways and tracks, signals such as stoplights, and, of course, the natural environment. An example of a rule would be driving on the right-hand side of the road. A still picture taken from above would show the structure. A moving picture would show the behavior of the various elements. At any given moment, these two things combine to yield the condition of the system. Change a behavior (for example, by a breakdown of a train at a crossing, an overturned truck on the highway, or a sudden snowstorm), and the condition of the system can change very rapidly. Change the elements (for example, take out some stoplights), and the system can go into gridlock and experience multiple crashes. Behavior is also governed by rules. Change the speed limit on an urban freeway from 60 to 25 miles an hour and gridlock occurs. Change it from 25 to 60 on a neighborhood street and there are likely to be lots of fatalities. A system is made up of elements, behavior, and rules.

How does this type of analysis help us to understand war? Wars are not just the result of specific historic causes, as a linear analysis might suggest. While each war does have specific causes, it is also the result of a particular social system that yields war as a normative result of dealing with conflict according to the rules, elements and behaviors present in the system. If that sounds tautological, it is. The war system has been in place in Western society for about 6000 years and has yielded so many wars that people mistake the behavior for human nature, but in fact it is a cultural phenomenon.

What is more, as Kenneth Boulding suggested, war and peace systems coexist along a continuum running as follows: Stable War — Unstable War — Unstable Peace — Stable Peace.[11] Under conditions of Stable War, war is the dominant norm, always present somewhere and frequently breaking out in several places at once. Small "peaces" are achieved by conquest, temporary truces, military alliances, and non-aggression pacts. Structural violence (or oppression) frequently prevails in these small "peaces." The effort to control war to some degree is vested in collective security (collective violence) schemes. Peace is, at best, an interval between wars. The economy is geared toward war, producing goods that destroy use value (bombs, bullets, land mines, etc.). Great inequalities of wealth and economic injustice exist in and between societies, and society is structured along dominator lines with overt or masked rule by elites.

In some regions, however, war has become an unstable system where institutions and norms of peace coexist with war, such as moves toward non-aggressive defense, campaigns for arms control and the inviolability of non-combatants, the existence of anti-war movements, institutions and practices of conflict resolution such as the International Court of Justice and the International Criminal Court, and peace education.

In a condition of Stable Peace, peace is the dominant norm and is prevalent throughout the whole social system. It is based on disarmament, civilian-based defense, nonviolence, peace education, nonviolence training, limited national sovereignty, a peace-based economy producing goods that enhance use value (infrastructure, cheap transport, health care, education, etc.), global concerns for economic justice and sustainable development, human rights, and peace building institutions. Society is structured along partnership lines with greater degrees of freedom and democracy.

My belief in writing this book is that while we have a long way to go, the world is clearly moving away from Stable War and in the direction of Stable Peace. My purpose in writing this book is to hasten our progress.

SECTION I. WAR

CHAPTER 1

Describing and Analyzing War

War is any conflict in which over 1,000 people are killed. The warfare we will be concerned with here kills many more; it kills in the tens and hundreds of thousands and even millions. It is important to understand that war does not simply "break out" as if it were some phenomenon of nature. It has causes that can be identified, sometimes reaching well back into history. The causes that lie behind the outbreak of a war may well be understandable and even seem justified, although that does not imply that there is reason to condone war as the means of remedying these causes. War can also be the result of mistakes sometimes, as in the current conflicts in the Middle East, mistakes that go back a hundred years.[1]

International war is a highly organized activity of nation states. Revolutionary wars or civil wars are the conflicts of large groups wanting to seize control of nation states or separate from them. Insurgencies, rebellions and guerilla wars are forms of civil war. Terrorism is, perhaps, a special case. In some forms, it ought not to be defined as warfare at all. Loretta Napoleoni points out that

> terrorism is elusive; each time someone believes he or she has found the correct definition, [someone] else proves it faulty. As a concept, it is hard to pin down because it is essentially a political phenomenon. What is the difference between a freedom fighter and a terrorist? It depends on the angle from which one is looking.... Even the qualifying observation that terrorism's victims are primarily non-combatants fails to isolate the uniqueness of this.[2]

She goes on to point out the well-known fact that modern war also kills civilians *en masse*, as in the terrorism exercised by the state in conventional warfare. Like Hitler's bombing of London, one of the aims of the Allied carpet bombing of European cities in World War II was to terrorize the civilian population of Germany so they would give up. And then there is the terrorism some state elites consciously manipulate against their own populations.[3] However terror is employed, or by whom, it is for the purpose of intimidating civilians and causing them to change their behavior in some way. Like large-scale conventional warfare, terrorism is not the spontaneous outbreak of rage by madmen, but in fact "a rational choice made by strategic thinkers."[4] The terrorist acts exercised by jihadists against the U.S. and European nations is carried out expressly for the purpose of getting them to change their Middle Eastern policies and to remove their military presence from the region.

But the "terrorism" we seem to be focused on in today's "war on terror" was traditionally defined not as war at all, but as a crime. Prior to the attacks on the World Trade Center the U.S. government defined terrorism in just this way. Napoleoni argues that "until 9/11, the judiciary had primarily addressed terrorism: the police persecuted [sic, pursued?] terrorists; who ended up being prosecuted in courts of law ... the core definition of terrorism rests, therefore, in a criminal act and thus the criminal nature of terrorism is its true emphasis."[5] And finally, two more aspects of terrorism are questionable; first, can one make war on an -ism? Bombs fall on people and objects, not on ideas. And second, does it work, or, like pouring water on a gasoline fire, does it just spread the fire? Professor Mary Kaldor argues that "the blunt instrument of war may further intensify a cycle of violence and attract new recruits to terror."[6]

In any event, large-scale war is never a spontaneous event. International war requires large bureaucracies on both sides, while the other forms of war require a large bureaucracy on at least one side at the beginning and, if the rebels hope to compete, they will quickly develop such a command and control structure themselves. It requires careful, advance planning of strategies, tactics, procurement, replacements, dealing with the wounded and veterans, promotions, training, and the psychological preparation of the civilian population through carefully constructed propaganda. Warfare defined in this way is a comparatively recent phenomenon in human history.

A Brief History of War

While modern *Homo sapiens* have been around for over 100,000 years, it is thought that for most of that period they did not make war on one another. For one thing, small groups of hunters and gatherers could not afford to lose a single person since all were needed for the survival of the group. This does not mean that there was no sporadic violence but we have very little evidence of it. Even after the emergence of village agriculture around 8000 BC in what is today called the Middle East, there is little evidence of warfare for about four millennia. While not universally true, most excavations do not turn up weapons or depictions of war or much evidence of destruction or of fortifications. This changed sometime after 4000 BC when nomadic groups invaded the Fertile Crescent and then made conquests along the shores of the Mediterranean Sea. Prior to this, it is thought that societies were organized along partnership lines — men and women had equal status and there was little social stratification.[7]

The new groups, in contrast, were intensely patriarchal, worshiped warrior gods, built hilltop forts, and in the excavations of their remains one finds many weapons and depictions of warfare. Along with the development of war came the development of hierarchical society (including slavery) and, of course, the perfection of a new social institution, the military state with its standing army. With these developments, warfare became endemic in the Middle East. Empires rose, were attacked and disappeared in quick succession, sometimes leaving barely a trace of their egotistical kings, a passing noted in the famous poem by Percy Bysshe Shelley.

> I met a traveler from an antique land
> Who said: "Two vast and trunkless legs of stone
> Stand in the desert.... Near them, on the sand,
> Half sunk, a shattered visage lies, whose frown,
> And wrinkled lip, and sneer of cold command
> Tell that its sculptor well those passions read
> Which yet survive, stamped on these lifeless things;
> The hand that mocked them, and the heart that fed;
> And on the pedestal these words appear;
> 'My name is Ozymandias, king of kings;
> Look on my works, ye Mighty, and despair!'
> Nothing beside remains. Round the decay
> Of that colossal wreck, boundless and bare,
> The level sands stretch far away."[8]

These societies have recently been named dominator societies in contrast to the partnership societies that preceded them. They were aggressively patriarchal. They operated on the basis of power over rather than power shared. But it was, and is, not only women who were dominated by men. Men were, and are, also dominated by other men in this hierarchical form of organization that ran through education, the religious institution, the state, and, of course, the most hierarchical of all organizations, the military. Full worth is achieved only by a few at the top. All others take orders and often suffer humiliation and restrictions on their freedom.

Those at the top freely used violence or the threat of it to maintain the social hierarchy and their control of wealth and production through the coercive power of the state. This new, coercive organization of society and production was efficient, if ruthless, and resulted in surpluses and burgeoning populations, resources that freed the rulers of the state from necessity and gave them the wherewithal for their armies.

The Parable of the Tribes

More than this, however, social-structural reasons dictated that the warrior society pattern would win out. As Andrew Bard Schmookler points out in *The Parable of the Tribes* "As civilization developed, humans confronted a situation in which the play of power was uncontrollable."[9] Lester Milbrath, in his book *Envisioning a Sustainable Society*, writes "In an anarchic situation like that, no one can choose that the struggle for power shall cease. But there is one more element in the picture: *no one is free to choose peace, but anyone can impose upon all the necessity for power*. This is the lesson of the parable of the tribes."[10] Milbrath then outlines this argument:

> The warlike eliminate the pacifistic and content. A tribe (society) that is confronted by an aggressive power-maximizing neighbor has only four options:
> a. It may suffer destruction; in a struggle for power the surviving society will be the one that employs power most effectively.
> b. It may be absorbed by the aggressive power and become transformed into a power-maximizing society.
> c. It may escape the compelling pressures of the intersocietal system by withdrawing beyond the reach of other societies. Only in the least accessible regions of the planet have the equalitarian and peaceful societies been able to survive into our time. All other societies were drawn into the power contest, or were eliminated by it
> d. If it chooses to defend itself against the aggressor, the peace-seeking society becomes the imitator of power-maximizing society. [And then he quotes Schmookler] "The tyranny of power is such that even self-defense mechanisms become a kind of surrender. Not to resist is to be transformed at the hands of the mighty. To resist requires that one transform oneself into their likeness. Either way, free human choice is prevented. *All ways but the way of power are blocked*."[11]

All of this presented a problem that still exists. What does a peaceful society that does not know or want war do when confronted by a warrior society that does? How do they respond to invasion? Do they submit, or transform themselves into the very kind of society they deplore in order to effectively resist? If all societies choose to live in peace, then they can, but if one chooses war, then the others must choose war or preparation for war, or submission, or, if possible, flight. In summing up, Schmookler writes:

> I have just outlined four possible outcomes for the threatened tribes: destruction, absorption and transformation, withdrawal, and imitation. In every one of

these outcomes the ways of power are spread throughout the system. This is the parable of the tribes.

The parable of the tribes is a theory of social evolution which shows that power is like a contaminant, a disease, which once introduced will gradually, yet inexorably become universal in the system of competing societies. More important than the inevitability of the struggle for power is the profound social evolutionary consequence of that struggle once it begins. *A selection for power among civilized societies is inevitable.* If anarchy assured that power among civilized societies could not be governed, the selection for power signified that increasingly the ways of power would govern the destiny of mankind. This is the new evolutionary principle that came into the world with civilization. Here is the social evolutionary black hole that we have sought as an explanation of the harmful warp in the course of civilization's development.[12]

Since there did not seem at the time to be any alternatives to these choices, most societies, though not all, adopted the dominator mode and became warfare states. This has led us to 6,000 years of warfare as competing states readily resorted to large-scale, organized violence, that is, to their armies.

In this way, the "war system" evolved and it flourished, and although some religious and ethical traditions deplored it, many succumbed to it. The norm was for the religious institutions to legitimate the state and its violence. In ancient Egypt, the pharaoh was passed off to the commoners as a god. In medieval Europe, warrior kings claimed to rule by divine right in the "Davidic tradition" as the agent of God on Earth. In modern times most peoples still believe that God is on their side in any war they undertake. In World War I the German soldiers had "Gott mit uns" emblazoned on their belt buckles and the Allied armies sang their *Te deums* after the victory in 1918.

The Historical Development of Conventional War

While it is true that the development of organized warfare in the third millennium BC resulted in a dramatic increase in violence when conflicts occurred, generally it was only for a short period of time, a day or two when the armies met and slaughtered each other on the battlefield or brutally sacked a town. This remained the pattern until modern times, when five developments vastly increased the level and the duration of violence. These were: (1) the development of the modern, centralized state; (2) the rise of nationalism; (3) the development of democracy; (4) the industrialization of warfare; and (5) the total organization of the economy, indeed, of the entire society, to support the killing on the battlefield.

For modern war to exist, the modern state had to be invented. In the early Middle Ages the central government, or state, was a weak institution.

Most power had fragmented and devolved to powerful land-owning lords in the hinterland. In tenth-century France, for example, the king controlled only the Isle de France, that little territory around Paris. But kings steadily increased both their control over territory and subjects, and the extent of their legitimate authority, until, by the seventeenth century, the monarchial state was the strongest institution in society. Thus, by the modern period, only the state had the legitimate authority to declare war and to require its subjects or citizens to risk their lives for its preservation, or expansion, and in the process to kill other humans.

The second development was the rise of nationalism or patriotism. Prior to the French Revolution in 1789, most armies were small and made up of professionals or even mercenaries whose loyalties were not fanatical, to say the least. Save for the early wars of Islam and the Crusades, armies were not fighting for powerful ideological motives, and even the Crusades degenerated into smash-and-grab raiding, not only against Muslims but also against fellow Christians; Muslim states fought Muslim states as well. The armies of early modern Europe were so expensive for kings to keep that often in war situations, they would maneuver and dance around each other to avoid a costly battle. But the French Revolution began the modernization of warfare. The ousting of the aristocrats left the French without a professional army, and when they were invaded by the Prussians and Austrians who wanted to reverse the revolution, out of necessity the French created a democratic army, a people's army, vast in size and fanatically loyal to the nation since, if defeated, they would lose the rights they had won from the aristocrats. Given this advantage, Napoleon walked over Europe, bragging that he could not lose because, as he warned the Austrian Chancellor Prince von Metternich, "I can spend 30,000 men a month."[13] Confronted with this, the other European powers had to imitate his methods to defeat him. Nationalism and democracy combined so that more was at stake than some king's professionals fighting against some other king's professionals for a small piece of territory. It raised the stakes and increased the size of armies so that wars were more violent and were fought over larger territories and over longer periods of time. Napoleon lost some 400,000 men in the failed invasion and then retreat from Russia, although most of these died of the winter weather.

Nationalism and democracy were the second and third developments. The trend toward greater violence continued during the American Civil War (1861–1865). In that conflict about 600,000 men were killed in battle, the result of the fourth development: the industrialization of warfare. This included the mass production of weapons and the development of steam-driven transport of armies by ships and railroad. It had begun in the early 1800s but accelerated dramatically in the second half of that century. Modern sci-

BRITISH TOMMIES RESCUING A COMRADE UNDER FIRE. This man was wounded on the first day of the Battle of the Somme in World War I, July 1, 1916, and is being carried through a trench by a comrade. Saved for the moment, he died 30 minutes after the photograph was taken. The British took 58,000 casualties on that day, one-third of them killed. The battle lasted three and a half months, and gained about six miles for the Allies at a total cost on both sides of 1,240,000 casualties, about 206,000 per mile gained. Adolf Hitler was wounded in this battle. (Imperial War Museum E AUS-001220)

ence, which placed so much power in the hands of manufacturing and modern methods of mass production, created the modern battlefield with its mass slaughter. The development of high explosives by Alfred Nobel in 1863, long-range artillery, the machine gun, and finally aerial bombardment all filled the air with flying metal and concussive explosions. This was perfected by 1914 and defined World War I as the first fully modern war.

World War I began in August 1914, and by Christmas 1,000,000 men were dead. In 1916, the British took 58,000 casualties on the first day of the Battle of the Somme.[14] Battles no longer lasted just a day as in the Middle Ages and early modern period, when armies met on a "field" and for a few hours there was terrible slaughter, sometimes even several thousand casualties. The fighting on the Somme lasted for almost eleven months and in the end the British, French and German casualties amounted to 1,240,000 men killed or wounded.[15] Over the course of the war in approximately the same time span as the American Civil War, eight to ten million died, a nearly 20-fold increase. Twenty years later, in World War II, so many died that the estimates vary from 50 to 100 million, in just five years. The Russians alone lost 20 million in World War II. The ultimate outcome of this trend in which science and technology were applied to modern war was the 20-megaton hydrogen bomb, capable of utterly obliterating the largest cities on earth in a fraction of a second.

The fifth development in the history of warfare was the invention of total war, in which the state takes control of all production and the other institutions of society and orients them toward the war effort. Some writers contend that total war was actually an outcome of the Enlightenment — a paradoxical result of the desire on the part of the intellectuals for total peace. They argued that war was unnatural and that "a new era of permanent peace was about to dawn ... and the fact that war hadn't ended could mean only that someone was keeping it from ending"; thus there had to be one final total battle so that total peace could ensue, and so followed what Gopnik calls "the long line of misery that led to the 'war to end all wars.'"[16] This certainly sounds like Woodrow Wilson's World War I rhetoric, but one must be careful when attempting to blame war on peace.

In any event, by the beginning of the twentieth century total war had come to be a fact, and none of these wars was worse than World War II, when everything was devoted to war production. Automobile companies were directed to produce tanks. The production of civil airliners gave way to war planes. But it goes much further; citizens were urged to plant vegetable gardens, the so-called "victory gardens," and even the film industry was mobilized to develop propaganda films. Rationing occurred so that certain materials, such as sugar, gas, tires, and cloth, would go toward the war effort.

The development of aerial bombardment also triggered another ominous change in warfare, and that was the change in the ratio of civilian to military casualties. The area bombing of whole cities in World War II, the first time that massive bombing became technically possible, was consciously designed to break the morale of the enemy by massive, deliberate killing of civilians. In fact, terror bombing did not break morale; instead, it heightened it, but at a terrible cost in the lives of non-combatants. In World War I, 80 percent of the casualties were military. Today, the reverse is true. Most casualties are civilians.

Modern war requires an immense amount of highly detailed advance planning. Modern military states have on file so-called contingency plans for fighting a wide variety of potential "enemies." Up until the 1930s the U.S. still had a contingency plan for war with Canada. The general staff is a group of experts who plan whole campaigns and individual battles and then, as events unfold, continually revise these plans. It is an immense bureaucracy reaching from just behind the lines in a conventional war all the way back to the war department in the home country. At this remote level, the war is abstract for those who are planning it and they may feel little emotion, certainly nothing like the actual troops engaged with the enemy. War at this level is much like a modern business with graphs, charts, lists, projections, reports, and, of course, maps.

A final development that should be noted is the rise of asymmetric warfare. While not new (it began in Spain during the Napoleonic Wars), the confrontation between large-scale, heavily-weaponed armies such as that of the United States, and lightly armed, small-scale guerrilla groups that can strike with surprise and then fade into the population and disappear, gives the poor states or groups a way of leveling the battlefield. The modern, massive army is ill-equipped and poorly designed for this sort of warfare and a third-rate power, such as a state or an insurrectionary force, can tie down even a superpower and prevent it from winning while causing it to suffer unacceptable casualty rates. Terrorism, such as suicide bombing or the airliner attacks on the World Trade Center, is a variant of asymmetric warfare.

The Nuclear Age

The most ominous development in the history of warfare has been the development of nuclear weapons. As Einstein said, "Since Hiroshima, everything has changed except our thinking."[17] Even before J. Robert Oppenheimer's scientists were trying to develop the atomic bomb, the mentality necessary for the age of nuclear terror had already been laid down by the decisions of Bomber Command late in World War II. The fire-bombing of Hamburg and Dresden is a dark topic even more than 60 years after the events. It was at Hamburg and Dresden that the mentality of the atomic age was born. The actual nuclear bombs that destroyed Hiroshima and Nagasaki came a few months later but they were mere technical devices, allowing us to do to those people in a split second what had taken three days and nights at Dresden. The breakthrough into genuine evil, where humans were willing to incinerate whole cities for a political cause, had already occurred over the old cities of Germany.

By the beginning of World War II in 1939 a handful of physicists had determined that it was theoretically possible to split the nucleus of uranium atoms and that doing so would release a monster explosion of such force as never before seen on the planet. Fissioning the atom is what happens in the sun. In 1939 Albert Einstein and Leo Szilard wrote to President Roosevelt urging a research program aimed at producing such a superweapon. Believing

that the other belligerent nations were working on an atom bomb, he initiated
the top-secret Manhattan Project, which by the spring of 1945 had readied
the first test of an atom bomb at a secret site in the New Mexico desert. The
blast came on July 16 and shocked even the scientists who had prepared it.
Prophetically, the project leader, J. Robert Oppenheimer, recited a line from
the Hindu epic the Bhagavad-Gita: "I am become death, destroyer of
worlds."[18] Oddly enough, or perhaps not so oddly, the test was named "Trinity." The first actual bombs were dropped on Japan — on Hiroshima on August
6 and on Nagasaki on August 9. The bomb that destroyed 100,000 people in
Hiroshima released the energy of just one gram of uranium. It was, as President
Truman observed, an unleashing of "the basic power of the universe."[19]
Jonathan Schell writes:

> The huge — the monstrous — disproportion between "the basic power of the
> Universe" and the merely terrestrial creatures by which and against which it
> was aimed in anger defined the dread predicament that the world has tried, and
> failed, to come to terms with ever since.[20]

The bombs that destroyed Hiroshima and Nagasaki were, relatively
speaking, tiny compared to those that were developed later. Measured in tons
of TNT equivalent, Hiroshima was about 12,500 tons or 12.5 kilotons. The
big bombs of World War II, called "blockbusters," carried about 8,000 pounds,
or four tons of explosives. The Hiroshima bomb was 3,125 times as powerful
and had the added lethality that came from searing radiation. The temperature
on the ground underneath the fireball was 6,000 degrees Kelvin, or hotter
than the surface temperature of the sun; for comparison, water boils at 315
degrees Kelvin. Later came 1-megaton and 5-megaton bombs (megaton = million tons), and even 10- and 20-megaton bombs. All the conventional explosives expended in World War II are estimated to be about three megatons
over six years. Thus a single 5-megaton nuclear bomb carries more destructive
power than all of World War II, to be expended on a single "target." Furthermore, there is a qualitative difference in that, in addition to blast and fire,
nuclear bombs release lethal radiation and electromagnetic pulse that destroys
all electrical systems in a huge area. Some forms of radiation can last over
50,000 years, poisoning the soil and water and those who try to live on them
for uncountable generations.

In a nuclear war we would see the complete collapse of the economy.
The results of conventional bombing in the First Gulf War (1990–1991) left
Iraq without basic services in electricity, clean water, waste disposal, health
care, transport, fertilizer production, and so on, resulting in hundreds of
thousands of deaths from malnutrition and disease. A nuclear war of just ten
one-megaton bombs, the equivalent of 800 Hiroshimas, would completely
destroy the economy of any large country.[21]

DEVASTATED HIROSHIMA. The bomb was dropped August 6, 1945. One second there was a city, and less than a second later there wasn't. One hundred thousand or so died. The lucky ones were vaporized; the rest died of severe burns or radiation sickness. "Everything has changed," said Einstein, "except our thinking." (New York World-Telegram & Sun Newspaper Photograph Collection, Prints & Photographs Division, Library of Congress, CL USZ62-134192)

The explosions of atomic and hydrogen bombs are unlike those of any other weapons in that they are exponentially more violent and more complex. Conventional bombs are chemical explosions made by igniting gunpowder or TNT and are an exercise of what physicists call the "weak force." A nuclear detonation utilizes what physicists call the "strong force," achieved only by splitting atoms (Hiroshima-type atomic bomb) or by fusing them (Nagasaki-type atomic bomb and hydrogen bomb). Prior to 1945 the strong force had never existed on the surface of the earth. It is the force that drives the sun. It is terribly difficult to bring off. A core of radioactive material is surrounded with an envelope of chemical high explosives that implode and either drive the atoms apart or fuse them together, releasing a catastrophic force. The first of the immediate effects is a blinding white light that can sear the eyeballs. This is followed by the "thermal pulse," a super intense blast of heat (6,000–7,000 degrees Kelvin) that can last several seconds as the fireball climbs in the air. The third effect is the blast wave, which can flatten large concrete and steel buildings. The fourth effect is EMP, or a release of electromagnetic force that knocks out all electrical and electronic devices. A 20-megaton bomb exploded 120 miles above Omaha, Nebraska, would disable all electrical devices in the United States, bringing the economy to a dead standstill.[22] The fifth effect is radiation, the release of materials that are sending out millions of invisible "bullets" that penetrate concrete, glass, wood, and the soft tissues of humans and animals. Radiation is a biocide that depresses life at all levels, depending on the dosage one receives. Large doses, such as would be experienced by anyone on the perimeter of the blast or immediately downwind, can kill rapidly as the internal organs disintegrate and hemorrhage. Lesser doses, miles and even hundreds of miles from the blast, can make one violently ill

and over time cause cancers.

The effects of a nuclear explosion over a city are horrific. The Hiroshima bomb was estimated to have the force of 12.5 kilotons (or 12,500 tons) of TNT. Eighty thousand people died immediately in that blast, the city was flattened, and thousands of others lay on the perimeter dying of radiation or burns. One moment Hiroshima was there and the next it wasn't. Such weapons are small compared to those in today's nuclear arsenals. The "average"-size weapons during the Cold War were in the megaton (million ton)

NUCLEAR WEAPON DETONATED AT BIKINI ATOLL. After removing the natives from their island in 1946, the U.S. conducted 22 nuclear explosions at this Pacific site and then in 1969 declared the island safe and returned it to the remaining natives, whose efforts to rehabilitate the ecosystem foundered in a radioactive desert. Sick, they had to leave in 1979 and it remains uninhabitable to this day, a prophecy of what would happen to major portions of the earth in a nuclear war. (Farm Security Administration to Office of War Information Collection, Prints & Photographs Division, Library of Congress, LC-USW33-059244)

range: one megaton, two, five. Some much larger weapons were also produced up to 60 megatons or 60 million tons of TNT equivalent.

A one-megaton bomb detonated 8,500 feet above Manhattan would flatten every building in an area of 61 square miles and severely damage the buildings in an area of 200 square miles. Broken glass and other debris would be hurled at hurricane force outward from the center for ten miles. Winds two miles from ground zero would approach 400 miles an hour, diminishing to 180 miles an hour at a distance of four miles. Large cities' downtown areas would be like canyons. Schell observes, "The walls would fall in and the ravines would fill up."[23] The fireball would be a mile wide and rise to six miles, broiling the city below, setting everything on fire in a radius of nine miles from the center. Cars, buses, lampposts, and everything made from metal and glass would melt. Darkness would prevail and radioactive rain would fall. Bomb shelters would be useless as all the oxygen would be burned from the air and toxic gases would infiltrate. Millions would die. Schell writes, "The people of New York would be burned, battered, crushed and irradiated in every conceivable way. The city and its people would be mingled in a smoldering heap."[24] Of course, in an actual nuclear war, New York and other large cities would be hit with several bombs, perhaps even in the five-megaton range. The destruction in the immediate area would be almost unimaginable, but the effects would spread far and wide as winds carried the radiation away, spreading it over areas not affected by the blast. Eventually it would circle Earth.

After even a limited nuclear war, the northern hemisphere, and possibly the southern, would experience nuclear winter. Most of the survivors would very likely die later in the cold and the dark and the radiation. Smoke from the burning cities and forests would hide the sun for months, creating a nuclear winter with temperatures close to zero in high summer.[25] All of the fuels and toxic chemicals stored in cities would be released into the environment and would make their way to ecological sinks — groundwater, lakes, rivers, oceans. Drinking water would be contaminated by radiation and by these chemicals. Crops would not survive the triple assault of radiation, cold, and darkness. Farm animals would die from the cold, lack of food, and thirst. The dead and dying forests would become fuel for fires far into the future. Since radiation is both a mutagen and teratogen, hideous birth defects, which have already been seen in the nuclear test areas in the Pacific islands, would also be the order of the day. The effects of the darkness and the radiation would include the destruction of the phytoplankton at the bottom of the food chain, resulting in a die-off of many or most of the animals on land and in the sea. A total breakdown of the social order, starvation and epidemic disease would be universal. At Hiroshima the whole city was wiped out, but help could and did eventually arrive from the outside. In a large-, or even not-so-large-scale nuclear war, there would be no outside from which help could come. These effects could come from a detonation of as little as 100 megatons in the northern hemisphere. Considering that the U.S. and the Soviet Union together had amassed 18,000 megatons of nuclear weapons in the 1980s, and still have several thousand, such a scenario, should a war break out, is not unlikely. Against these weapons, and their delivery systems, there is simply no defense. The intercontinental missiles come in on a very low trajectory at 10,000 miles an hour. Even if, and it is highly unlikely, an anti-missile system could be developed that would be 90 percent effective (high for complex technical systems), still the warheads that would get through would equal hundreds of World War IIs, with the added complications of radiation and nuclear winter.

One is compelled to ask, how did it come to this? The war system, which will be described in detail in chapters 3 and 4, led inevitably to these weapons. In a zero sum game such as the presently constructed international relations, the choices are win or lose. Since one's enemy or potential enemy may develop highly destructive weapons, one must do the same and hope they will act as a deterrent. Arms races are an inevitable result. The efforts to manage them, and somehow to limit them, are ineffective over the long run, since there are always ways around the treaties. For instance, when the U.S. and the Soviet Union agreed to limit the megatonnage that could be hurled at one another by limiting the number of launchers, ways were found to miniaturize the warheads and to put up to ten independently targetable warheads on a single launcher. A single missile could kill ten cities and they became faster, more accurate. The cruise missiles were equipped with terrain reading radar so they could come in almost at ground level and thus escape detection until exploding. Efforts to contain the number of nations that possess nuclear weapons were enshrined in the Nuclear Non-proliferation Treaty, whose signators agreed that they would not acquire nuclear weapons if the states that already had them (initially the United States, Soviet Union., Great Britain and France) would take steps to get rid of theirs. They never did and the "nuclear family" grew to include Israel, India, Pakistan, China, North Korea and probably soon Iran.

The world came very close to a nuclear holocaust in the 1980s as irresponsible leaders played brinksmanship with the fate of the earth in their hands. In response to the Soviet Union setting up SS-20 missiles in Eastern Europe that could quickly strike France and England, the U.S. retaliated with new kinds of delivery systems in Europe: the lightning fast and highly accurate Pershing missile in Germany and cruise missiles in England. The Pershings were so fast and accurate that within a few minutes of launch they could be racing down the smokestacks of the Kremlin. These weapons could be used as first-strike nuclear weapons and they gave the Soviet Union no choice but to launch on warning when and if their radar picked them up at all. Soviet radar defenses were outdated, operating on vacuum tubes, and even more prone to false alarms than were the American defense radars of NORAD, which often gave indications of nuclear attacks underway. Technical glitches could have set off accidental launches, initiating the end of civilization. Today the probability of a nuclear holocaust has shrunk, but the monster is not dead. It still lurks in the back of the cave. And the Nuclear Non-proliferation Treaty is collapsing as non-nuclear powers see the double standard being played out, and see that nuclear weapons may give them deterrent power, assuming everyone acts rationally. Arms races are built into the present international system, which is why it is so dangerous

Today, many people think that the nuclear threat is over, that the big powers have renounced nuclear weapons or even dismantled them. It is true that some weapons were dismantled after the end of the Cold War and their launchers destroyed. But those warheads remain, stored away where they can be refitted to new launchers. And both the U.S. and Russia maintain overwhelming active nuclear arsenals, enough to end civilization in an afternoon. For example, the U.S. still maintains three active nuclear weapons missile launch sites on alert status: one at Minot, North Dakota; one at Great Falls, Montana; and on the Wyoming/Colorado/Nebraska border. The U.S. still has 1,374 ICBM warheads, any one of which can destroy a large city, 2,410 submarine launched ballistic missile warheads, 176 bombs on jet bombers, and 1,100 nuclear armed cruise missiles.[26] And, too, there is the threat of a nuclear war breaking out between India and Pakistan, Iran and Israel, or elsewhere. The nuclear monster has not been slain. It is alive and well and still stalking humankind.

The Essential and Timeless Nature of Battle: Simone Weil

While the technology and sociology of war have changed dramatically in the last few centuries, some aspects have not changed since ancient times. What war does to the human soul as the fortunes of battle ebb and flow has been constant. The essence of battle is a combination of violent force, exhaustion, rage and fear. Simone Weil writes about its effect on those caught up in it. "Force turns whoever comes under its sway into a thing ... it makes a person a thing in the most literal sense: it makes him into a corpse."[27]

It is not only lethal force that turns a person into a thing; the threat of imminent death turns him into a thing even before he has been killed. "A disarmed and naked man at whom a weapon is leveled becomes a corpse even before he is touched [and] though he is still breathing he is no longer anything but inert matter."[28] And those who, for the moment, exercise this power over another, become intoxicated with it. But, she points out, "No one ever really possesses it or thinks he possesses it."[29] The fortunes of battle shift, the counterattack is mounted, and the powerful become the terrified running for their lives. It is no longer a game. And in the end, the act of killing turns the killer into a thing as well: "The conquering warrior is like a scourge of nature: maddened by war, he has turned into a thing and words have no more power over him than they have over inert matter."[30] In the days of Troy it was only the oncoming enemy that could induce the fear and the rage, but in modern war, the enemy might be well out of sight at least sometimes, but the threat is not.

The Modern Battlefield

From the time of the *Iliad* down to the seventeenth-century warfare stayed pretty much the same. Two armies met in a specific place and fought

THE BIG GUNS. The cannon were lined up for miles along both sides of the front line in World War I. About 1.5 billion shells were fired on the Western Front alone. It was an orgy of death and destruction and when it was over, not many knew why it had happened at all. What they did know is that it would soon lead to another and even worse war where the high explosives were not only fired from cannon but also dropped from the bomber fleets. (Drawing [1914–1918] by Wladyslaw T. Benda [Cabinet of American Illustration, Library of Congress])

a battle on a given day with swords and pikes, bows and arrows, and it was terrible but soon over. Gradually, around the fifteenth century, gunpowder came into use in Europe in smooth bore muskets and primitive cannons, which had very short range and even worse accuracy than the long bow, but were deadly if you were hit with the lead ball, and their noise and smoke were frightening. It was in the nineteenth century that dramatic changes began to occur in the technology and duration of war. The Crimean conflict and the American Civil War went on for years. But even in those conflicts, death came almost always from an enemy one could see. The most dangerous weapons were the rifled muskets, deadly only under 200 yards, and the short-range black powder cannon. Still, some 600,000 men died in the American conflict. But it was to get much worse.

Swedish scientist Alfred Nobel had invented high explosives in 1863 by combining nitroglycerin, which was an extremely high explosive but also extremely volatile, with silica to make a paste that, while more stable, could be detonated by his patented detonator cap. Production began in 1865 primarily for the mining industry, but the world's militaries were quick to see another obvious use. By 1914 they were ready with the awful dismembering cannonades of World War I, with the entire battlefield being torn up into craters and mounds of earth. Tens of thousands of shells would be fired prior to the charge out of the trenches. World War I saw the use of long-range artillery, capable of launching a shell over several miles. Massed over miles of front, these guns were armed with Nobel's high explosives and with poison gas shells. The high explosives were both concussive and scattered shards of hot steel (shrapnel) over a wide area. The explosions made the ground tremble. An artillery barrage is perhaps the most terrifying experience a human can undergo. By 1918 at sea, naval guns were capable of hurling 500 pounds of high explosives some 20 miles. Submarines could lurk underwater and destroy unsuspecting ships with high explosive torpedoes, causing horrendous, violent explosions and frequently sinking the target in a few minutes with total loss of life as men burned alive, were blown to bits, or drowned in the oily sea.

In World War I the artillery was complemented by another mass killing device, the machine gun. It was invented by Hiram Maxim in 1881. By World War I, a later variant, the Vickers machine gun, could fire 600 bullets per minute over a range of 4,500 yards. Mounted on pivots, these guns could sweep a battlefield with a hail of metal. The machine gun accounted for 90 percent of the casualties on the Western Front.[31]

World War I also saw the first use of aerial bombardment, both from Zeppelins and from light aircraft. The damage was of little consequence, but by World War II, only 20 years later, fleets of up to 1,000 heavy bombers, Lancasters and Liberators, flying at 15,000 feet and at speeds of over 200 miles per hour, would appear over a city and devastate it with high explosives and fire bombs made of jellied gasoline (napalm), and with white phosphorus.

"In the Second World War," Winston Churchill said, "every bond between man and man was to perish."[32] Perhaps it was not the first time that it had happened, but it had never happened in such a preplanned, consciously cruel way, nor had the break ever been as extensive. The ultimate "perfection" of the technique of city-killing was a firestorm. It happened first, rather by accident, to Hamburg on the night of July 28, 1943, when the Royal Air Force accidentally created a firestorm that engulfed the center of the city, burning at temperatures of 800 degrees Fahrenheit.

> Seventy thousand people died at Hamburg the night the air caught fire. They were mostly women, children and the elderly since those of soldiering age were generally at the front. They died horrible deaths, burning and suffocating.[33]

Nineteen-year-old Kate Hoffmeister was caught up in the raid.

> The rain of large sparks blowing down the street, were each as large as a five mark piece. I struggled to run against the wind but could only reach a house on the corner of the Sorbenstrasse.... We couldn't go on across the Eiffenstrasse because the asphalt road had melted. There were people on the roadway, some already dead, some still lying alive but stuck in the asphalt. They must have rushed onto the roadway without thinking. Their feet had got stuck and then they put out their hands to try to get out again. They were on their hands and knees screaming.[34]

Next it happened to the beautiful old German city of Dresden, where Bomber Command finally got it right, what they had been intending all along — a planned firestorm that the Germans still recall. English and American commanders, knowing that Dresden was not a significant military target by any stretch of the word, a city filled with refugees and art works, calmly and coolly planned the sequence of bombing. First they sent in a wave of bombers dropping high explosives to blow the roofs off the houses and apartment buildings. Then the second wave dropped incendiaries to get the city burning. Then, when they knew the fire crews would be out, they sent in the bombers with high explosives, killing the fire crews. As Bomber Command had planned, the whole city coalesced into a single fire of enormous proportions, with hurricane-force winds blowing inward toward the center, — in short, a firestorm. No one knows how many tens of thousands died at Dresden. Days later, when relief workers tried to open the basement bomb shelters, they were so hot that the inrush of oxygen burst into flame. And it remains crucially important to understand how those normally decent young men who flew the Lancasters and the Liberators, who knew exactly what was going on down there below their planes, under their bombs, could have acquiesced to such utter slaughter.

The air fleets of World War II were attacked by the defenders with anti-aircraft fire, filling the air around the planes with explosions showering shrapnel, and with fighter planes firing machine guns and cannon. The skies themselves became a killing field. In World War II casualties in British Bomber Command were the highest of any other sector in the war: of every 100 men who flew these missions, only 24 survived.[35]

On the ground, World War I had stagnated in trench warfare for four deadly years as the commanders tried again and again to hurl massed infantry against machine gun and artillery positions.[36] Life in the trenches was dreadful, especially in the rainy seasons when men lived in knee-deep mud. The area between the trench lines, "no man's land," was bare of trees, blasted away by artillery and pocked with shell craters that filled up with liquid mud and water and in which men drowned during attacks. It was littered with decaying corpses. The trenches themselves were inhabited not only by soldiers but also by millions of rats that fed on the corpses. By contrast, World War II was in large part a war of movement, pioneered by the German Blitzkrieg or lightning war, in which fighter bombers and massed tanks quickly overran enemy positions and achieved breakout. In both wars, soldiers were in for the duration — until it was over or until they were wounded severely enough to be sent home, or until they were killed. It is no wonder that so many of them had "shell shock," a euphemism for going insane. Some of the more egregious weapons used to mutilate and kill humans in the twentieth century and on into the present one are land mines, depleted uranium weapons, and fuel-air bombs. Land mines are small explosive devices that are buried a few centimeters under the surface and explode when stepped on, tripped by a trigger wire, or when rolled on by vehicles, indicating the two types — anti-personnel and anti-tank.[37] In tiny Cambodia there are as many as ten million mines still buried as a result of the Pol Pot regime, the Sihanoukists and the Vietnamese invaders. Eighteen countries have been identified as the manufacturers, including the United States. There are 40,000 amputees in Cambodia and an estimated 40,000 more died before they could get to help. "The rural poor are especially at risk: they can be killed or mutilated in the simple act of trying to get water or wood."[38]

More than 100 million mines remain buried in 70 countries around the world, left over from past wars. Anti-personnel mines of the blast type are designed to destroy a person's foot or leg into fragments, causing secondary damage of infection or amputation in addition to the initial injury. A second type, the bouncing mine, is ejected a few feet off the ground before exploding in order to cause injury to the chest or head. Fragmentation mines release small bits of metal, killing at close range and causing injury up to 200 meters away. Land mines can remain active for fifty years after they were planted in the ground, and most minefields were never mapped in the first place, leaving them as hidden dangers to civilians long after the wars have ceased. More than a million people, nearly all civilians, and a high percentage of them children, have been killed or maimed by mines in the last 30 years.[39] Some mines, such as the butterfly mines used by the Soviets in Afghanistan, look like toys, and children frequently pick them up and, if lucky, live maimed for life. Children are often illiterate, especially in developing countries, and can't read the signs that warn of known minefields. They are also far more likely to die from mine injuries than adults, and even if they live and can get medical help, few will receive prostheses that can keep up with their growing limbs. UNICEF describes land mines as "particularly savage weapons."[40]

A weapon more recently introduced is the depleted uranium explosive shell. According to the World Health Organization:

> Uranium (U) is used primarily as a fuel material in nuclear power plants. However, most reactors require uranium in which the 235U content is enriched from its naturally occurring concentration. The uranium remaining after removal of the enriched fraction is referred to as depleted uranium.[41]

It remains radioactive. Its extreme density makes it useful as armor penetrating shells, as well as for armor plate, and it has been used extensively in recent wars, primarily by the U.S. military in Iraq, Kuwait, Bosnia, Kosovo, Serbia, Afghanistan and Montenegro. The total number of rounds fired in these conflicts is approximately 1,335,340, leaving in place on the ground approximately 665,208 kilograms of radioactive material,[42] most of it fragmented into dust.

Another lethal weapon that modern science has bequeathed to warfare is the fuel-air bomb. This device is released from an airplane that sprays an atomized form of a volatile liquid like gasoline or a powder such as zinc over an area up to a mile long, followed by a detonator that causes the entire mass to flash and explode. The oxygen in the air is ignited in a massive fireball that kills everything in a one-mile radius. The explosions are less rapid than TNT bombs but their slowness allows them to penetrate underground bunkers, killing by concussion or suffocation as they use up all the oxygen. In addition to this horror, a great deal of scientific research has been commanded and funded by various governments in the quest to develop chemical and biological weapons. Of course, poison gas, the most common chemical weapon, was used in World War I, and killed in horrendous fashion, burning out the linings of the lungs. Chemical weapons are limited to the area where they are detonated. Biological weapons, however, literally have a life of their own and can spread and cause epidemics in whole populations. These weapons are laboratory-upgraded (that is, made more virulent) forms of classic viruses and bacteria such as cholera, tuberculosis, and filo viruses, such as Ebola, that cause hemorrhagic fevers. The victims in the latter case literally decompose alive over a period of several days as all of the vital organs and the mucous membranes are attacked. For many of these laboratory supercharged bioticals there is no antidote and no cure.

War Wounds

While gruesome to contemplate, it is crucially important to be honest about what happens to the human body in battle. Before the modern era wounds were caused by edged weapons such as swords, arrows, and pikes, and by clubs such as the mace and the war hammer. They were awful. Homer describes them graphically in the *Iliad*.

> First Antilochus slew an armed warrior of the Trojans, Echepolus, son of Thalysius, fighting in the foremost ranks. He struck at the projecting part of his helmet and drove the spear into his brow; the point of bronze pierced the bone, and darkness veiled his eyes; headlong as a tower he fell amid the press of the fight, and as he dropped King Elephenor, son of Chalcodon and captain of the proud Abantes began dragging him out of reach of the darts that were falling around him, in haste to strip him of his armour. But his purpose was not for long; Agenor saw him hauling the body away, and smote him in the side with his bronze-shod spear — for as he stooped his side was left unprotected by his shield — and thus he perished. Then the fight between Trojans and Achaeans grew furious over his body, and they flew upon each other like wolves, man and man crushing one upon the other. Forthwith Ajax, son of Telamon, slew the fair youth Simoeisius, son of Anthemion, whom his mother bore by the banks of the Simois.... Therefore he was named Simoeisius, but he did not live to pay his parents for his rearing, for he was cut off untimely by the spear of mighty Ajax, who struck him in the breast by the right nipple as he was coming on among the foremost fighters; the spear went right through his shoulder, and he fell.... Thereon Antiphus of the gleaming corslet, son of Priam, hurled a spear at Ajax from amid the crowd and missed him, but he hit Leucus, the brave comrade of Ulysses, in the groin, as he was dragging the body of Simoeisius over to the other side; so he fell upon the body and loosed his hold upon it. Ulysses was furious when he saw Leucus slain, and strode in full armour through the front ranks till he was quite close; then he glared round about him and took aim, and the Trojans fell back as he did so. His dart was not sped in vain, for it struck Democoon, the bastard son of Priam.... Ulysses, infuriated by the death of his comrade, hit him with his spear on one temple, and the bronze point came through on the other side of his forehead. Thereon darkness veiled his eyes, and his armour rang rattling round him as he fell heavily to the ground.[43]

And further, in Book 5 of the *Iliad*:

> The spear of Agamemnon caught him on the broad of his back, just as he was turning in flight; it struck him between the shoulders and went right through

his chest, and his armour rang rattling round him as he fell heavily to the
ground. Meriones overtook him as he was flying, and struck him on the right
buttock. The point of the spear went through the bone into the bladder, and
death came upon him as he cried aloud and fell forward on his knees. Meges,
moreover, slew Pedaeus.... The son of Phyleus got close up to him and drove
a spear into the nape of his neck: it went under his tongue all among his teeth,
so he bit the cold bronze, and fell dead in the dust.[44]

After the invention of gunpowder, wounds could also be caused by shot,
shrapnel, concussion, and poison gas. Machine guns were aimed low in order
to cut off men's feet. There are accounts of World War I battles in which running men kept going for some yards on stumps after their feet had been shot
off, and other accounts of two men standing, locked together in death by
their bayonets driven into each other's bodies. The modern rifle or machine
gun also provides penetrating wounds to all areas of the body. It is not uncom-
mon for a man to be shot in the chest, penetrating his lung so he drowns in
his own blood, or in the heart, or in the stomach or intestines. Other victims
suffer having their jaws shot off, or bullet wounds to the head, causing, if they
live, severe brain damage.[45] Wilfred Owen, a poet and soldier in the British
Expeditionary Force,[46] described one such comrade in "Dulce Et Decorum
Est."[47]

> Bent double, like old beggars under sacks,
> Knock-kneed, coughing like hags we cursed through the sludge
> Til on the haunting flares we turned our backs,
> And toward our distant rest began to trudge.
> Men marched asleep. Many had lost their boots
> But limped on, blood-shod. Many went lame, all blind,
> Drunk with fatigue, deaf even to the hoots
> Of tired, outstripped five nines that dropped behind
> Gas! Gas! Quick boys — an ecstasy of fumbling,
> Fitting the clumsy helmets just in time.
> But someone was still yelling out and stumbling
> And flound'ring like a man in fire or lime....
> Dim, through the misty panes and thick green light
> As under a green sea, I saw him drowning.
> In all my dreams, before my helpless sight,
> He plunges at me, guttering, choking, drowning.
> If in some smothering dreams you too could pace
> Behind the wagon that we flung him in,
> And watch the white eyes writhing in his face,
> His hanging face like a devils sick of sin;
> If you could hear, at every jolt, the blood
> Come gargling from the froth-corrupted lungs,
> Obscene as cancer, bitter as the cud
> Of vile, incurable sores on innocent tongues,

My friend, you would not tell with such high zest
To children ardent for some desperate glory,
The old lie, Dulce et Decorum est,
Pro patria mori.

Paul Fussell, an historian who fought in a rifle company from Normandy all the way to the end of the war in Europe, writes about "the bizarre damage suffered by the human body in modern war."[48] While soldiers were often shot with rifles and machine guns, the wounds they feared the most were those that dismembered their bodies. Concussion and shrapnel could tear a man's body to pieces and sometimes that is all that would be found by comrades. Heads would get blown off, as well as hands, fingers, testicles, and legs. Sometimes only the trunk of a man was found. Fussell quotes Captain Peter Royle, a British artillery observer:

> I was following about twenty paces behind when there was a blinding flash in front of me. I had no idea what it was and fell flat on my face. I found out soon enough: a number of infantry were carrying mines strapped to the small of their backs, and either a rifle or machine gun bullet had struck one, which had exploded, blowing the man into three pieces — two legs and head and chest. His inside was strewn on the hillside and I crawled into it in the darkness.[49]

Examples like this are multiplied hundreds of thousands of times in the history of modern combat. Often a man would be wounded through being struck by a buddy's head, or another man's lower leg or some other body part. Wounds and death by crushing as buildings blew up and fell in on defenders were also common in the house-to-house fighting, whether in France in 1918, or Germany in 1944, or Fallujah in 2006. Concussion could also suck the oxygen from around a man and he would suffocate for lack of air. A General Hackett, who had seen plenty of these sights, wrote, "It was like being in a strange and terrible nightmare from which you longed to wake and could not."[50]

It is not in the least surprising that recruiting literature, or, indeed, most of what is written about military life, does not describe the wounds soldiers suffer or the ways in which they die. Another soldier poet who fought and survived World War I wrote:

Lost in the swamp and welter of the pit,
He founders off the duck-boards; only he knows
Each flash and spouting crash, — each instant lit
When gloom reveals the streaming rain. He goes
Heavily, blindly on. And, while he blunders,
"Could anything be worse than this?"— he wonders,
Remembering how he saw those Germans run,
Screaming for mercy among the stumps of trees:
Green-faced, they dodged and darted: there was one
Livid with terror, clutching at his knees...

Our chaps were sticking 'em like pigs ... "O hell!"
He thought — "there's things in war one dare not tell
Poor father sitting safe at home, who reads
Of dying heroes and their deathless deeds."[51]

Those who survive their wounds live on, often maimed, with terrible burn scars, missing noses and ears, prosthetic legs, or arms or hands. Others live on with severe mental and emotional damage.

Modern conventional warfare requires extensive pre-planning and advance preparation. It is a cataclysmic event that is often drawn out over years and results in huge numbers of dead and even more wounded. The advent of non-conventional warfare (nuclear, chemical, biological) promises even more casualties and destruction and perhaps the end of civilization itself, if humanity does not invent and adopt new ways of dealing with conflict. These will be suggested in Section II. But first, we need to ask the question "How do we get young men to kill and to endure battle, and what are the psychological consequences they endure?

CHAPTER 2

The Psychology of Killing

How do nation states get normally decent young men to kill, what are the psychological impacts of being in that situation, and how do these impacts follow combat soldiers when the wars are long over? And there is a more sinister question: is there a hidden psychodynamic at the collective level that explains the very existence of war?

Contrary to popular opinion, there is a powerful psychological predisposition against killing even in combat situations. Killing is actually a very difficult act for nearly all people except psychopaths, even when under fire. Lt. Colonel David Grossman writes in his book, *On Killing,* that "there is no doubt that this resistance to killing one's fellow man is there and that it exists as a powerful combination of instinctive, rational, environmental, hereditary, cultural and social factors. It is there, it is strong, and it gives us cause to believe that there may just be hope for mankind after all."[1]

There are paradoxes associated with war and peace, and sometimes it is difficult to disentangle them because they are often held by the same person. It is true that humans are by nature peaceful. It is, in some ways, hard to make them fight and kill each other. There is no better example than the Christmas Truce of 1914. On Christmas Eve in the first months of World War I, even after a million men had been killed in battle, a spontaneous truce occurred in some sectors of the Western Front. British soldiers, hearing Germans just a few yards away in their trench singing *Stille Nacht* (Silent Night), were touched in that part of the mind where empathy resides. They began singing and trading carols back and forth. Then, bit by bit, they ventured out of the trenches into no man's land and shook hands, traded cigarettes, shared food and drink, showed each other pictures of their families, and even organized games of soccer. It went on for almost 24 hours before the officers could get the men back into their trenches. Even after the terrible slaughter of the previous months, they were able to recognize their common humanity.

Or perhaps because of that slaughter they could see that the other infantrymen were just poor guys caught up in the same meat grinder, like themselves, at the mercy of forces beyond their control. To say the least, officers up the chain of command were horrified and made it clear that any future fraternization would be severely punished. Fraternization is an interesting word — it is a Latinate version of the word brother: to "brotherize" is unacceptable in warfare because, if universal, it would eliminate warfare.

Many commentators have suggested that warfare is inevitable because of the structure of the human mind. Countering this idea is the "Seville Statement on Violence,"[2] drawn up in 1986 by 20 prominent social and behavioral scientists and since signed by more than 100 national and international scientific societies and associations. It states a number of propositions. First, that "it is scientifically incorrect to say that we have inherited a tendency to make war from our animal ancestors," pointing out that while there is predation in nature, intra-species attacks are extremely rare, and going on to say that "the fact that warfare has changed so radically over time indicates that it is a product of culture." The second clause begins, "It is scientifically incorrect to say that war or any other violent behavior is genetically programmed into our human nature," pointing out that genes provide only a developmental potential that must be activated by the social environment. Clause 3 states, "It is scientifically incorrect to say that in the course of human evolution there has been a selection for aggressive behavior." Cooperation has played a more significant role in the evolution of human society. Clause 4 states, "It is scientifically incorrect to say that humans have a 'violent brain.'" Our higher neural functions enable us to interpret and filter stimuli rather than react to them automatically. Clause 5 begins, "It is scientifically incorrect to say that war is caused by 'instinct' or any single motivation," and the statement concludes that "biology does not condemn humanity to war."

The result is that in order to kill, one must be heavily conditioned. The World War I troops who fraternized across enemy lines on Christmas Eve of 1914 had not been conditioned in the way that modern soldiers are. The Seville Statement concludes that "the technology of modern war has exaggerated traits associated with violence both in the training of actual combatants and in the preparation of support for war in the general population. As a result of this exaggeration, such traits are often mistaken to be the causes rather than the consequences of the process."

So we have the paradox that there is some natural inhibition to do violence, and yet it is easy to overcome this inhibition with the right psychological manipulation or conditioning. We are by nature peaceful, but that nature is easily overcome by employing certain cultural practices. One of these is the inculcation of hatred. The use of propaganda to arouse fear of another people whose language and religion and customs are different, and to dehumanize them, leads to the kind of atrocities committed by Americans against the Native Americans at Wounded Knee, by the Turks against the Armenians, by the Nazis against the Jews, by Lt. William Calley and his soldiers in Vietnam at My Lai, by the Serbs against the Bosnians in the Balkan wars of the 1990s. In the last case, systematic rape of women and girls and the executions of groups of unarmed men and boys were consciously used as a prolonged strategy by the Serbs to humiliate and defeat the Bosnians. But this is not to single out a few nations as morally worse than others. In warfare all nations commit atrocities. Bombing from the air and land mines are atrocities. As General Harris, head of Bomber Command in World War II, said when questioned about the intentional incineration of Dresden, "Tell me one act of war that is moral."[3]

The other cultural method that shuts off the higher brain and its moral sense is the method used by modern armies in their training programs — psychological conditioning: stimulus-response, punishment or reward, repeated almost endlessly. What makes humans reluctant to kill each other is both a strong sense of empathy and a rational calculation of prudence. The former is the more important of the two. Empathy is that ability to feel another's pain and suffering as if it were your own. You know what grief, fear, sorrow they are going through, and you know you would not want to go through that yourself. You feel compassion for them and would not want to be the cause of inhumane deeds that put them in that way. It is the origin of what Christians call the golden rule: do unto others as you would have them do unto you; and of the Buddhist teaching that one is not only one's brother's keeper, in a very real sense one is one's brother since all things are interdependent and cannot flourish without each other. Then, for many, there is the strong conviction that all people are children of God, just like oneself, and deserve the right to life and liberty.[4] Prudence is the rational calculation that if you bomb someone's town and destroy it, they are going to want to do the same to you. Analytical reason leads people to want to raise questions and to process and evaluate answers. These sentiments or mental processes, empathy and reason, lie in the forebrain, the latest part of the brain to develop and that which sets us aside, to a very real degree, from the animals. Hatred and conditioning turn off or bypass that part of the brain. This is why we often describe men who brutalize others as animals, although this is hardly fair to the animals, among whom organized warfare is almost unknown. Turning off this part of the brain, honestly stated, is the goal of those who wish to turn boys into soldiers, who want the recruits to automatically, instantly, without question or evaluation, obey the order to kill. An effective combat soldier does not have empathy and does not think about the moral aspect of what he is going to do to another human being.

This is not to say that reason plays no part in modern warfare. To the contrary, it is essential to modern warfare, but only for the staff, the planning and command bureaucracy, not for the frontline soilders. The staff, which must prepare battle readiness even when there is no war, which plans for several different types of future wars and enemies, which plans overall battle strategies and must plan long in advance for complex avenues of supply and re-supply, requires the advanced use of strategic reasoning of a problem-solving sort, but this is not the same as moral reasoning. It is also true for the so-called defense intellectuals, those academics in think tanks such as the Rand Corporation or the Cato Institute who study and plan for wars and grand strategies. At this level, empathy appears to be entirely lacking. The problem to be solved is purely technical. Of course, physical distance from the actual gore and shrieks of the battlefield makes this much easier.

But not totally easy, for the paradox often sits in the mind of one and the same man at this level. Therefore there must be some rational justification for the war because, while it is obvious that these men would be horrified if some homicidal maniac raped and dismembered a child in the town where they live, they know they are setting in motion the killing of thousands of children, women, and old men as well as enemy soldiers. This is doubly true for those men who plan the targeting in a potential nuclear war, knowing they will cause the death of millions. Hence the need for powerful rationalizations for war that make it possible for them to compartmentalize their minds and tolerate the astronomical levels of brutality that comprise modern war. Just war doctrine, which in some form or other every nation appeals to before it goes to war, supplies the anesthetic. In Judeo-Christian doctrine, it makes an appeal to moral values. The secular version of it is simply an if-then calculation — do it to them before they do it to you. For both, however, there is the unquestioned assumption that wars have always existed and are inevitable in the future, so it's better to win them than to lose them, whatever level of brutality it takes.

Getting Men to Kill

The closer one is to another person, the harder it is to kill and the more traumatic the resultant psychological damage to the killer. Physical proximity often inhibits killing, even on the battlefield. There are numerous first-person narratives like the one that follows, recounting a group of American soldiers in World War II who jumped into a ditch during shelling only to find armed Germans sheltering there as well.

> And lo and behold there were about five Germans, and maybe four or five of us, and we didn't give any thought to fighting at first.... Then I realized, they had

their rifles, we had ours and then shells were landing and we were cowering against the ditch, the Germans were doing the same thing. And then the next thing you know there was a lull, we took cigarettes out and passed 'em around, we were smoking, and it's a feeling I cannot describe, but it's a feeling that this was not the time to be shooting at one another. They were human beings, like us, they were just scared.[5]

Killing is so difficult that the Army found in World War II that only 15 to 20 percent of the infantry fired their guns at the enemy in battle.[6] Many did not fire at all; others fired up in the air. In his exhaustive study of killing, psychologist and career army officer Lt. Colonel Dave Grossman observes "that there is in most men an intense resistance to killing their fellow man. A resistance so strong that, in many circumstances soldiers on the battlefield will die before they can overcome it."[7]

Of course, hundreds of thousands and even millions are killed in modern warfare. So if the infantry is not firing, who is? The main answer is that most casualties come either from a few men killing many with machine guns, or from artillery and bombing, where the enemy is at such a distance that he or she cannot be seen and the common humanity not felt. The explosion of a single artillery shell or 500-pound bomb can kill and maim many victims in an instant. Artillery crews are firing at "grid references," submariners are torpedoing "ships," bomber crews unloading on "targets." They can pretend they are not killing human beings. At close range, where you can see their eyes, it is almost impossible to kill unless the soldier has gone through powerful operant conditioning during training.

Geographic distance equals emotional distance. Snipers are seemingly able to kill with no problems, especially if they are using mechanical devices like long-range scopes or night scopes. For example, "Night-vision devices provide a superb form of psychological distance by converting the target into an inhuman green blob."[8] As one Israeli tank gunner wrote, "You see it all as if it were happening on a TV screen.... It occurred to me at the time; I see someone running and I shoot at him, and he falls, and it all looks like something on TV. I don't see people, that's one good thing about it."[9] This statement shows our amazing capacity for conscious self-deception, as in "I know what I am doing but I am going to pretend that I don't." The human mind is very complex.

Also, artillery are served by squads of men, and it seems that in groups the guilt or resistance factor is reduced by diffusing it through the unit. Grossman writes about "Group absolution: The individual is not a killer but the Group is."[10] Also, men are more likely to kill if ordered by a higher authority, hence the aim in all military training is to get men to obey orders instantly and without question.

After the results of the World War II studies were known, armies learned how to effectively condition recruits to overcome their innate resistance to killing. In Vietnam, the firing rates of the infantry were between 90 and 95 percent.[11] How did they achieve this? The world's militaries learned to adopt the techniques developed by psychologists for training or programming lab animals for automatic responses, such as Pavlov's famous experiments with dogs. Ring the bell, and dogs salivate. Provide the right stimulus and response training, and men attack automatically.

Grossman explains the techniques that led to the dramatic increase in firing rates in Vietnam: "Psychological conditioning was applied *en masse* to a body of soldiers, who, in previous wars were shown to be unwilling or unable to engage in killing activities."[12] Three methods are used in basic training: desensitization, conditioning, and denial defense mechanisms.

The first process is desensitization. How we name things is extremely important. It is through words that we mediate reality to our minds. Two kinds of naming, or language, are employed to desensitize: the positive, or euphemisms, which neutralize horrifically violent acts with deceitful terminology, and the negative, which justifies killing by dehumanizing the other. Both make doing violence or accepting violence done in one's name easier. Euphemisms are used in basic training to cloak the reality of what the recruits are preparing for. Firing at the enemy is not killing, it's "servicing" or "engaging the target," as if killing a man was providing him with a service or somehow akin to a man and a woman promising to marry. But euphemisms are more commonly used in communicating with the civilian population in order to mask the horrors they are expected to support. For example, after World War II, the U.S. War Department became the Defense Department. The concomitant slaughter of civilians in battle against enemy soldiers is called "collateral damage." A second bombing run on a city is called "revisiting the target." The word "invasion" is now frowned upon and replaced with "incursion." The 1983 airborne attack of the U.S. military on the tiny island of Grenada in the Caribbean was titled a "pre-dawn vertical insertion" and dead enemy soldiers are "decommissioned enemy quantum."[13] A bullet hole in a human being is a "ballistically induced aperture in the subcutaneous environment." Soldiers are just "doing their jobs," as though their "work" were no different from that of a bank clerk. The neutron bomb, a form of nuclear weapon in which the blast is minimized (insofar as that is possible), and the lethal radiation is maximized, is called by the Pentagon a "radiation enhancement device." And nuclear holocaust is called a "nuclear exchange."

Grossman writes that

the language of men at war is full of denial of the enormity of what they have done. Most soldiers do not "kill," instead the enemy was knocked over, wasted, greased, taken out, and mopped up. The enemy is hosed, zapped, probed, fired upon…. Even the weapons of war receive benign names — Puff the Magic Dragon [an AC 47 aircraft with tremendous rate of fire used in Vietnam], Fat Boy and Thin Man [the atom bombs that incinerated Hiroshima and Nagasaki] — and the killing weapon of the individual soldier becomes a piece or a hog, and a bullet becomes a round.[14]

Some of the military's euphemisms seem to be just silly. For example, a shovel is called a "combat emplacement evacuator," and a toothpick a "wood interdental stimulator." A parachute is an "aerodynamic personnel decelerator" and a zipper an "interlocking slide fastener." A pencil is a "portable hand-held communications inscriber." But this is not silly at all. These terms serve the function of setting off the soldier from the civilian population by means of a private language that gains more weight by appearing to be scientific and precise.[15]

Negative depictions are used to dehumanize the enemy. This works by extending the emotional distance between killer and killed. The men to be killed are not husbands, fathers, sons, teachers, and medics, but "gooks," "nips," "towel heads," "huns," "slants," "animals," "krauts," "vermin" and on and on. In the First Gulf War, the Iraqis were sometimes called "sand niggers." Hate is cultivated. And this hate and dehumanization easily spills over to the civilian population.

Richard Holmes writes in *Acts of War* that

A soldier who constantly reflected upon the knee-smashing, widow-making characteristics of his weapon, or who always thought of the enemy as a man exactly as himself, doing much the same task and subjected to exactly the same stresses and strains, would find it difficult to operate effectively in battle…. Without the creation of abstract images of the enemy, and without the deper-sonalization of the enemy during training, battle would become impossible to sustain.[16]

In explaining the preparation that led up to the atrocious massacre of civilians by American troops at My Lai, led by Lt. Calley, during the Vietnam War, Grossman refers to their basic training, when, in the words of one veteran, "his drill sergeant bellowed in his ear, 'Dinks are little shits. If you want their guts, you got to go low. Crouch and dig.'"[17] And Grossman quotes Holmes' book, *Acts of War*: "the road to My Lai was paved, first and foremost, by the dehumanization of the Vietnamese and the 'mere gook rule' which declared that killing a Vietnamese civilian did not really count."[18] This, combined with the heavy casualties the troops had been taking, and, according to one witness, the express order of their officer, Captain Medina, to "kill everything" (when asked if he meant women and children, he repeated the order), resulted in the massacre.[19] The purpose of dehumanization is to convince the soldier that there is a distinction between killing the "enemy" and murder. As we shall see in the section on psychological impacts of killing, it doesn't work very well.

Classical conditioning is carried out by thousands of repetitions, each successful trial being immediately rewarded. A Vietnam vet recalled his basic training: "We'd run PT (physical training) in the morning and every time your left foot hit the deck you'd have to chant, 'Kill, kill, kill, kill.'"[20] Grossman refers to such practices, which are thoroughly institutionalized in basic training, as the "boot camp deification of killing," and writes that what other observers have missed "is the role of (1) Pavlovian classical conditioning and (2) Skinnerian operant conditioning in modern training."[21]

> Instead of lying prone on a grassy field calmly shooting at a bulls-eye target, the modern soldier spends many hours standing in a foxhole, with full combat equipment draped about his body looking over an area of lightly wooded rolling terrain. At periodic intervals one or two olive-drab man-shaped targets at varying ranges will pop up in front of him for a brief time, and the soldier must instantly aim and shoot.... When he hits a target it provides immediate feedback by instantly and very satisfyingly dropping backward — just as a living target would. Soldiers are highly rewarded and recognized for success in this skill and suffer mild punishment ... for failure to quickly and accurately "engage" the targets — a standard euphemism for "kill."[22]

Some firing range "targets" are more realistic — three-dimensional with simulated blood that explodes when hit. Grossman goes on to say that "Every aspect of killing on the battlefield is rehearsed, visualized and conditioned."[23]

Of course, all of this is easier because, for the most part, the men being trained to kill are not men at all, but teenage boys. Armies recruit young adolescents because they are easier to train than older men. They have had very little experience of life. They want desperately to fit into a group and be accepted. They want to show that they are tough. And they are generally in dire need of reassurance from the authority figures who will guide and push them through a rite of passage that is hard but not insurmountable — that is, boot camp — and after which they will be welcomed to full manhood in elaborate graduation ceremonies. As former naval officer and now international journalist and documentary filmmaker Gwynne Dyer, said in his PBS series, *War*, "Anybody's son will do."

> The armed forces of every country can take almost any young male civilian and turn him into a soldier with all the right reflexes and attitudes in only a few weeks. Their recruits usually have no more than twenty years' experience of the world, most of it as children, while the armies have had all of history to perfect their technique.[24]

Basic training is designed to humiliate these young men, induct them into a dominator society *par excellence*, make them part of a mass, and separate them from "mere" civilians. Perhaps, as we will see later in the final section of this chapter, it is to set them off as the victims whose sacrifice is necessary to hold the society together. For example, Marine Corps recruits always arrive at camp in the dark, in the small hours of the morning after a long bus ride. This is by design so they will arrive tired and disoriented. As they are getting off the bus the drill sergeants are already yelling at them and harrying them along. Their civilian clothes, that which identifies each of them as an individual, are taken away, as is their hair. The verbal humiliation continues. They are told that they are just boys, mere weaklings—but the Marine Corps is going to make them into men. Over the next weeks they are given successively more difficult tasks to perform, although the bar is never so high that most eighteen-year-olds can't get over it.

Basic training is a carefully designed psychological program to break down their self-esteem and individual wills and then, by carefully calibrated stages, to build it up again but within the confines of this highly disciplined hierarchical society. They go through hours and hours of close-order drill, which is of no earthly use on the modern battlefield but which inculcates movement as part of a mass according to unquestioned orders. The military is the most extreme subset of dominator society allowed in our democratic culture and is in direct opposition to it. Basic training is a rite of passage and at the end the reward is a sense of manhood—very carefully prescribed and defined manhood—involving the willingness to kill and to die for one's country. They were boys; now they are men, men who will kill on command. And they are sent off to their "duty stations," to "do their job," as the accepted euphemism has it.

While modern conditioning has made it easier to kill in battle, nevertheless the killing of other enemy soldiers and civilians is not done without producing, in many cases, severe emotional trauma that often follows the soldiers for the rest of their lives.

Wounds to the Heart and Mind: The Psychological Damage of Combat

Having successfully conditioned the mass of soldiers to kill in combat, what have been the psychological effects on these men? In combat, men are forced to do and see things they never expected as they were growing up. When one does blow another's brains out, or cut him in half with a machine gun, or in hand-to-hand combat bayonet him in the belly or cut his throat or club him to death with the butt of a rifle, the impact on the psyche is severe, at least for many men. Also, the prolonged fear of being maimed or killed is traumatic, as is seeing the devastation wrought on cities and villages and knowing you were responsible. And then there is the indelible image of the bloody body parts all over the battlefield, and not only of soldiers — in modern war it is very often the remains of women and children. And there is the problem of dealing with a new and frightening knowledge about oneself and one's murderous rages. And, too, there is survivor guilt on the part of those who saw the buddy standing next to them decapitated while they went unscathed. A soldier can come out of a war without a single visible injury wound and nevertheless be wounded for life.

If a soldier spends long enough in battle, he will become a psychiatric casualty. The chances of this are greater than becoming a victim of enemy fire. In World War II over 800,000 men in the American army were classified unfit for military service due to psychiatric reasons, and, at one point, more men were being discharged for such causes than the Army was recruiting. A study by Swank and Marchand of World War II combat "determined that after sixty days of continuous combat, 98 percent of all surviving soldiers will have become psychiatric casualties of one kind or another," and the remaining 2 percent are likely to be psychopaths to start with.[25]

The soldier experiences an acute roller coaster of adrenaline rushes and subsequent backlashes. He can't flee but he can't overcome the danger or easily reconcile the guilt that comes either from killing another human being or refusing to do so and exposing his comrades to mortal danger. Grossman writes, "A soldier in this state will inevitably collapse from nervous exhaustion — the body will simply burn out."[26] The fear, exhaustion, and guilt produce familiar psychiatric symptoms: mental fatigue, crying fits, extreme anxiety or terror, hypersensitivity to sound, sweating, palpitations of the heart. Another result can be psychotic disassociation from reality, a confused state in which the soldier no longer knows where he is: symptoms include delirium, manic depression, and even Ganzer's syndrome, in which he makes jokes and acts silly. Amnesia, convulsive attacks, or curling up in the fetal position are also witnessed, as well as hysteria, extreme dramatic religiosity, and schizoid trends.[27]

In Vietnam the military resorted to tranquilizing drugs and phenothiazines to numb the frontline soldiers to the effects of the horrors of combat so that they could quickly be sent back into battle. But these drugs only treat the symptoms and do not deal with the long-term effects of extreme psychiatric stress. In fact, according to Grossman, they may well "supersede the development of effective coping mechanisms, resulting in an increase of long-term trauma…. At their best, these drugs only served to delay the inevitable confrontation with the pain, suffering, grief and guilt that the Vietnam veteran repressed and buried deep inside himself. And at worst, they actually increased the impact of the trauma suffered by the soldier."[28]

Even though all the conditioning works and soldiers are now enabled to kill other soldiers and sometimes civilians almost automatically, it still produces severe reactions because it is so far divorced from everything they learned before coming into the military. One U.S. Marine, upon breaking into a house where a sniper had been firing on his platoon, had this reaction:

> I was just absolutely gripped by the fear that this man would expect me and would shoot me. But as it turned out, he was in a sniper harness and he couldn't turn around fast enough. He was entangled in the harness so I shot him with a .45 and I felt remorse and shame. I can remember whispering foolishly, "I'm sorry" and then just throwing up…. I threw up all over myself. It was a betrayal of what I had been taught since a child.[29]

Vomiting is a common reaction for soldiers after killing another human being.

Following the Vietnam War, mental health professionals began to recognize and name a long-term psychiatric disturbance termed post-traumatic stress disorder or PTSD. Clinically it is defined as "a reaction to a psychologically traumatic event outside the range of normal experience."[30] It can involve a variety of symptoms, including recurring and intrusive nightmares, flashbacks, emotional deadening, social withdrawal, sleep disturbances and difficulty initiating and maintaining intimate relationships. The Vietnam War left somewhere around a million men with PTSD and they have a far higher than normal rate of heart disease, drug use, divorce, marital problems, alcoholism, high blood pressure and ulcers. They make up a large share of the homeless population and have a higher than average incidence of suicide. Often men suffering PTSD deny their pain and try to bury their grieving beneath a shell. They seldom join veterans' organizations. They tend to be loners. And they tend to be forgotten and even condemned by society. Psychiatric war casualties last a long time and it is not just the ex-soldiers who suffer. Their families and friends also pay the price of their broken lives.

Modern warfare is horrendously intense, violent and brutal. When you ask young men to violate everything they have ever been taught as right and good, and to murder and mutilate other young men and (inevitably) civilians, their minds will suffer and their behavior may well be distorted for the rest of their lives. It doesn't matter whether they believe the cause for which they were fighting was just or in vain. PTSD strikes in either case. Many soldiers coming home from the Iraq and Afghan wars are experiencing the same symptoms and are also finding that the military medical system is grossly underprepared to help them. Casualties continue.

Captain Shannon Meehan (U.S. Army, Ret.), a veteran of the war in Iraq, ordered the shelling of a dwelling that housed enemy insurgents, only to find out afterward that the insurgents were not there. He courageously shared his experience in an article in the *New York Times*:

The strike destroyed the house and killed everyone inside. I thought we had struck enemy fighters, but I was wrong. A father, mother and their children had been huddled inside. The feelings of disbelief that initially filled me quickly transformed into feelings of rage and self-loathing. The following weeks, months and years would prove that my life was forever changed. In fact, it's been nearly three years, and I still cannot remove from my mind the image of that family gathered together in the final moments of their lives. I can't shake it. It simply lingers. For many soldiers, what follows a killing is a struggle of the mind. We become aware that what we've seen has changed us. We can't unlearn it, and we continue to think of those innocent children. It is not possible to forget.[31]

Captain Meehan fell into the same emotional spiral that has afflicted so many returning soldiers.

War erodes one's regard for human life. Soldiers cause or witness so many deaths and disappearances that it becomes routine. It becomes an accepted part of existence. After a while, you can begin to lose regard for your own life as well. So many around you have already died, why should it matter if you go next? This is why so many soldiers self-destruct when they return from a deployment. I know something about this. The deaths that I caused also killed any regard I had for my own life. I felt that I did not deserve something that I had taken from them. I fell into a downward spiral, doubting if I even deserved to be alive. The value, or regard, I once had for my own life dissipated.[32]

He has found some relief in the joyous birth of his own son, but nothing is forgotten, nor should it be, he writes. "In recent months I've been trying to honor the lives I took by writing and speaking in public about my experience, to show that those deaths are not tucked neatly away in a foreign land. They may seem distant, but they are not. Soldiers bring the ghosts home with them, and it's everyone else's job to hear about them, no matter how painful it may be."[33]

It is disturbing to consider the ways in which the minds of young men are manipulated using psychological techniques in order to get them to kill and the ways that killing disturbs their minds. But there is an even more disturbing hypothesis about psychology and the very existence of war itself. Scholar Richard Koenigsberg and others argue that war is the result of an unconscious desire on the part of a society as a whole to kill its own young men in order to prove the very existence of a meaningful society that can confirm our existence. War, they say, is a mass psychopathology the subconscious origins and motivations of which we refuse to recognize.

Koenigsberg has recast the perception of war from its traditional explanations as normative, glorious and honorable.[34] He argues that we are delusional if we think the colossal slaughter and maiming of young men and civilians of all ages can be characterized in that way. The emperor has no clothes. War is about the mass production of corpses and mutilated bodies. War is a sickness, a psychopathology that grips whole nations and yet one to which they remain blind. War arises out of the irrational subconscious mind of the collective. While men say they go to war for honor, or territory, or self-defense, or empire, or whatever political or economic cause, in fact they go to war to prove that the nation is real and the only way to do that is to show its power by its ability to sacrifice human beings to itself. And, he asserts, not only those of the "enemy," but even more so, its own young men. In fact, we go to war in order to get our own boys killed. Then we can feel a meaningful emotional relationship to the nation. That, he argues, is what patriotism is all about.

He extrapolates from the sociologist Emile Durkheim, the psychiatrist Sigmund Freud, and the anthropologist René Girard. In brief, Durkheim argued that the nation, like other institutions, is a mental construct, an invention of convenience to counter the centrifugal forces that would, if unchecked, tear society apart. In reality, living within these continually shifting boundaries are different classes and ethnic groups and religious sects and individuals with different interests, all divided from one another in varying degrees of competition and even hostility. Advanced industrial societies especially require a "common faith, a common *conscience collective*, if they were not to disintegrate into heaps of mutually antagonistic and self-seeking individuals."[35] So what holds them together? The myth, or totem, of the nation. Durkheim believed that God is society writ large, and hence our identification with society is emotionally extremely powerful, especially since this nation-state god requires ritual sacrifice.

The social psychologists who make this argument also rely on Freud, who believed that our conscious life is in fact determined by infantile unconscious desires and fears. During the nineteenth century, the dominant trend in Western thought was positivism, which subscribed to the belief that people could ascertain real knowledge concerning themselves and their environment and judiciously exercise control over both. Freud, however, suggested that such declarations of free will are in fact delusions; we are not entirely aware of what we think and often act for reasons that have little to do with our conscious thoughts.

Girard argues that this disparate conglomerate of people and groups we call society, or our nation, can only continue to exist in some semblance of unity if it identifies a scapegoat, a sacrificial victim, and so deflects violence outward, as the Germans did with the Jews, just to take the most famous case. We know who we are and we validate who we are by destroying the enemy. "We" are not "them" and define ourselves in contrast to them. Koenigsberg argues that war is also just such a case of sacrificial victimization, but, and here is where he is original and not derivative, he argues that the necessary sacrifice includes a society's own young men as well as the "enemy." War exists because it satisfies a powerful psychological need, the need to believe that there is something greater than the individual self, something worth making sacrifices for, as it were. In short, the enemy only provides a convenient excuse to kill our own young men, and they provide the mask or taboo that prevents us from recognizing what we are doing.

Like all three of the theorists on whose arguments he builds his own, Koenigsberg and others who make this argument are irrationalists — that is, they believe the forces that cause and perpetuate war are the dark, unrecognized forces of the violent and irrational subconscious, demons that do not want to be exorcised. Perhaps this might account for the extreme anger that some people feel when others protest against a particular war or weapons system, or even against the flag that is the symbol or totem of the nation. They feel threatened at the very core of their beings, thinking perhaps as follows: "Because, if my child did not die or suffer mutilation for something great and honorable, then this mutilation of a life is a meaningless waste and I helped kill my own beloved. And what does that make me?" It would require too much emotional and psychic pain to risk thinking along these lines, and so the real generator of war is beyond rational control. The implication of this hypothesis is that trying to control or eliminate war by showing how irrational or dysfunctional it is in economic or political terms, or by trying to create institutions such as the United Nations or the International Criminal Court for genocide, is a waste of time. This hypothesis also explains why peace advocates often become the enemy, and sometimes the sacrificial victims. They must be discredited if we are to go on with our comforting beliefs and not wake up to the fact that we are butchering our children for no good cause.

The great paradox here, encountered first by Freud, is that using reason one discovers how irrational we are. Freud thought, of course, that by elevating the irrational to consciousness, it could be dealt with — hence psychoanalysis on the individual level. One supposes that the same is true at the level of the collective. However, the cure rate of psychoanalysis has not been encouraging. We do not want to know what we are doing. Koenigsberg points out that we are only able to believe in honor and noble sacrifice if we do not look at the bodies of the soldiers who have been so horribly mangled. For instance, in World War II American journalists were prohibited from photographing our own dead, and in the wars against Iraq, the U.S. government prohibited the photographing even of flag-draped coffins coming home. But wouldn't his thesis actually require that? The bodies are the proof of the great value of the nation and of our belonging to it.

And what about the fact that so many millions went willingly over the top and walked into certain death being spewed by the machine guns? Had they taken on the role of sacrificial lamb, internalized it as ones set apart? Koenigsberg believes the answer is yes. Somehow it is assumed that soldiers will "do their duty," even to the extent of forfeiting their lives. Yet what a radical form of behavior this was — walking into machine-gun fire. The behavior of soldiers in the First World War contradicts what biologists and psychologists tell us about the instinct for survival.[36] It must be something very powerful. Jean Elshtain believes that these sacrifices are part of "modern state worship."[37] The state has taken the place of God. "In war, actual human bodies are sacrificed in the name of perpetuating a magical entity, the body politic. Sacrificial acts function to affirm the reality or existence of this sacred object, the nation. Entering into battle may be characterized as a devotional act, with death in war constituting the supreme act of devotion."[38] It is, after all, what Lincoln said at Gettysburg — "the last full measure of devotion" — and we commonly call it the "supreme sacrifice." How close are we to admitting the truth of this terrible hypothesis?

Certainly Koenigsberg and others are right to unmask war, to show it to be a profoundly stupid enterprise. And he is right to raise the question of, why men willingly sacrifice themselves, as the millions did in World Wars I and II. Why do our children buy into this self-destructive myth? Surely there is something profoundly irrational about modern war, about tolerating inevitable deaths and mutilations in the millions.

The hypothesis might also go far in explaining how followers of Christianity, whose God preaches nonviolence and compassion, can deny the obvious rational application of their central teaching and instead endorse the slaughter of countless others of God's children. And Robert Bellah's thesis about the existence of a civil religion that is a conjoining of religious and political myths ("In God We Trust," laying a hand on the Bible to be sworn in to high office, military chaplains, etc.) is empirically demonstrable.[39] Just as certainly the state seems to trump the church.

Nevertheless, there are some serious problems with Koenigsberg's thesis, and there are some alternate explanations for the seemingly inexplicable behavior of generals who send boys off to slaughter, the boys who go, and the civilians who endorse it.

To begin with, it is a nondisconfirmable hypothesis. He points to a phenomenon that cannot be seen. One cannot disprove the non-existence of the unseen and unseeable, the collective unconscious. A person could say that modern war is caused by invisible demons, and while patently false, there is no way to prove it is not so. Second, there are anthropological considerations that weigh against it. If it is necessary to have mass slaughter of a nation's young men in order to keep the nation from flying apart, what about those societies that do not indulge in modern warfare: the Swedes, the Norwegians, the Costa Ricans (who do not even have an army), and many others? The Koenigsberg thesis is a universalizing hypothesis but it does not cover all the cases.

There are other problems. In his favorite example, World War I, the French army did finally mutiny and refused to leave the trenches. The German navy mutinied at Kiel. And the Russians actually left the trenches and walked home in 1917. Also, the vast number of psychological casualties, the so-called shell shocked, were another case of refusing to participate in the insanity, albeit by becoming passively insane. And even this was very difficult, not because of some mass psychosis, but simply because for soldiers to refuse to attack requires a great deal of coordination and planning, which are not only unlikely on a battlefield but also prevented by the officers, who, under nearly all circumstances, would shoot anyone on sight who proposed it. That is why soldiers who are about to mutiny shoot their officers.

It is far more reasonable to propose that people put up with the insanity of modern war because their cultures provide them with no alternative, with no peace system, no other means to settle differences, no knowledge of the reality of peace. Their governments lie to them about the reality of war, both its nature and its necessity. Living in a society that is dominated by a war system — its institutions, norms, beliefs, all supported by the media and educational system — gives them no other way to think. This is a more positive approach to the problem of war and offers a surer way out. But Koenigsberg makes us think, makes us realize that the task of turning humanity around to a society characterized by a peace system will not be easy. Nevertheless, there is plenty of explanatory power in that which is visible and empirically verifiable without needing to resort to an unseen, and very sick, collective subconscious.

So how do we break out of this iron cage of warfare so that we do not have to do this any longer? What does a peace system look like, and how do we move from the no-longer-functional war system to a culture of peace in which there will be no more mass violence, death, and PTSD?

First, we have to understand how the war system self-perpetuates.

CHAPTER 3

The War System, Part 1

Why do we have war after war after war? Wars do not really, as the common parlance has it, "break out." They are not accidents or departures from the norm in our peculiar type of social system. Just as moving large amounts of oil around dangerous oceans in tankers will inevitably result in a certain percentage of major spills, so, too, will a system of conflict management such as ours inevitably produce war. While it sounds contradictory, war is a necessary by-product of the security system we have become used to. Robert Holmes observes, "The problem isn't so much a lack of desire for peace as it is a commitment to institutions that make peace impossible.... As a result, we today have inherited a world deeply committed to war."[1]

By war I mean war as we know it — highly organized, institutionalized, violent conflict managed by sovereign states in which large-scale killing takes place as a result of strategic planning and conscious tactics, primarily for appropriation of territory, resources, or the top place in the pecking order, or as a response to aggression aimed at one of these ends. At least since 1648 such wars have taken place in a war system. A war system is a set of ideas, values, institutions, behaviors and hardware (weaponry) exercised by sovereign states in a mutually reinforcing relationship with one another so that the normative outcome is war. It is an institutionalized method of dealing with interstate and intrastate conflict using violence that becomes self-fueling and self-perpetuating, a system characterized by positive feedback.

The answer to the question of why we have war is this: we have war because we have war. War is overdetermined; its supporting norms are self-fueling and robustly redundant. Wars produce the conditions for future wars. How does this social system work?

Much of the thinking that guides policy-makers and ordinary citizens in their decisions about war and peace follows very traditional lines. The traditional thinking in academic fields such as international relations, political science, and government has been in a very deep rut for a very long time. It is often based on unquestioned assumptions and proceeds according to linear analysis. The most common of the unquestioned assumptions are these: first, that war has always been with us; second, that it is the common and usual condition of humans; third, that it is rooted in human nature; and fourth, that, unfortunate as it is, it can't be changed. Self-proclaimed "realists" avow that they understand these conventional truths and argue that those who disagree with them are not even legitimately in the discourse. Those who disagree are disparaged as utopians, sentimentalists, or dreamers whose views can be ignored.

This is the box inside which we have caged our thinking for centuries, perhaps millennia. Thus we approach conflict in terms of military strategies. In particular, wars are fought, won or lost. The general, overall result is continual warfare, which exacerbates and perpetuates conflict. We think only about particular wars, and how to prevail in them. The thinking is all tactical and strategic. It is never systemic. We do not think much about War (with a capital "W"), and how to end it. What we humans now need to do is think outside the cage. We need to break out from this conventional thinking, draw back, and look at it from a distance. We do this by asking new questions.

To start with, two very basic questions need to be asked about the so-called realist position. The first is whether or not this is indeed an accurate description of reality, and the second is whether or not it is functional, whether or not it works to provide genuine security for all.

It is not accurate. As discussed earlier, many historians now think that war is a fairly recent invention in terms of the overall history of humans. Fully modern humans have been around for at least 160,000 years or maybe longer, and war as we understand it — that is, as the preplanned, highly organized, strategic use of mass slaughter in battles carried out by the state — has been with us only for a few thousand years. Its origins in Western civilization go back to around 4000 BC. Hunters and gatherers did not know war and it now appears that neither did the first agriculturalists. So war has been with us for less than one twentieth of our existence as a species. Modern war, or total war, by which I mean the industrialized mass slaughter carried out by mobilizing whole societies for killing, has been with us only since World War I, or roughly one sixteen-hundredth of our history as a species. War is not innate.

What is more, war is not the common condition of humankind; it is the exception. Most people never experience a war. Most nations do not experience war for very long periods of time. And while we Americans live in one of the exceptions to this rule, even the U.S. is generally not at war with most of the other nation states. We have never been at war with Peru, New Zealand,

Australia, Algeria, Egypt, Israel, Malaysia, South Africa, Venezuela, and so on. We have not been at war with Mexico since 1848 or Canada since 1815. While we fought Germany twice in the previous century, we fought only for 6 of its 100 years. And so while there is always some war somewhere in the world, peace is the general condition of humanity. If war were rooted in human nature, genetic, as we say these days, then all humans would be fighting all the time. Since they are not, all we can say is that the tendency toward individual aggression may be genetic, but so is the tendency toward cooperation. A particular society can encourage and reward either tendency. War is a social invention, one that happens to be strongly encouraged by the modern, national security state. Therefore, war is not inevitable, but it is an endemic social system of the type analyzed in the Introduction. The war system can be analyzed at two levels: the level of the nation state and, above that, the world level where nation states compete, often violently. In each case we can observe the elements, rules and behavior that stabilize the system and perpetuate the practice of warfare and how each of these strengthens the others.

The War System at the World Level

At the world level the main elements are nation states arrayed against one another. This is the so-called state of nature made famous by the seventeenth-century English philosopher, Thomas Hobbes, in his Latin epigram, "*bellum omnium contra omnes*," the war of all against all.[2] Hobbes said that before there was any government to keep the peace, each person and group was potentially at war with every other person or group. While this probably does not describe prehistoric society before the emergence of central governments, it definitely describes the historic and current international condition — almost two hundred sovereign nation states and no government over them to make them keep the peace. It is a condition of anarchy. The overriding rule in this war system is national sovereignty, that is, no state recognizes a legitimate authority beyond itself unless to do so appears to be in its self-interest. This makes for the second rule as well — the rule of competition, a competition that is seen as a zero sum game. If nation A gains power, it is because nation B lost it. The nature of conflict is perceived to be either win or lose. While not all of them play the deadly game, many do, and at differing levels of power. Since each nation sees its neighbors as potential enemies, as a threat, it arms itself and acts as tough as it can. Seeing such behavior, the other nations conclude that their neighbor is a potential enemy and they arm and act tough, confirming the suspicions of the original nation. Each tries to achieve security by preparing for war and feeds the fears of the others. This is called the "security dilemma." In systems terminology, it is a strength. It helps perpetuate the war system.

The Romans knew this game and played it until it killed them. The Romans put it similarly: "*Si pacis, para bellum,*"[3] if you want peace, prepare for war. But, of course, it didn't work, since war breeds war. The wars they fought and the domination they sought eventually backfired on them.

Because conflicts are adversarial and sometimes escalate to war, there is enough war in the system to sufficiently frighten everybody into staying as armed as they can. Thus, in a war system, peace gets narrowly conceived of as security and security gets defined as a military problem. Of course, this perpetuates the entire system. It runs on the basis of self-fulfilling prophecy. That is one of the reasons it looks so inevitable. It is a circle of self-perpetuating violence. It is as if we were all standing in a circle, each with our little pile of treasures at our feet (land, oil, minerals, doctrines and dogmas), afraid that everyone else wants our little pile, since we know we would like theirs. So we all have guns pointed at each other. No one has the courage to be the first to put his down. So we stand there, age after age after age, and every once in a while the guns go off. People are blown to bits. Fear is multiplied. Revenge takes root and thrives. This armed anarchy is a system strength. It perpetuates the war system.

Another dimension of this system strength is that national security states must always be as prepared as possible, ready for any contingency. Since they do not know what their rivals may do, they prepare for the worst and do so on the basis of their rival's military capabilities, or what they believe them to be. In short, national security planners and operatives are always looking for and preparing for the next war and they see it everywhere. At one point in the Reagan administration, the secretary of defense, Casper Weinberger, described the relationship with the Soviet Union as a "state of permanent pre-hostility." This, of course, confirmed the Soviet's fears of U.S. hostility and potential war. Even 20 years after the Cold War ended, the United States was seeking to place an anti-missile defense system on the borders of Russia.

In a war system, even peace gets defined in terms of war. The cynical American humorist, Ambrose Bierce, was not far off the mark when he defined peace in his *Devil's Dictionary* as "in international affairs, that period of cheating between two periods of fighting."[4] The United States military picked up on Weinberger's unfortunate phrase and often refers to peace as "permanent pre-hostility."[5] Its euphemism for war is "violence processing."[6]

But more telling is the Latin meaning of "pax," as in *Pax Romana* or *Pax Americana*. It refers to the kind of treaty that the victors impose on the losers, a dominator's peace, an order of the subjugated called, in the terminology of peace studies, "structural violence." Peace treaties are documents signed at the end of a war. Thus the feedback in the system is positive, perpetuating it with threat and counter-threat, fear, suspicion and revenge. The most obvious case in modern history is the treaty signed at the end of the Franco-Prussian War of 1870, when the Prussians took the Alsace and Lorraine provinces from France, so that, in 1914, the French were eager for World War I in order to get them back, which they did. And the dictated peace that humiliated Germany after that war led inevitably to Hitler and World War II.

In addition, the mentality of the operators of the international state competition is Machiavellian. It is based on a worst-case estimate of human nature and the behavior of states. The operators assume that their rivals will go to any lengths and will ruthlessly employ any means — lying, cheating, stealing, killing, and so on — to gain advantage in the power struggle. And, since the maintenance of the state is the *ultima ratio* for these national security managers, they will likewise go to any lengths to protect their state. Any values that get in the way of this will be ignored when push comes to shove, even if it be a long tradition of human rights or democracy. They all believe that the end justifies the means. All morality falls by the wayside. They are all willing to use terror. And, in this aspect of the war system as well, the self-fulfilling prophecy works. We have seen recently that even in a well-established democracy such as that of the United States, the suspension of the rule of trial by law (*habeas corpus*) and the legalization of torture will be used when the threat to the state seems great enough to the elites in power.

Suspecting the evil behavior of its neighbor, a national security state seeks to protect itself by employing the same amoral or immoral methods, thus proving to its neighbor that it too must adopt such Machiavellian methods. The entire system operates at the lowest possible level. The Soviet Union used spies and executed spies, and the U.S. did the same while each proclaimed the moral high ground to their citizens. The Nazis bombed open cities from the air and the Allies did the same in response, slaughtering millions of innocents.

Another link in the war system at the global level is between the political and economic systems. The most obvious example here is the link between the national security state and the export of arms by private manufacturers. The state, in an eternal quest for revenues and for economic growth, coordinates and facilitates the sales of arms to other states. The arms manufacturers participate in this for the obvious reason — immense profits. The result is that more and more arms come into the system. But the arms do not flow into the system uniformly — that is, arms of the same destructive power are not distributed everywhere simultaneously. The streams are uneven and variously timed. This upsets the distribution of power and creates fears and suspicions. This is especially true because, given the logic of the system, a nation must not take the risk of calculating its own preparedness needs on its assessment of the intent of its neighbors, but on the basis of their military capabilities. If a neighbor in the region has suddenly acquired a large tank army, or medium-range missiles, then the other states in the region must assume they might use them, and so they prepare by acquiring more arms or arranging new military alliances. For example, the United States has poured billions of dollars' worth of arms into Egypt, Iraq under Saddam Hussein, and Iran under the shah, and Israel as well. The Soviet Union did the same for its Arab client states. Pouring more high-tech weapons into the Middle East is clearly a destabilizing factor that has raised suspicions and unbalanced the equilibrium of power and made the wars fought there all the more destructive.[7]

In such a climate, achieving technical superiority over one's rivals is highly desirable. It is self-evident that a nation must try to develop better weapons than its potential enemies, weapons that are more destructive and/or whose delivery to target is more assured. As nation A sees nation B engaging in this kind of research and development it will follow suit, initiating an arms race that is, nevertheless, futile. Technology is not susceptible to secrecy, at least not for very long. After World War II, when the United States was the sole possessor of the atomic bomb, it was believed that the Soviet Union would not develop such a weapon for at least 25 years. In fact, they exploded their first atom bomb in 1949, just four years after the U.S.. The efforts to prevent other nations from getting the atom bomb if they wanted it have also failed in spite of the Nuclear Non-proliferation Treaty.[8] Once India had the bomb, Pakistan had to have it. And the soon-to-be Iranian bomb is a response to the Israeli bomb. And so nation B will get the same weapons after a little while, which will then prod nation A to acquire even more lethal weapons. This part of the system is also self-fueling, resulting in each successive war becoming more deadly than the last. The nuclear arms race between the Soviet Union and the United States culminated in the absurdity of 50,000 warheads or the equivalent of 6000 World War II–size catastrophes capable of being detonated in a single afternoon.

The war system is so robust that even the supra-national institutions created to control it, such as the United Nations and the World Court, are instead designed so that they will be subservient to it. The United Nations is an international body made up of sovereign national security states and its approach to conflict, while not a national security approach, is a collective security approach. Conflicts are still solved, as a final resort, by appeal to war, although the great powers make it very difficult even for this deviation from national security to operate through their control of the Security Council veto. Responding to popular demands at the end of the Second World War for an end to war for good, the managers of national security states were unable and unwilling to conceive of and implement a genuine peace system. They were too insecure and unimaginative to give up the model of the sovereign national security state. They did not outlaw war, they outlawed aggression, and since any nation that wants to make war will concoct an excuse that their attack is defensive (Hitler claimed in 1939 that the Poles had invaded Germany), the Charter was flawed at the start.

National security states are in competition for the world's resources. To be effective at the "game" of industrialized warfare requires oil and strategic minerals and the ability to ensure their flow to one's own country. This is done through trade, but behind the velvet glove of trade is the mailed fist. In the nineteenth century the British navy made sure that the advantages of so-called free trade flowed to England. Since World War II, the U.S. navy has done the same. The carrier attack groups that sailed to the Gulf in 1990 were not on a pleasure cruise. That war and the subsequent one were principally about control of oil, regardless of the propaganda that was promulgated to whip up public enthusiasm for the conflicts. These wars, as is always the case in a war system, raised the level of fear, hostility and violence in the region, making future peace more problematic.

To reiterate Schmookler's thesis, in a state of international anarchy just one aggressive national security state can force otherwise peaceful states into a war system by limiting their choices. They can submit and be absorbed by the aggressor. They can choose to fight, but only by imitating their enemy, and win or lose, the mode of violent conflict is established in the system. Or they can flee and leave the field to the aggressor, although today there is nowhere on earth to flee to. In the absence of a robust peace system, one state can force war on the system, and the others are powerless to choose peace. This is how the system currently functions at the international level and how it has functioned for some 6000 years. It is the iron cage of war. Quite possibly this would be enough to perpetuate war in the absence of a peace system. But the war system receives even further positive feedback from militaristic institutions and norms within the national security state.

How the War System Functions Within the State

At the national level — that is, inside national security states — there are many elements that provide positive feedback to the nation state's aggressive posture and militaristic behavior. The most important set of institutions comprise the national security apparatus, an interlocking directorate made up of those elected and appointed officials whose jobs are to keep the nation ready to be an actor in the Hobbesian anarchy. In the case of the U.S., this includes

THE PENTAGON. The nerve center of the world's largest war-making organization houses 26,000 defense workers in 6.5 million square feet of office space linked by 17.5 miles of corridors. Here are coordinated the hundreds of billions of dollars' worth of annual procurement and payout operations and all the war planning and contingency planning for the globe, which the U.S. army has divided into five military commands, each headed by its own general. (Theodor Horydczak Collection, Prints & Photographs Division, Library of Congress, LC-H814-T-W02-005-A)

the president in his role as commander-in-chief, his national security advisor, the National Security Council, the National Security Administration, the Secretary of Defense and directly under him the Joint Chiefs of Staff, the vast Pentagon bureaucracy, the Director of the CIA and all of the bureaucrats in that organization, and the Department of Homeland Security. In addition there are the so-called Service Academies: West Point, the Air Force Academy, and the Naval Academy, the various war colleges including the Army War College and the Naval War College, and what was formerly called the "School of the Americas," now renamed the Western Hemisphere Institute for Security Cooperation, at Fort Benning, Georgia, where Latin American military personnel have been trained in how to suppress their own people using violence. Among others, Manuel Noriega was a graduate.

In a state like the U.S., these vast bureaucracies involve tens of thousands of positions, not including actual fighting men and women, the soldiers, sailors and air force personnel. This huge, interlocking social system is geared toward keeping the war system functioning. It knows no other purpose, never questions the assumptions of the war system, and is prone to the phenomenon of group think where non-conventional ideas almost never come to the surface. Every major power and many minor ones have this kind of official war bureaucracy. Within the system, all the rewards, including the promotions, salary increases, status, reputation, and pension levels, go toward maintaining and strengthening the system. These organizations have access to huge economic resources. And finally, they are all followers of Hobbes and Machiavelli.

The Military Industrial Complex

If this were all there was to the intra-state features of the war system it would perhaps be enough to maintain war in the world, but the war system is far more robust than this. In addition to its official bureaucracy, there are other layers of institutions in the society that support war in various ways. In the U.S., one of the systemic features is the so-called iron triangle, a mutually supportive relationship between the Pentagon, Congress, and the corporations that manufacture and supply weapons and other war materiel. Based on its worst-case scenarios of the international situation, the Pentagon asks for as much money as it can get from Congress. Congress is only too happy to accede to its demands, and sometimes exceeds them. This is because each member can then go back into his or her district and claim to the voters that they have brought jobs and economic growth into the district, as the military contracts go to manufacturers and suppliers. The Pentagon is only too happy to make sure that the contracts for large weapons systems such as the new F-22 fighter planes, are divided out into hundreds of congressional districts in order to create support for the appropriation and for the military approach to international conflict in general.[9] The manufacturers and suppliers are delighted with the system since they get the inflated contracts. Voters are pleased because they get jobs. Again, nearly all the feedbacks are positive. There are few, if any, negative feedbacks and the system accelerates out of control. In a wealthy nation like the U.S., it provides a level of armaments out of all proportion to any rational assessment of genuine need and so wars have to be "found" to justify the expenditure. This alliance of national security bureaucrats and weapons manufacturers can be found in all major powers in forms peculiar to their particular societies. In the old Soviet Union it was known as the Metal Eaters Alliance.

The military industrial complex is an impressively large operation not only in the U.S. but also worldwide. It dwarfs such sectors as public health, education, or environmental protection in nearly all countries.

War making is the world's biggest business. The U.S. military is itself a major multinational with assets equal to half of all U.S. manufacturing corporations combined. Nearly 40 percent of industrial plants and equipment is devoted to military manufacturing; about 30 percent of all U.S. industry output was purchased by the Pentagon in 1989.[10]

Almost every major corporation in the U.S. is involved in military contracts. General Electric, whose slogan is "We bring good things to life," made nuclear weapon components for decades until a boycott forced it to sell the business to another contractor. The links between government and the arms manufacturers were made clear by the tax preferences given to the latter. For example, in one year GE made profits of $6.5 billion and not only paid no corporate income taxes but also received tax refunds of $238 million.[11]

Major military contractors in the U.S. include Lockheed Martin ($17 billion in 1992), Boeing ($16.6 billion), Northrop Grumman ($8.7 billion), Raytheon ($7 billion), General Dynamics ($7 billion), United Technologies ($3.6 billion), Science Applications International Corporation ($2.1 billion), TRW ($2 billion), Health Net ($1.7 billion), L-3 Communications Holdings ($1.7 billion).[12] Also making significant money out of tax dollars were Honeywell, Inc., Hughes, Rockwell, and Textron. The Department of Defense Office of Public Affairs announces on their website the contracts awarded each day. As a typical case, eleven contracts were awarded on April 22, 2010, totaling $279,290,000. Two samples were as follows:

American Science and Engineering, Inc., Billerica, Mass., was awarded on April 20 a $48,818,439 firm-fixed-price contract. This contract is to procure up to 37 backscatter van military trailer scanner systems for entry control points in Afghanistan. Work is to be performed in Billerica, Mass., with an estimated completion date of Jan. 17, 2011. One bid was solicited with one bid received. Research, Development & Engineering Command, Natick Contracting Division, Orlando, Fla., is the contracting activity [W911QY-10-C-0078].

M&H Enterprises, Inc., dba Martin-Harris Construction, Las Vegas, Nev., was awarded on April 20 a $41,573,312 firm-fixed-price contract for the construction of the Lackland Airman Training Center Dormitory #2. Work is to be performed in Lackland Air Force Base, Texas, with an estimated completion date of April 30, 2012. Bids were solicited on the World Wide Web with 16 bids received. U.S. Army Engineer District, Fort Worth, Texas, is the contracting activity [W9126G-10-C-0021].[13]

To influence the government into maximum spending many of these companies have formed and support three lobbying associations: the Aerospace Industries Association, the Electronics Industries Alliance, and the National Defense Industrial Association.

General Dynamics employs 86,600 people worldwide and has four divisions: Aerospace, Combat Systems, Marine Systems, and Information Systems and Technology. They build battle tanks; infantry fighting vehicles; mobile-bridge systems; armor, chemical and biohazard detection equipment; and much more. In 2007 the U.S. administration was preparing a sale of arms to Saudi Arabia totaling $20 billion, including advanced satellite bombs, upgrades to its fighters and new naval vessels. To "balance things out" in the Middle East, they promised the Israelis $30.4 billion worth of military aid over the next ten years.[14]

Worldwide, almost $2 million was spent each minute on the military in the late twentieth century. During the 40 years of the Cold War, the U.S. and Soviet Union spent astronomical sums on their militaries. As of 1995, six years after the Cold War was over and the Soviet Union had collapsed, the U.S. was still spending $820 million a day. But these expenditures were not confined to big powers. The poor, third-world country of Ethiopia, which periodically experiences famines caused by desertification, could have reversed its environmental deterioration by spending some $50 million a year for reforestation. Instead, the government in Addis Ababa pumped $275 million per year into its military between 1975 and 1985.[15] Uganda spent half its gross domestic income on arms, Peru 30 percent of its budget, Afghanistan and Pakistan about 40 percent. For comparison, these nations spent about 2 percent of their income on health and education.[16] War is a big business.

The executive branch is also involved. Since "defense" is such a sacred cow, presidents and presidential candidates can sound patriotic and virtuous by inflating the military budget. And, of course, the weapons manufacturers' lobbies are able to provide campaign contributions to those candidates, most of whom are incumbents who look with favor on inflated military budgets. It is all wrapped in the flag and, on a darker note, undergirded by stimulating fear. As captured Nazi war criminal former Air Marshall Hermann Göring pointed out to his captors shortly before his death in a Nuremburg prison:

> Naturally the common people don't want war; neither in Russia, nor in England, nor in America, nor in Germany. That is understood. But after all, it is the leaders of the country who determine policy, and it is always a simple matter to drag the people along, whether it is a democracy, or a fascist dictatorship, or a parliament, or a communist dictatorship. Voice or no voice, the people can always be brought to the bidding of the leaders. That is easy. All you have to do is to tell them they are being attacked, and denounce the pacifists for lack of patriotism and exposing the country to danger. It works the same in any country.[17]

The fact is that the U.S. military budget is the largest in the world, nearly larger than those of all other nations combined. According to the Department of Defense, the 2010 Pentagon request was for $663.8 billion, more than the entire world spends on international aid.[18] This does not include the budget for nuclear weapons, which is housed in the Department of Energy. But in a social system geared to war, it is simply disloyal and political suicide to ask "How much is enough?"

Prior to the Iraq war, the Strategic Integrated Operating Plan of the Pentagon claimed that the U.S. could be ready to fight two World War-II-size wars and an Iraq-size war simultaneously. This proved to be a preposterous fantasy because fighting a modern war is fabulously expensive, as the United States has learned to its dismay in Iraq. The economic cost of attempting to defeat a counter-insurgency and control a civil war in a third-rate power such as already-defeated Iraq is running into hundreds of billions of dollars, requiring deficit financing on a scale never before seen. Counter-insurgencies and asymmetric wars may be more expensive, kill per kill, than a conventional war on a set battlefield. So there can never be enough money appropriated from the people.

In addition to the obvious benefit to politicians and defense contractors, there are immense benefits for military officers in keeping the budget large and the programs for weapons development going. If a procurement officer

CHILDREN PLEDGE ALLEGIANCE TO THE FLAG. One of the first loyalties children learn is to the state. They are taught the pledge in a peer pressure situation long before they receive any education in critical thinking, and by the time they do, these loyalties are deeply imprinted and resistant to reason. (Stock Photo)

or program development officer is successful, he is likely to receive promotion to a higher rank, which brings not only greater prestige but also comes with a higher retirement pay. Additionally, after retirement, some of these officers find lucrative employment with the very weapons contractors to whom they assigned contracts or with whom they worked on various programs.

The system grinds on and on. In a recent note, in April 2010, the White House asked Congress for $250 million in start-up funds to develop the "Prompt Global Strike" system, "a new class of weapons capable of reaching any corner of the earth from the United States in under an hour and with such accuracy and force that they would greatly diminish America's reliance on its nuclear arsenal.... In theory, the weapon will hurl a conventional warhead of enormous weight at high speed and with pinpoint accuracy, generating the localized destructive power of a nuclear warhead."[19] Final cost for development and deployment is unknown. If successful, it will facilitate the Pentagon's doctrine of "full spectrum dominance" of the world, arousing further fears in the minds of our neighbors.

There are other elements and feedback mechanisms internal to the nation that help support and perpetuate the war system. The educational institution is a major element, teaching and reinforcing patriotism and loyalty to national symbols in the lower grades before children can reason. In many schools in the U.S., the Pledge of Allegiance is required at the beginning of the school day and classrooms display the American flag. Also, the way in which history is taught is both war-ist and chauvinist in most countries, undergirding and perpetuating into the next generation the belief that war is an inevitable norm and therefore the only thing to do is to win it when it comes, and that our nation is always on the side of right. There is almost no critical thinking about the war system in the lower grades and high school. Children take their cultural cues from the adults. An especially disturbing picture appeared in the *Washington Report on Middle Eastern Affairs*, showing young Israeli schoolgirls inking messages onto artillery shells that may well have blown young Lebanese girls to bits in the following weeks of July 2006.[20] The Israeli girl whose face we can see is obviously enjoying herself, unaware in any conscious or empathic way of what she is doing.

At the university level, nearly all research programs and coursework in international relations adopt the Hobbesian and Machiavellian view of the world, never questioning traditional assumptions. A tremendous amount of intellectual effort goes into studying things as they are. Almost no one thinks outside the box. Only very recently has a small portion of the university community established research and coursework in the study of peace. The system of private military academies also perpetuates the war-ist mentality. Here one will frequently find the sons (and now the daughters) of traditional military families whose members can proudly point to several generations of military service.

High schools and universities cooperate in training young people to be soldiers through the ROTC programs. There are 273 college ROTC programs and, in 2009, 513,259 high school students were enrolled in Junior ROTC[21] The military is planning to penetrate even further down the grades in 2010 with middle school programs. These programs are advertised euphemistically as "leadership training." Also, administrators at the high school and college levels actively encourage military recruiters to come onto campus. The military plugs into this subsystem by offering money for college tuition in return for enlistment. Again, all the feedback loops are positive, reinforcing the system.

Another powerful and dynamic element in the war system is the media. The news media are, by and large, uncritical and unsophisticated when it comes to international relations. The fact that most Americans who actually follow the news are presented with only half-hour news programs, half of which is taken up with commercials, leaves them with a very incomplete and vague understanding, not only of the events, but also of the underlying causes and conditions of world affairs, and as a result, these viewers are easily manipulated. The media provide almost no critique of the war system and, when conflicts break out, they fall all over themselves to deliver the government's view of things. When this happens in other countries, Americans call it propaganda. During the First Gulf War, they willingly acceded to government censorship and the evening news anchors became cheerleaders for the war rather than objective reporters. Also, like the managers of the war system, newsmen and women tend to have earnestly adopted a Machiavellian or security-realist view of the world. They almost never question its assumptions. Many years ago during the Cold War, I asked a prominent American newsman who had been Moscow bureau chief for a major American news service, how he thought the Cold War could be ended. He replied with surprise, "I've never thought about it." The news media are, by and large, part of the system both through their overt reporting and editorializing, and through what they leave out.

A further disturbing trend is a developing confusion of news and entertainment that trivializes important issues. There is less and less in-depth reporting as the news media cut the number of their foreign correspondents. And finally, the penchant for depicting the world in stark, bipolar terms is growing, obscuring the complexity of many important issues. By and large, Americans and others remain innocent of any sophisticated knowledge about the nature of the international system and of the difficult conditions in which so many people around the world live. The fact that after the attack on the World Trade Center in September 2001 Americans had to ask "Why

LEARNING OF GERMAN RETREAT, FRENCH WOMAN RETURNS TO FIND HER HOUSE IN RUINS. The war system is not an abstraction. This universal scene of a woman in the midst of ruin and loss, her misery probably compounded by knowing her son or husband is lying dead somewhere in the mud, ought to be on the wall of every living room in the world to remind us of the real consequences of the war system. (Library of Congress, LC-USZ62-115012)

do they hate us?" indicates a huge vacuum of knowledge about the impact of U.S. policy and, in general, the history of the last 200 years in the Middle East.

Much of our view of reality, including conflict and the most effective ways to deal with it, comes to us from television and movies, where the use of violence is almost the only way that conflict is presented. For example, a television show very popular in the era 2001—2007 was 24. This counter-terrorism drama had as its story line the desperate struggle of counter-terrorism agent Jack Bauer to defuse an imminent threat to the United States. Jane Mayer writes, "The twisting story line forces Bauer and his colleagues to make a series of grim choices that pit liberty against security."[22] Frequently, the choice is to torture the suspects, who are "beaten, suffocated, electrocuted, drugged, assaulted with knives, or more exotically abused," and, of course, they divulge the secrets that let the heroes save the nation. In 2006 the program won an Emmy Award for Outstanding Drama. Its creator, Joel Surnow, freely admits that he is exploiting the fears that arose in America after the 9/11 attacks. While the show does occasionally show a character who objects to the torture, that character is always portrayed as naïve, weak and ineffectual. The show is indicative of a trend in which scenes of torture on TV have increased from an average of four a year to more than a hundred, as those committing the acts have changed from the villains to the heroes.[23] It is apparently unimportant to the show's creators that the torture in which America's saviors engage on the show is illegal in both U.S. and International Law. In addition to this program, many other programs on television support the idea that justice requires overwhelming force, often beyond the bounds of the law. One cannot look at evening television, or even the ads for the programs, without seeing fist fights, guns, and explosions.

The movie industry contributes to this pervasive view of the world with its nearly ubiquitous violence in offerings that are euphemistically called "action films." And while a few war movies are now somewhat more realistic in portraying actual violence on the battlefield, they present war almost as a phenomenon of nature as inevitable as the tides. In the U.S., one can find such overt examples as the Rambo movies, or, more subtly, such films as *Saving Private Ryan*, *Blackhawk Down*, and *We Were Soldiers*, which, while they are graphically honest about what happens to soldiers in war, still perpetuate the enemy stereotype and the use of violence as the only way to deal with conflict. Joseph J. Paczelt has analyzed these three films in an insightful essay, "Upon St. Crispin's Day."[24] They portray war almost entirely in terms of the individual soldier and leave out the historical and political context of the conflict, "jacking up the cult of the warrior."[25] No attempt is made to explain the historical context or the justness or unjustness of the war depicted. In *BlackHawk Down*, "combat is a phenomenon unto itself"[26] without political context. We don't get to know why wars happen. In *We Were Soldiers*, "war is something that happens."[27] These more recent films are individualistic and survivalist narratives that reinforce the special nature of combat soldiers, something that can't be understood by mere civilians. As a result, "this message demands extreme reverence for all veterans."[28] Instead of the enemy, civilians become the other and war is an "un-explained natural occurrence; perpetual war is justified."[29]

In addition to films and television, there is an entire genre of war magazines glorifying war, such as *WWII History*,[30] which can be picked up in grocery store checkout lines. The articles relive the historic and minor battles and fawn over various kinds of weapons. They also advertise the Military Book Club ("Join now. Don't miss any of the action."), some of whose recent titles include *Battle for the Ruhr, Jump Into the Valley of the Shadow, Sea of Thunder, Sniper* and countless others. They also offer such guided trips as "Russian Military History Tours," and an endless array of weapons and replica weapons, uniforms, gear, and models of weapons. It does not matter which side they are portraying, as the article "SS Elite Battle for Bastogne" indicates. In a war system, these magazines promote the cult of the warrior.

Countless violent video games portraying real and imaginary wars are another product of the media. The video game, *Battle of the Bulge*, offered by Close Combat, allows the player to reenact the bloody World War II battle in which 181,000 men were killed or wounded. A game reviewer wrote, "In fact, it's so fun that Close Combat: Battle of the Bulge will prove to be one of those games that you'll fire up again and again, and each time you'll come away having enjoyed yourself tremendously."[31] Many of the games are first-person shooter style in which the player actually manipulates weapons and blasts away at the "bad guys." A game called *100 Bullets* is, according to its review on a game site, "Part hard-boiled crime story, part paranoid espionage thriller ... [it] follows what happens when people from all walks of life meet Agent Graves, a mysterious figure who offers his 'clients' the opportunity of a lifetime: an attaché case containing the proof, the gun, and the carte blanche immunity to exact revenge on a person who's done them an irrevocable wrong."[32] Games such as this and countless others are played by most middle school boys and by many girls. Another, *Grand Theft Auto 4*, "has been labeled as one of the most violent video games in the market criticized for depicting excessive violence including beatings, carjackings, drive-by shootings, drunk driving and prostitution."[33] A *Washington Post* writer interviewed a player: "'It's awesome,' said ... a Washington computer network administrator. 'You can carjack any car, go to the seedy part of town, beep the horn and pick up a prostitute. Then you take her to a dark street and the car starts shaking. When the prostitute jumps out, your money is down but your energy is full.' Players can get their money back by killing the woman."[34]

It is likely that playing these games increases aggression in young men. According to the American Psychological Association, "Playing violent video games like Doom, Wolfenstein 3D, or Mortal Kombat can increase a person's aggressive thoughts, feelings and behavior both in laboratory settings and in actual life," according to two studies appearing in the April issue of the American Psychological Association's (APA) *Journal of Personality and Social Psychology*. Furthermore, violent video games may be more harmful than violent television and movies because they are interactive, very engrossing and require the player to identify with the aggressor, say the researchers. "'One study reveals that young men who are habitually aggressive may be especially vulnerable to the aggression-enhancing effects of repeated exposure to violent games," said psychologists Craig A. Anderson, PhD, and Karen E. Dill, PhD. "The other study reveals that even a brief exposure to violent video games can temporarily increase aggressive behavior in all types of participants."[35]

It is intriguing that the "U.S. Army spent eight million dollars developing a realistic video game that's free for downloading and makes war entertaining so youth will want to enlist. The Pentagon tracks who scores well, so it can target them for recruiting later."[36]

Play is a powerful force for socialization. The international war toys industry is an important source of positive feedback for the war system. Examples alone would fill a book. The "Awesome Kids" series of toys, according to its website, was "founded by an entrepreneur who was concerned about the growing trend of toys attempting to leave no room for imagination in play, especially in the early ages of 3 to 8 years. Her concept of 'Toys in a Box' provided the basis to cover many areas of play with a single basic box. The boxes were to be portable, packable, and stackable to allow the young child the freedom to play anywhere and clean up with a minimum of effort. This concept also allows the parent to teach the responsibility of cleaning up after oneself without the need for great pressure and to teach children to be neat and organized besides imagination play."[37] While this sounds totally innocuous, the description of its Civil War toy box is totally bloodless: "All the excitement of the War Between the States comes to life in this box. Here's a collection of the most significant men and machines of the war. You can stage land battles (like Gettysburg) with infantry, horsemen and artillery. You can even re-enact the great first battle of the ironclad ships." This toy is for three-year-olds. The most famous of all war toys is GI Joe who over the years has come in countless numbers and up-to-date uniforms and weapons. The "action figure" "GI Joe Military Metal — Hot Drop Zone" is described by the manufacturers as follows:

> This sculpture depicts a U.S. Army Airborne Infantry Sergeant vigorously securing a "Hot LZ (Landing Zone)" during a helicopter troop insertion. During the Vietnam War, the U.S. Army used the Huey helicopter to insert and extract combat troops into hostile areas. The Trooper is using his M-60 Light Machine Gun and is dressed in standard issue jungle fatigues. This sculpture is displayed on a 6½ inch oval simulated wood base. Each includes a certificate of authenticity.

Price is $29.99, available at Wartoyz.Com. Another toy, "GI Joe: Unforget-table Military Moments — Story of Victory," tells the child: "The mission is over. Now is the time for the crew of the Air Force F-4 Phantom to exchange their views on today's air combat sortie over North Vietnam. The pilot is seated and using his hands to describe to his Radar Intercept Officer (RIO) how he was able to shoot down the MIG. The sculpture is 8 inches high, and comes on a 8 × 6 inch oval simulated wood base for easy display." GI Joe does not come with a bloody stump where his arm should be, or lying in a hospital bed with his eye shot out. War and soldiers are sanitized and mythologized. But not always. Perhaps the most extreme war toy yet on the market is Forward Command Post, or the bombed-out dollhouse, where we do see the devasta-tion of war and the heroic soldier defending the ruin with his automatic weapons. We are not informed if Barbie has become a refugee or if she is a decaying corpse still inside. Forward Command Post is recommended for children five years and up, as is the GI Joe Long-Range Army Sniper.[38]

War toys "attribute a positive value to hurting, killing and threatening others. Permission to have in the home toys that convey this value implies parental approval of this value," according to Darlene Hammell, MD, and child psychiatrist Joanna Santa Barbara. They go on to say that playing with these toys teaches children that "war is a game, an exciting adventure, killing is acceptable, even fun, violence or the threat of violence is the only way to resolve conflicts, and the world is divided into 'goodies' and 'baddies' where the bad guys are devoid of human qualities and their destruction is desirable."[39]

Another social factor that is a strength in the system is the presence of many veterans, the result of many wars. American Legion clubs and Veterans of Foreign Wars posts are found in almost every small town, and one can not drive through these villages without seeing a large tank or cannon in the town park. There are war memorials in almost every town. The professional veterans' associations keep alive the idea that being a soldier is, as the euphemism has it, being in "the service," and their national organizations lobby for a strong military and an aggressive posture in foreign relations. Very often veterans create organizations around their former units or their ships. For example, a website for the Second Armored Division Remembrance Group provides a meeting ground replete with photographs, including several showing what must be their grandchildren in full military uniform and hefting World War II weapons they are barely big enough to hold.

Other organizations, such as the Navy League, adopt the same view of the international system and lobby effectively for perpetuating the war system and for absurd levels of preparedness. Additionally, there are large groups of citizens enthusiastically participating in battle reenactments where, unlike reality, no one ends up mutilated or dead.

One final institution remains to be examined and requires a long section of its own. The ways in which religion supports the war system are many and complex, but first it is important to clarify the discussion of "terrorism" and war because some observers think that we have entered a new era with a new kind of war, one that, conveniently for many, will be ongoing and un-endable.

After the end of the Cold War in 1989 many people thought that an era of peace would follow. Since the war system had not ended, only a particular though long-standing conflict, that thinking was naïve. Still, many people were surprised by the outbreak of conflicts based in ethnicity, and especially by the ferocious level of violence associated with them, as the former Yugoslavia broke up, accompanied by vicious terrorist mass murders and rapes. And shortly thereafter, it seemed, the rise of international terrorism came to the fore with the attacks on the World Trade Center in New York. In fact, ethnic cleansing and terrorism are old practices, as anyone who has not forgotten the Nazi Shoa is well aware.[40]

Ethnic cleansing ought to be familiar to Americans from a reading of their own history. The violent removal, and in some cases extermination, of the Native American nations and the confinement of the survivors to enclaves or reservations was echoed later in South Africa, where the apartheid system created the Bantustans. In between, at the beginning of the twentieth century, was the massacre and genocide of the Armenians by the Turks. And subsequently we have seen genocidal practices in Rwanda and the Sudan. All of these are a form of war.

Most if not all acts of war are, from a moral point of view, despicable. Terrorism is especially so. But it is nothing new and is simply one method used by all sides in modern warfare. By terrorism I mean the deliberate attack on civilians in order to cause fear and panic and to break morale. Indian attacks on settler villages during the frontier period of American history were terrorist attacks. Terrorism comes in two forms. First, there is the kind usually employed by the non-state actors, almost always the weaker side in a conflict since they lack the expensive means to fight the enemy on its own terms. This is true of suicide bomber attacks by Palestinians on Israeli civilians. If the Palestinian Liberation Organization had American-supplied F-15 fighter bombers, as the Israelis do, they would use them. But they don't. Putting justice considerations aside for the moment, the exceedingly one-sided conflict between the U.S., a superpower, and groups of radical Muslims provokes this kind of terrorism. The second kind of terrorism is state terrorism, where sovereign states use overwhelmingly violent attacks on civilians to break the morale of the enemy. The Germans began the practice of terrorizing whole cities from the air when they bombed the city of Guernica in the Spanish

Civil War, a scene caught by Pablo Picasso in his painting of that name. They carried it on when they bombed Rotterdam in World War II. The much-vaunted campaign of "shock and awe" that initiated the American attack on Iraq had the same aim. All sides use terrorism in military conflicts. The Viet Cong and North Vietnamese carried out assassinations of village leaders and teachers as part of a deliberate terror campaign and the U.S. military proclaimed free-fire zones where they killed any human that moved. The Contras, a tool of the United States, carried out similar terror attacks on villages of civilians in Nicaragua in the 1980s. The Israelis use collective punishment, another form of terrorism and a violation of international law, in their struggle with the Palestinians.

It is of particular interest, however, that in the recent era religion has become closely associated with this kind of warfare. We turn now to an examination of religion and war, modern mercenaries, the impact of war on the natural environment, the failure of war to bring peace, and global domination.

CHAPTER 4

The War System, Part 2

The complex social system that yields wars as a normal result of its operations has several additional components, including a religious dimension, the new phenomenon of private armies, the military's impact on the environment and, finally, the structural violence that is associated in our time with globalization.

Religion as a System Strength

Religion is a complex phenomenon that functions both as a strength and a strain on the war system. Elise Boulding writes that "every religion then contains two cultures: the culture of violence and war and the culture of peaceableness."[1] Each religion has many facets, often including doctrines and teachings that compete with one another for allegiance. It would be all too easy to oversimplify the case here, as J. Milburn Thompson points out: "Since religion pertains to core values, it can inflate the intensity and intractability of ethnic conflict.... Most analysts, however, have concluded that while religious divisions can be a contributing factor, religion itself is seldom the root cause ... for ethnic conflict."[2] Nevertheless, religion does play an important part in the war system. Religion has been a cause of war, though not frequently. More often it supports the war system as a justification and as a solace. But it can lead to extremes, especially in the paradoxical case of Christianity. In his book *When Religion Becomes Evil*, Charles Kimball puts forward a disturbing assertion that "A strong case can be made, in fact, that the history of Christianity contains considerably more violence and destruction than that of most other religions."[3]

For a case in point, during the Cold War there were even some Christian preachers who hoped for nuclear holocaust. One such was quoted as saying,

"Why don't you do it tonight, Jesus? ... If you're ready to go, it would be fantastic."[4] Obviously this is on the fringe of Christian views on war: nonetheless this writer was inspired, he believed, by the fiery end of the world prophesied in Revelation. But it is not necessary to go to the fringe elements to see the problem. In World Wars I and II good German Lutherans and good American Lutherans, with the aid and comfort of their military chaplains, killed one another savagely. All of this was made possible by a pillar of Christianity, St. Augustine, who long before in the fourth century had provided an elaborate philosophical justification for war. Just how does religion justify violence?

First, Judeo-Christian scripture is full of violence and the justifications for violence. And it is not just in Christianity, but also in Judaism and in Islam, the other "religions of the book"—the Old Testament, in Christian parlance. Jews, Muslims and Christians believe that God acts in history and that therefore the events of history, including the warfare of nations, are to be understood in terms of God's will. Nor is religious violence confined to these three. Hinduism condones violence and even Buddhism, with its powerful pacifist bent, was melded with the warrior cult of the samurai in Japan. But it is the three religions of the book that have been primarily responsible for condoning or inspiring religious violence over the past three thousand years, and it is on this book that many Christians, Muslims and Jews draw for their justifications for supporting the war system, even if they are often unaware of it. As Jack Nelson-Pallmeyer correctly points out, "Like plutonium, theological distortions have an after life."[5]

The Old Testament is filled with violent images of God, which are conveniently forgotten by most Christians and Jews until they need to justify their nation when it decides to go to war or to commit some other act of violence. For instance, God orders parents to murder their disobedient children. The Lord spoke to Moses, saying, "All who curse father or mother shall be put to death" (Lev. 20: 102a), and in Deuteronomy he commands the community to stone to death rebellious sons (20: 18–21). He orders extreme violence and terrorism as the method by which the chosen nation of the ancient Hebrews is to usurp the land of the Canaanites.

> And when the Lord your God gives them over to you and you defeat them, then you must utterly destroy them. Make no covenant with them and show them no mercy [Deut. 7: 1–2].

These troubling images are multiplied hundreds of times in the Old Testament. In the Hebrews' battle with King Og of Bashan the Lord orders Moses to commit genocide.

> But the Lord said to Moses: "Do not be afraid of him; for I have given him into your hand, with all his people and all his land. You shall do to him as you did

to King Sihon of the Amorites, who ruled in Heshbon." So they killed him, his sons, and all his people, until there was no survivor left; and they took possession of his land [Num. 21: 34–35].

Similarly, in Deuteronomy genocide is divinely sanctioned: "But as for the towns of these peoples that the Lord our God is giving you as an inheritance, you must not let anything that breathes remain alive. You shall annihilate them" (Deut. 20: 16–17). The feast of the Passover is celebrated in remembrance that God killed all the firstborns of the Egyptians, a true slaughter of the innocents. All of this and much more because "The Lord is a warrior" (Exodus 15: 3). And in the book of Joshua we read:

> And it came to pass, when Israel had made an end of slaying all the inhabitants of Ai in the field, in the wilderness wherein they chased them, and when they were all fallen on the edge of the sword, until they were consumed, that all the Israelites returned unto Ai and smote it with the edge of the sword. And so it was, that all that fell that day, both of men and women, were twelve thousand, even all the men of Ai. Only the cattle and the spoil of that city Israel took for a prey unto themselves, according unto the word of the Lord which he commanded Joshua. And the King of Ai he hanged on a tree until eventide [Josh. 8: 24–29].

But it is not only the enemies of the Hebrews that are ordered to be slaughtered. When the chosen people themselves are seen to fall away, they too are the victims of divine violence. Isaiah 13: 15–16 reads:

> Whoever is found will be thrust through, and whoever is caught will fall by the sword. Their infants will be dashed to pieces before their eyes: their houses will be plundered and their wives raped.

The ancient Hebrews understood their own subjugation by the empires that successively ruled the region as divine punishment for their sins. But nevertheless, they expected divine vengeance to be visited upon the oppressor. When under the rule of the Babylonian Empire, the Psalmist wrote, "O daughter Babylon, you devastator! Happy shall they be who pay you back what you have done to us! Happy shall they be who take your little ones and dash them against the rock!" (Ps. 137: 8–9).

As astonishing as these verses are, they are not unusual. In fact, biblical scholar Raymund Schwager has noted that

> there are six hundred passages of explicit violence in the Hebrew Bible, one thousand verses where God's own violent actions of punishment are described, a hundred passages where Yahweh expressly commands others to kill people, and several stories where God irrationally kills or tries to kill for no apparent reason.[6]

The writers of the Old Testament believed that God achieved justice (e.g., liberating the Jews from Egypt) or the good society, punishing those who fell away from the covenant, by extreme and bloody violence. "Thou shalt not kill" does not apply to those out of favor with God as seen by the writers of the Old Testament. The ancient Hebrews were, in fact, one of many warrior-god tribes that flourished in the ancient Middle East, a prime example of a patriarchal, dominator society carrying out divinely sanctioned holy war. It is no surprise that women were allowed no meaningful role in their society other than as wives and bearers of children.

By the end of the first millennium BC the Hebrews were under the imperial heel of the most successful of the ancient dominator societies — Rome. By this time the theologians, prophets and popular preachers had developed a doctrine of the end times. Much of this doctrine was borrowed from Zoroastrianism, where it was prophesied that history would end with a cosmic battle between the forces of good and the forces of evil, between God and Satan. In this final struggle not only would thousands of humans be killed in battle but there would also be a final judgment in which those found wanting would be sent to everlasting torment in Hell and the earth itself would be destroyed. When the end times were put off again and again, anxiety and fear rose to feverish heights. Thus in late Palestinian Judaism we have both a violent and angry God and his enemies. Coupled with the holy-war motif of the Old Testament we see the rationale and the role models for violence. All of this was a legacy bequeathed to the future, adopted both by Islam and, oddly enough, by Christianity with its seemingly pacifist Jesus.

There is much in Judeo-Christian doctrine and history that can be used to support a peace system, but it is so far a minor current.[7] The main stream has adopted the violent, dominator mode of late Palestinian Judaism with its foundation in Old Testament holy war. It is a somber fact of history that in the name of Christ men have murdered and condoned murder, tortured women and children, slaughtered in war, and executed each other without remorse. The Crusaders saw Jesus in terms of their own society, that is, as their feudal lord who called them to recapture his patrimony, the Holy Land.[8] Thus it made sense to them to kill all the Jews they could find as they wended their way to the East.

But even for modern Christians who do not want to carry out pogroms, but in fact to fight against regimes characterized by structural and overt violence, such as the Nazi Empire, Christianity can be adapted to support unspeakable violence, often in the name of protecting the soldiers themselves. In York Minster, the great church at York in England, there is a chapel dedicated to the Prince of Wales' Own Regiment of Yorkshire, and one can find there the Regimental Order of Service in the pews. The Lord is the God who helps the Regiment. It reads, "Praised be the Lord daily: even the God who helpeth us." Psalm 15 is cited, on the purity of "He that hath used no deceit in his tongue or done evil to his neighbor." Then they quote St. Paul's Epistle to the Ephesians: "Put on the whole armor of God, that ye may be able to stand against the wiles of the devil," and so on. All of which seems innocent enough if one does not recall whose service this is. And then the Regimental Hymn: "Thy Kingdom come, O God / Thy rule, O Christ begin / Break with thine iron rod / the Tyrannies of sin.... Men scorn by sacred name / And wolves devour thy fold.... O'er heathen lands afar/ Thick darkness broodeth yet." It is not difficult to see that the task of breaking the iron rod of tyranny in dark heathen lands is vested in this regiment. The service closes with the Regimental Prayer:. "O Lord God, the shield and buckler of all who trust in thee: Grant to our Regiment in its battalions and ranks the strength that feareth no evil tidings, no desperate endeavour, and no foe bodily or spiritual; but advanceth in thy righteousness, through all rough places, under the Captain of our Salvation, Jesus Christ our Lord, Amen." The image of Jesus as a captain was echoed by the Argentines who fought the British in the Falklands Island War in 1982. I recall that in that conflict Mary was made an honorary captain in the Argentine air force.

What we are seeing here is a Manichean picture of the world — the battle between good and evil — and the militarization of Christian imagery. But it is perfectly understandable because men in battle are placed in desperate and fearful conditions and naturally seek the protection and sanction of the God in whom they believe, even at the cost of gross cognitive dissonance.

There seem to be four reasons for this obvious deviation from the teachings of Jesus. First, Christians adopted the Old Testament as sacred scripture because they saw it as a prophecy of the coming of Christ. Along with it came the violent Yahweh. Second, many who followed Jesus understood the eschatology in the old way in spite of his teachings. Christianity became more of a religion about Jesus than a following of his religion. This was enshrined in the two major creeds that say nothing about his life and teachings but skip from the virgin birth to the crucifixion. Third, for many, Christianity is a highly legalistic and creedal religion in which believers are required to assent to certain religious formulae. Those who do not are heretics. Those who are not with us are against us in the cosmic struggle between God and Satan. It is a short step from that reasoning to the violent conversions of pagans, the Crusades, the fires of the Inquisition, and the Christian justifications for war and even nuclear war in the twentieth century. And fourth, Christianity was captured by the state in the fourth century and has, for the most part, remained there ever since. A deal was struck between the Byzantine emperor and the bishops, in which the latter would sanction his wars in return for making Christianity the only legal religion. One of these bishops preached a sermon in which he said, "Give me, my prince, the earth purged of heretics, and I will give you heaven as a recompense. Assist me in destroying heretics, and I will assist you in vanquishing the Persians."[9] In AD 346 the pagan temples were closed and the death penalty decreed for anyone found performing the old rituals.[10] The unholy alliance was forged, and it has continued to this day.

In the ninth century the Emperor Charlemagne waged many brutal campaigns for the conversion of the pagans. In 1099 Pope Urban II preached a crusade, a holy war, against the Muslims who had taken over the Christian cradle lands, initiating hostilities that that lasted several hundred years and are clearly remembered by those who live in the Middle East as being instructive for the conflicts with the West that have flared up again in the last hundred years.

While the Old Testament tradition is unambiguously in support of holy war, the teachings of Christ, upon which Christianity is founded, provided a sea-change — for a time. "You have heard that it was said, 'An eye for an eye and a tooth for a tooth.' But I say to you, 'Do not resist one who is evil. But if any one strikes you on the right cheek, turn to him the other also.' ... 'You have heard that it was said, You shall love our neighbor and hate your enemy,' but I say to you, 'Love your enemies and pray for those who persecute you'" (Matt. 5: 38–45). And as he was being arrested by the Roman imperial authorities, he advised Peter, "For all who take the sword, perish by the sword" (Matt 26: 53). Based on these and other scriptures, early Christians appear to have been mainly pacifist and the saying "I cannot fight, I am a Christian" was commonplace. But as the Vandals were invading North Africa in the fourth century, St. Augustine, who was bishop of Hippo, was part of the movement that turned Christianity on its head. Like Nestorius, he condoned war for Christians, but his influence was far more long-lasting because he was the first to formulate the Christian doctrine of just war, and it continues to be the norm into the twenty-first century. Augustine said that war was forbidden to Christians *except under certain circumstances.* These were as follows: it had to be a defensive war, begun by the other side; it had to a measure of the last resort; it had to be declared by a legitimate authority; there had to be a reasonable hope of prevailing; it had to have as its aim the restoration of a just peace; it had to be fought with only enough force to overcome the enemy; it had to avoid attacking non-combatants; and it had to be fought in the spirit of love for the enemy. No war could be just for both sides. Every one of these conditions had to be met in order for Christians to fight. It sounds perfectly reasonable but it has aided and abetted the incinerations of Dresden and Hiroshima. Religion was placed in the service of slaughter.

In Augustine's view, Christ's teachings were not meant for this fallen age of sin; the kingdom was not yet come.[11] And so in the "real world," it is all right to kill humans in war. Modern Catholic teaching follows this line, as does much of Protestant thought. Vatican II stated, "As long the danger of war persists and there is no international authority with the necessary competence and power,[12] governments cannot be denied the right of lawful self-defense, once all peace efforts have failed."[13]

In addition to the obvious hypocritical deviation from the teachings of Jesus, there are practical problems with such a stance. First, every side considers itself to be the offended party. Even the Nazis had some measure of just claim as a result of the unjust Peace of Versailles. Furthermore, just-war doctrine is a return to the Old Testament position that justice may be achieved by violent means. Currently Islamic terrorists believe sincerely that their society has been offended and attacked by Western imperialists with our secular culture. In short, everyone can and does claim that their war is just. Even when openly violating the prohibition of preemptive war, as George W. Bush did in his attack on Iraq, the claim of self-defense was put forward to provide the rationale. Every nation or group that initiates violence believes that war is forced on it by the other side and so turn to just-war doctrine to explain the atrocities they are about to inflict on their fellow humans.

Another problem with just-war doctrine in modern times is that modern weapons cannot be used indiscriminately. The terror bombing of German and Japanese cities in World War II was a clear violation of just-war doctrine, ignored by military chaplains. Even when one tries, with so-called smart bombs, to target only other soldiers, there have been horrendous civilian deaths, euphemized as "collateral damage."[14] Apologists for just-war doctrine have tried to weasel out of this by arguing that if it was not intended to kill civilians, then the doctrine is not violated. This, no doubt, is of little comfort to the dead or to their families.

In this way the Catholic Church and many Protestant denominations supported the Vietnam War as a just defense of freedom against the Communists and even supported the preparation for and threat of nuclear holocaust in which hundreds of millions of non-combatants would be slaughtered. Just-war doctrine can easily be twisted and rationalized even by devout Christians when the state is the principal institution in society and, it seems, the object of their primary loyalty. The American flag has a prominent place at the front of the sanctuary in almost every church in the U.S. and nationalistic songs are included in the hymnals.

The Old Testament idea that one's nation is chosen by God for domination dies hard, if at all. The chosen nation shall use domination to redeem the world by violence. For example, during the era of the U.S. wars of dispossession against the Indians and during the Spanish-American war, Senator Albert Beveridge repeated this sentiment in his justification for the violence.

God has ... made us the master organizers of the world to establish system where chaos reigns. He has given us the spirit of progress to overwhelm the forces of reaction throughout the earth. He has made us adept in government that we may administer government among the savage and senile peoples. Were it not for such a force as this the world would relapse into barbarism and night. And of all our race He has marked the American people as His chosen nation to finally lead in the regeneration of the world. This is the divine mission of America.[15]

And later, President Woodrow Wilson, son of a Protestant minister, initially opposed entry into World War I but then took the U.S. in, paradoxically, to fight the war to end war and bring on the millennium of peace. Again, redemptive violence justified all the killing. Somehow, the peaceable kingdom would be achieved as a result of ten million deaths. Interestingly, prior to the U.S. entry in 1917, most Protestant ministers were pacifist. Then they turned 180 degrees and we find such assertions as "We must help in the bayoneting of a normally decent German soldier in order to free him from a tyranny which he presently accepts a his chosen form of government."[16] One clergyman asked and answered, "Would He [Christ] fight and kill? There is not an opportunity to deal death to the enemy that He would not shirk.... He would take bayonet and bomb and rifle and do the work of deadliness against that which is the most deadly enemy of His Father's kingdom in a thousand years."[17]

But one need not go back to World War I. President Bush, a self-avowed born-again Christian, refused to meet with a delegation of ministers from his denomination who wished to persuade him not to initiate a war against Iraq. Instead, he went ahead to try to recreate the Middle East in our own American image. What appears to be happening in these cases is that the ideology of messianic nationalism is a system strength that trumps the teachings of Jesus, even for devout Christians. And additionally, a dominating patriarchy is also trumphant in the examples of Christian violence, for the Catholic Church and the fundamentalist Protestants have been historically and remain overwhelmingly an institution of men and a dominator form of religious government, which may help to explain why the Church was so easily socialized into the norms of violence in spite of its founder. Thus, in Western history, "The violence of God is used to justify the claims of followers whose recourse to violence is rationalized as part of faithful service to God and in pursuit of God-sanctioned goals."[18]

But Judaism and Christianity hardly have a monopoly on religious violence. Islam is an outstanding example of it as well. It is important to note that Islam, like the other religions of the book, has a peace tradition, all of which will be examined in a later chapter. Islam is a religion revealed to Mohammed in the seventh century AD but it rests on many biblical traditions — many of the stories are the same and Jesus is recognized as a prophet, though not as

God. Like Christianity, it too was born in an era of strife, but unlike early Christianity, it did not eschew violence. Mohammed was a political leader as well as a spiritual leader and in the contest for the hearts and minds of Arabia, his young movement was attacked violently and persecuted and he and his followers fought back successfully with arms. Thus, while in Western society one must explain the subordination of the church to the state, in Islam there has never been a separation and Muslims are somewhat baffled by the distinction between sacred and secular. Islam was a theocracy from the start and expansionist warfare spread the religion to the pagans. Note that Christians and Jews were, in the main, not required to convert; only the pagans were.

Imam Dr. Abdul Jalil Sajid points out that the well-known concept of jihad simply means "struggle," and may easily be understood to be the interior struggle between one's own worse and better natures. But it also means war. He is quick to point out that there is no doctrine of holy war in Islam — that is, war is not to be undertaken for purposes of converting the defeated. But there is clearly a concept of just war and the sources of this tradition are the Old Testament, the Qur'an, and the Hadith. "Islam confirms almost all Biblical and Hebrew Prophets as the Prophets of Islam and their messages as the messages of Islam as long [as] it is confirmed in the Qur'an."[19] It is the obligation of all Muslims to help in creating an Islamic state, for, it is believed, it is only within such a political and social framework that moral values can be upheld. Still, preemptive war and the killing of civilians are forbidden, as is suicide, and hence suicide bombings.[20] He writes:

> Peace in Islam does not mean the absence of war, but the absence of oppression, corruption, injustice and tyranny. Islam considers that real peace can only be obtained when justice prevails. Islam therefore justifies war against regimes that prevent people from choosing their ideals and practicing their beliefs.[21]

And he goes on to say that, unlike Christianity, citing Jesus' dictum to turn the other cheek, "for Muslims, injustice would be triumphant in the world if good people were not prepared to risk their lives in a righteous cause. It [defensive war] is not an act of aggression for the sake of material interests or a wanton display of national or tribal power, but it is a sacred duty assigned to every Muslim in the interests of humanity so that there should be peace and justice in the world."[22] As hard as it is for Americans to understand, Osama bin Laden and his supporters see what they are doing as a defensive war to rid the Muslim world of corruption so that peace and justice, as they define it, can prevail. Theirs is a defensive jihad. Loretta Napoleoni has analyzed this phenomenon at some length.

> Islamist leaders today address packed mosques using rhetoric similar to that of Pope Urban II when he launched the first Crusade.... Islamic fundamentalism

has presented itself as a cohesive force, the sole power able to rid the Muslim world of Western economic hegemony. Emerging merchant, trading and banking classes see in the modern jihad an opportunity to remove the impediments to business and economic growth imposed by Western domination. The masses see it as a chance to rid the Muslim world of parasitic elites and dictatorial regimes, opening up economic opportunities and restoring dignity to the Muslim world. The religious elites see it as a means of regaining political control.... The modern jihad is a brew of Islamist revolutionary ideology, a Muslim search for identity, and socioeconomic aspirations. Yet the rhetoric is all religious.[23]

Given the ability of people to broadly interpret when they have been unjustly treated, it would appear that the Muslim doctrine of just war, or just jihad, is very similar to Augustine's. In short, there is a lot of wiggle room to understand one's own war as divinely sanctioned, even required. And when one side is technologically disadvantaged in armed struggle, it will use whatever means come to hand. As Peter Ustinov has bluntly pointed out, "Terror is the war of the poor, and war is the terrorism of the rich."[24] And people often understand their fears in the language of religion. Jack Nelson-Pallmeyer sums it up:

> Violence continues to plague the monotheistic religions that uphold sacred scriptures in which God is linked to superior violence.... The just and violent God often becomes an instrument or justifier of human revenge. Lurking behind the reality of superior violence is the idea of redemptive violence, the belief that violence saves.[25]

Consequently, those who are working for peace have much to fear from religion, but, as we shall see, much to hope for as well.

Because of the very nature of war — its death and destruction that inspire terror, its losses that inspire grief— and with the necessity of commiting horrible acts of violence that give rise to guilt and bring on the need for justification (and its acute uncertainties), it is no wonder that people turn to religion for solace, absolution and meaning. Religion's involvement with war is both cause and effect. Most if not all wars today are fought primarily for political and economic reasons. But religion is almost always in the mix somewhere, playing a supporting role.

Modern Mercenaries

Directly opposite war undertaken for religious reasons is war undertaken for money. While the phenomenon of mercenaries did not completely die out when the Peace of Westphalia (1648) made nation states the chief actors in international relations, it had all but disappeared by the twentieth century.

In the last several hundred years, it has been primarily the state, or revolutionary groups who claimed to be the legitimate state or wanted to secede and set up their own states, that mounted armies. But armies for hire never completely disappeared from the battlefield. During the era of decolonization in the 1950s and 1960s, and the subsequent instability in Africa, private militias such as Executive Outcomes, a force made up of ex–Union of South Africa troops, fought in several African states in the various civil wars and insurrections.[26] Private militias, a slightly different phenomenon, reappeared first in the Balkan wars at the end of the twentieth century, but by and large these men were fighting for ideological reasons, not for pay, as are the Muslim militias in Iraq and Palestine today. But with the outbreak of the U.S. Afghan and Iraq wars, we have seen a major increase in armies for hire, employed in this case by the United States. At one point the U.S. had almost 125,000 "private contractors" in Iraq, provided by the so-called security firms such as Halliburton, Brown and Root, Blackwater, and Custer Battles.[27] Many of these men were hired on as cooks and truck drivers but as many as half were in private uniforms carrying weapons. They protect military bases such as the Green Zone, provide interrogation, guard key personnel, provide armed escorts for convoys, act as civilian police, train Iraqi soldiers, and gather intelligence. Close to $4 billion has been spent on private security forces from over 100 different firms.[28]

The existence of paramilitary forces hired by states raises several issues. The first is loyalty. Private military forces are loyal only to the company that is paying them and they have been known to leave when the fighting gets too tough, and they have also been known to turn on the state that is employing them, and even to fight each other.[29] Another issue is accountability. It is unclear that the mercenary soldiers are held to the same standards as regular military in terms of responsibility. For example, they take no oath to the Constitution and are not bound to the military's rules of engagement for operating in any theater. Nor are they subject to the military's Uniform Code of Military Justice. Ben Cash, a former soldier serving in Iraq, asks, "Who is keeping track of these civilians with firepower?"[30] Additionally, it is problematic to turn civilian control of the military over to corporations whose operations are kept secret and that are often subsidiaries of other, larger firms in completely different fields. For example, Executive Outcomes was just one subsidiary of the Branch-Heritage mining consortium.[31] Brown and Root is a subsidiary of Halliburton, one of the world's most powerful oil and gas corporations, with business operations in many other industries as well.

Modern mercenary organizations exist for several reasons. They do not need to be kept around and ready when the fighting is over and they often downsize rapidly while waiting for another contract. Second, the all-volunteer army of the United States has trouble recruiting, and especially retaining, enough personnel to fight a protracted war, a problem made worse by the fact that once a soldier has served his enlistment term he can quit the army and, hiring out as a mercenary, find the same work for much higher pay. Also, in areas where Congress has restricted the role of U.S. military to advising foreign troops, the executive branch can hire mercenaries, who have much greater freedom of operation in such areas as, for example, the drug wars in Latin America. Cash concludes his study writing "Private militaries have existed for centuries, but at no time before has so much power been concentrated in such a small group of people."[32] They constitute a small, but significant, strength in the modern war system.

The Military Impact on the Environment

The entire war system has a debilitating effect on the natural environment. As war became more destructive of life in the twentieth century, it also became more destructive of the environment, depleting resources and degrading ecosystems. Artillery and aerial bombardment took a heavy toll. In 1914 the French planned for an output of ten to twelve thousand shells per day. By the end of the war they were detonating two hundred thousand per day, and the Americans, British, Germans, Austrians, and others, were contributing their own massive barrages, all of which churned up the land on the battlefronts, leaving crater holes that exist to this day as well as thousands of unexploded shells. In World War II the heavy bomber fleets obliterated whole cities in Europe and Japan, releasing all the chemical toxins stored in them as well as turning their oil, gas, buildings, and forests into greenhouse gases. Naval warfare degraded the marine environment in both world wars.

According to William Thomas, the Vietnam War was

> the first time military technology was employed to destroy the environment of an entire country. Carrying a 20-ton bomb load into the stratosphere, a B-52 could strike from 30,000 feet without warning, turning herds of water buffalo into writhing masses of gore or sending entire villages leaping in sudden eruptions of flaming sticks, human limbs and thatch.... By war's end, these behemoths of the Strategic Air Command had dropped 13 million tons of bombs on North and South Vietnam, Cambodia, and Laos — triple the total tonnage dropped in World War II. Their ferocious carpet bombing left at least 26 million craters in a country the size of Washington.[33]

The aerial bombing was augmented by an artillery bombardment that exceeded that of either of the world wars and roughly doubled the tonnage of high

WAR AND THE NATURAL WORLD. Australian troops walk across the explosion-churned mud on duckboards in the pitiful remains of Chateau Wood during the Third Battle of Ypres, October 29, 1917. Thousands of high explosive shells were fired every day in World War I. War destroys the natural world as well as the lives and psyches of men. (Imperial War Museum photograph E AUS-001220)

explosives detonated in the limited area of Indochina. The millions of craters made farming either impossible or very reduced in scale over large areas, and they also served as ponds in which disease-bearing mosquitoes bred, bringing malaria, dengue fever, filariasis, and encephalitis to the population. The U.S. air force also modified the weather over parts of Vietnam, seeding clouds in an effort to wash away the Ho Chi Minh trail, over which military supplies were being moved south to the Viet Cong. But the most severe impacts came from the chemical warfare employed by the U.S.

The chemical defoliant known as Agent Orange was a 50–50 combination of 2,4,5-T and 2,4-D, both phenoxy herbicides designed to kill plant life by causing it to grow out of control until it dies. The former contains TCDD dioxin, one of the most toxic substances known. It is carcinogenic, teratogenic and mutagenic. It was sprayed first on rice crops but that resulted in starving America's Montagnard allies instead of the enemy troops. Then President Kennedy ordered it sprayed over the forests. By 1966, the U.S. had destroyed 850,000 acres of rainforests and crops, and by 1967 they were destroying 1.5 million acres per year. All told, some 72.4 million liters of Agent Orange were misted down over the tropical forests and wetlands of Vietnam.[34] These biocides were sprayed over 8 million acres of forest and 3.8 million acres of cropland. Southwick writes:

> Single exposures caused trees to lose their leaves and crops to wither; repeated applications actually killed trees and poisoned agricultural fields for many years. Forests were targeted in both the central highlands of Vietnam and mangrove coastal zones. Land destruction in Vietnam involved 80 percent of all forest land and over 50 percent of coastal mangrove habitats.[35]

More of these chemicals were sprayed on Cambodia, covering 170,000 additional acres with poison. A rain of spontaneous abortions and birth defects ensued and continued through the rest of the century. The dioxin proved to be persistent and bioaccumulative in the environment. By comparison, the use of "Rome Plows," or 20-ton bulldozers, to scrape villages and rice paddies off the surface of the earth was a crude operation but one that was carried out nonetheless, destroying over one million acres. The U.S. forces also drained 39,000 hectares of sedge marshes and then torched the dried plant material with flame-throwers, and they napalmed mangrove swamps, killing off half of these nurseries of the sea in the region. In total, "5.4 million acres of tropical forests had been reduced to blackened rubble," leaving "almost lifeless Savannahs."[36] Much of the area grew back to dramatically less desirable species of weedy tropical plants such as imperator grass, Lantana, or bamboo, all of which are graze resistant. Much of the wildlife was destroyed and those rare and endangered species left were scattered into isolated little pockets of habitat land.[37] So much of Vietnam's natural capital was destroyed that observers believe the extreme poverty of the post-war period will continue well into the twenty-first century. What few areas of forest that did survive the war were, of necessity, exploited heavily to rebuild the nation's homes, schools, and other infrastructure after the war was over. The water table dropped in many areas. The International Union of Conservation reported in 1985 that "forests have never recovered, fisheries remain depleted, wildlife has not regenerated, cropland productivity is still below former values and [there is] a great increase in toxin-related diseases and various kinds of cancer."[38]

In the Iran-Iraq war of 1981–1989 the Norwuz offshore oil facility was bombed and spilled four times as much oil into that shallow sea as the Exxon Valdez spill. Dugongs,. a manatee-like animal, were entirely killed off, the shrimp fishery collapsed and sea bass and snappers had deadly levels of petroleum contamination. In the First Gulf War, sewage plants, water treatment plants, power plants, and dams were deliberately targeted, destroying the water-purification capabilities of Iraq and leading to contamination by fecal and other materials that caused a major epidemic of disease and took tens of thousands of lives.[39]

Practicing for and carrying out wars eats up large amounts of resources, especially petroleum. A high-performance F-14 fighter plane uses eight gallons of fuel per second. A two-seater F-16 fighter bomber burns 900 gallons of fuel in less than an hour, almost twice as much as the high-consuming American motorist burns in a year. During the Vietnam War, the F-4 Phantom jets burned 1680 gallons each hour and the standard heavy bomber of the U.S. fleet for several decades, the B-52, guzzled 3,612 gallons of fuel per hour while in flight. In the 1990s, the aircraft carrier U.S.S. *Independence* required 100,000 gallons a day to keep it on station.[40] Steaming from its U.S. port to the First Gulf War, the carrier burned two million gallons of fuel. The mechanized units of the land armies required whole fleets of fuel tankers to follow them at close range. During the First Gulf War a single armored division required 600,000 gallons of fuel per day to operate in the field. And the war *in toto*, fought to preserve control of oil supplies for the northern industrial nations, cost 20 million gallons of oil per day over its 46 days.[41] In a single average year, the U.S. military uses enough fuel to run the entire mass transit system of the nation for 22 years — 1.589 trillion BTUs — and that does not count the energy used to manufacture military hardware. And as these vehicles operate they spew forth greenhouse gases. Carbon emissions by the world's militaries totaled about 140 million tons a year by the end of the century, a figure equal to that of the entire nation of Great Britain. In order to burn these colossal amounts of fuel the aircraft needed to burn oxygen as well. A military 747 cargo plane, the same plane flown on long-range civilian flights, uses up in the first five minutes of its takeoff more oxygen than a 44,000-acre forest produces in a day. The stealth bombers used in the Gulf wars used ozone-depleting chemicals to cool their jet exhausts in order to mask their infrared signatures and conventional aircraft were regularly doused with halon fire retardant, another ozone-eating substance.[42]

The military was also a major consumer of minerals. A single jet engine for an F-16 fighter bomber requires four and a half tons of titanium, nickel, chromium, cobalt, and aluminum. William Thomas writes in *Scorched Earth* that "worldwide militaries consume more aluminum, copper, nickel, and platinum than all the developing nations."[43]

As stunning as the ecological impacts of modern war were in the twentieth century, the impacts of war preparation were even more dramatic and were not confined to the battlefield or even to the enemy country. They affected ecosystems and populations at home. Almost no legislation was allowed to interfere with the single-minded obsession with national security. For example, until 1992 it was not legal in the United States for the Environmental

Protection Agency to levy fines against military polluters. As J. Seager wrote in 1995 in the foreward to *Scorched Earth*, "The environmental costs of militarized peace bear suspicious resemblance to the costs of war…. Everywhere, military strategy is shaped by common assumptions about the use of the physical environment as a stage for the exercise of male power. Everywhere, militaries share a contempt for civilian environmental regulation, placing themselves and their 'national security' above the law."[44] For example, in the U.S. and elsewhere, large ecological and cultural systems were degraded by spent and unexploded munitions, and churned by tanks in large-scale practice maneuvers covering hundreds of square miles, while wildlife and people were agitated by the noise of aerial training missions.

Practice bombing is carried out on a massive scale by the world's air forces, especially the U.S. Carried out by high-performance aircraft, these bombing and strafing practice runs create sonic booms that disturb both wildlife and humans. In ten minutes' time an F-18 flying at supersonic speed can boom more than 5000 square kilometers with its explosive concussion. In some instances the booms can tear roofs off houses. Such booms have caused structural damage and behavioral changes in wildlife and especially stressed flocks of migratory birds in their rest and feeding periods. One of the principal ranges for such flights was the Quebec-Labrador peninsula, where 10,000 flights a year were made until the NATO command increased the number to 40,000 in 1992.[45] The increase was the result of a shift from Germany, where complaints and protests over the 100,000 flights a year had grown too vocal for the military. In all, World Watch reports, somewhere between 700,000 and a million military aircraft sortie each year. These military flights annually emitted more than ten million tons of carbon monoxide, nitrogen oxides, hydrocarbons, sulphur dioxide and soot, more than 60 percent of it at altitudes nine kilometers above sea level, thus exacerbating the atmospheric effects. These greenhouse gases were also augmented by the persistence of water vapor exhaled from the jet engines.[46]

The chief U.S. bombing range was Nevada, where 70 percent of the state's land area was reserved for military practice, although this amount was not quite enough. The Pentagon had to close off an additional 275 square kilometers after finding 1,389 live bombs and 28,138 rounds of ammunition accidentally dropped outside the Air Force bombing range.[47] Many of the artillery and bomb test sites are too dangerous to clean up and will have to be abandoned as national sacrifice areas.

After World War II, tons of military toxins were dumped in the ocean. Examples include 15 boxcars carrying 400 tons of mustard gas, intact bombs, and other ammunition dumped in the Pacific off Vancouver Island. For 20 years, the biologically rich breeding grounds off the Farallon Islands were used as a repository for more than 1000 barrels of nuclear and chemical waste as well as explosives. "Today," writes Thomas in *Scorched Earth*, "the sediments and surround waters contain plutonium, cesium, and heavy metals which accumulate in higher concentrations as they move up the marine food chain into human tissues."[48] And on the other side of the globe, in the shallow waters between Scandinavia and the Baltic republics, the victorious allies dumped 5000 tons of old munitions and 350,000 tons of poison gases.

The manufacture of weapons and munitions contributed huge amounts of toxic materials to the environment, especially in the U.S. and the former Soviet Union. For example, the Department of Defense produced more than 8.5 million tons of wastewater in the year 1989. Military wastes included fuels, heavy metals, pesticides, solvents, acids, cyanide, explosives, TNT, PCBs, nerve gas, and other chemical warfare agents. Many of these were leaking and contaminating groundwater off base. The U.S. Department of Defense itself identified 17,482 toxic sites on 1,855 bases in the country. Ninety-seven of these were so heavily polluted as to have been placed on the EPA's Superfund list. The military contractor Boeing Corporation dumped 24 million gallons of contaminated waste into two Seattle-area landfills.

At the Hughes Aircraft plant in Tucson, Arizona, trichloroethylene degreasers were allowed to leak into the aquifer and were found in concentrations of 480 ppb or 80 times higher than permitted by federal and state laws. The state had to close wells serving almost 50,000 people. Directly below the plant, concentrations stood at 16,000 ppb.[49] At the Aberdeen Proving Grounds in Maryland, officials were found guilty in court of dumping more than 200 chemicals, including hydrazine rocket fuel, "one of the world's deadliest contaminants."[50] The groundwater at and around the Kirtland Air Force Base (New Mexico) and at the community of Mountain View was found to contain heavy concentrations of nitrates at 50 times the legal limit, resulting in the situation described by one resident: "We can no longer grow our gardens, we can no longer safely bathe, and we have no water to drink."[51]

All in all, 21,272 toxic sites have been identified on military bases and as of 1995 some 400 had been cleaned up, often by merely moving drums of waste to other existing sites. By the middle of 1990, the total estimated cost of toxic cleanup on military bases was $1.5 trillion.[52] That was more than the U.S. spent on defense from 1798 to 1980.

In recent times, the U.S. military produced more toxic pollution annually than the five largest U.S. chemical companies, some 500,000 tons each year.[53] That figure does not include the toxins coming from the nuclear weapons program. Examples abound. Otis Air Force base in Massachusetts polluted the groundwater with trichloroethylene, a known carcinogen. Biologist Charles Southwick writes, "In adjacent towns, lung cancer and leukemia rates are 80 percent above the state average."[54] Rocky Mountain Arsenal, just outside Denver, was the repository for more than 100 chemical residues from nerve-gas production. Much of this was dumped into open reservoirs. Waterfowl landing on these died by the thousands.[55] The cost of decontaminating that site was estimated at $1 billion. At the Picatinny Arsenal in New Jersey, the groundwater shows trichloroethylene at 5000 times EPA standards and, in addition, heavy concentrations of lead, cadmium, PCBs, phenols, furans, chromium, selenium, toluene, and cyanide. The Army Corps of Engineers calls it the "most contaminated square mile on earth."[56] The region's major aquifer is badly polluted. At the Norfolk Naval Shipyard in Virginia there are high levels of copper, zinc, and chromium in the discharges polluting the Chesapeake Bay. At Tinker Air Force Base in Oklahoma, concentrations of tetrachloroethylene and methylene chloride in drinking water greatly exceed EPA standards, and the concentrations of trichlorethylene (TCE) in the surface waters are the highest ever recorded anywhere in the U.S. At Hill Air Force Base in Utah, heavy concentrations of volatile organic compounds, TCE, barium, lead, arsenic, and other chemicals were found. At McClellan Air Force Base in California, heavy metals were found in the nearby municipal drinking water wells. At McChord Air Force Base in Washington State, benzene, a known carcinogen, is found in concentrations 1000 times the state's safe limit.[57]

The contamination of nuclear weapons construction sites would fill a book of its own.[58] An ironic outcome of the recent nuclear disarmament treaties is the freeing up of large amounts of plutonium warheads that will need to be processed so the material can be used to fuel nuclear reactors. However, many problems abound, including the fact that the factory to process them will not be completed until 2016, and at a cost of $4.8 billion. There is a backlog of 34 tons already that will take 15 years to process, there is a flaw in the design of the fuel assemblies that yet has to be worked out, the facilities are not particularly happy about having to take this fuel, and, finally, there is not enough money to process it all anyway.[59] Managing conflict in a war system leads to myriad collateral problems, many of which the military wishes to ignore. As one American base commander who spoke at a community hearing in Virginia said in response to criticism, "We are in the business of protecting the nation, not the environment."[60]

The Failure of War to Bring Peace

If, as we have seen, war is so destructive of humans, cities, and the natural environment, why does it go on? The answer appears to be that many people who nonetheless abhor war believe it is the only way to peace and security. This assumption has been tested in the past century and found to be false. War, as the record shows, brings humanity neither negative nor positive peace.

Even in conventional terms, war does not produce its intended outcome, victory and supposedly some kind of satisfactory social system (i.e., peace for at least 50 percent of the participants). All of those going into a war expect to win but, in fact some lose horrendously. Sometimes both sides lose, as in the case of the Iran-Iraq war of 1981–1989, a stalemate with horrendous casualties on both sides (one million total) and severe environmental destruction. The destruction of communities is horrendous, even on the winning side, as in France in World War I. And the dead lose, even those on the winning side. Military cemeteries with their thousands and tens of thousands of crosses sprout where the old battlefields were. And in every one there are graves holding only bits and pieces and the inscription "Known only to God."

The best that can be said of war over the past century is that it has brought temporary truces, such as the 20-year truce between World Wars I and II. Of course, it is impossible to cover all of the conflicts of the twentieth and early twenty-first centuries in a few pages. What follows is a portion of the highlights.

The twentieth century really opened in 1897 with the American war to wrest Spain's remaining colonies away from her, which the Americans did with ease. Having initially promised freedom to the liberated peoples, they quickly set up dominator societies. Cuba was occupied and forced to accept a U.S. right to intervene militarily, making Cuba a U.S. protectorate, safe for the domination of United Fruit and other U.S. companies and for the corrupt governments that ended with the socialist overthrow of Fulgencio Batista in 1959 and the subsequent U.S.-Soviet struggle over Cuba where, in 1962, the world came to the brink of nuclear holocaust.[61] In the Philippines, the native peoples rebelled and after several years of brutal war were subdued by the U.S. army. A series of corrupt dictators then followed, culminating in the regime of Ferdinand Marcos, who understandably openly welcomed the great U.S. naval base at Subic Bay.

In 1917, Woodrow Wilson proclaimed that World War I was to be the "war to end wars." Ten million died in the slaughters of that war. Twenty million more died from the epidemic of flu that started in the trenches and subsequently ravaged the globe. The tsarist regime in Russia came apart as the German war effort weakened it and the Germans transported Lenin from Switzerland to the Finland Station in St. Petersburg to drive in the final spike. The Russian civil war resulted in the victory of a brutal dominator society that achieved never-before-seen levels of cruelty under Stalin and that lingered on until 1989.

At the end of World War I, the Germans were humiliated in the "peace treaty" they were forced to sign at Versailles, and from the beginning some in Germany planned to "right this wrong." Germany rearmed and carried out a trial war by intervening in the Spanish Civil War in 1936–1939, as did the Soviets. The Fascists under General Franco won and Spain lived under a dictatorship until the 1960s. The rise of the Nazis and the outbreak of World War II was the direct result of World War I. Hitler proclaimed the "Thousand Year Reich." It lasted twelve years. Every city in Germany was bombed into rubble and the country was divided and occupied by foreign troops for 50 years. Also in the inter-war period, Mussolini attacked Ethiopia, machine-gunning civilians from the air, as a part of his self-proclaimed revival of the Roman Empire. He allied with Hitler in World War II and Italy suffered defeat at the cost of thousands of American lives. The Florence American Cemetery is today a peaceful place where, in the hypocritical parlance of military cemeteries, 4,402 young men "sleep in peace." According to an inscription at the monument, another 1,209 remains could not be found, and are still up there in the hills somewhere. In some of the World War I French cemeteries there are 30,000 and 40,000 burials and these cemeteries are dotted all along the old trench lines from the Atlantic to Switzerland.

Another long-term failure of war that was born in World Wars I and II was the set-up for the Arab-Israeli wars. In an effort to garner whatever help they could in World War I, the British had made vague promises to the Jews of Europe in the Balfour Declaration that after the war they could return to their ancient homeland, Palestine, long since populated by Muslim Palestinians who were not asked about the arrangement. They also promised the Arabs who were under the rule of the Ottoman Empire that they could have free and independent states. These promises were never intended to be kept, as revealed when the Sykes-Picot agreement, a secret treaty between the British and the French laying plans for their dominance in the region, was made public by the new Soviet Union. The British and French carved up the Middle East according to where the oil was and set up puppet states. While some Jews emigrated to Palestine in the inter-war period, the great migration occurred when the Jews who had survived the Nazi Shoa left Europe. While the Middle Eastern question is complicated, the upshot was that two peoples tried to occupy the land one had lived in before. Hostilities broke out in 1948 and have become ever more deeply entrenched and the two sides intransigent, and, of course, they were supported with money and arms by the Cold War superpowers. As soon as the Jews proclaimed the state of Israel on the heels of the retreating British, the surrounding Arab states attacked in the first Arab-Israeli war (1948–1949). In 1956, the British, French and Israelis conspired to invade Egypt in the Suez Crisis. In 1967, fearing an imminent Arab attack, the Israelis launched a preemptive war against Egypt and Syria, the Six-Day War. In 1973 the Egyptians attacked Israel in the Yom Kippur War. The superpowers took sides in these wars and, while the British and French were forced to call off the Suez invasion, the Israelis basically won the battles for the control of Palestine. They instituted a military occupation and civilian settlement of Palestinian lands that continues to this day, with an armed truce between Israel and its neighbors. Peace did not come to the Middle East after World War II.

In the Far East, the patriarchal Japanese were on the winning side in World War I and were determined to imitate the European colonial powers by becoming a dominator society themselves. Thwarted by the colonial powers who had conquered much of East Asia in the eighteenth and nineteenth centuries, they invaded Manchuria in 1931 and China proper in 1937. The Americans, seeing this as a threat to their power in the region, denied them oil and critical minerals. The Japanese, knowing they would not achieve industrial prosperity without the raw materials of the Pacific Rim and that the U.S. navy stood in their way, attacked Pearl Harbor in 1941, setting off World War II in the Far East. The results for Japan were devastating — every major city either firebombed or incinerated by nuclear blast, their air force nonexistent, their navy at the bottom of the sea, and their army mostly killed. Then they were occupied.

World War II also exacerbated the civil war in China between the corrupt Nationalists under Chiang Kai Shek and the brutal Communists under Mao Tse-tung. The victory of the Communists led to a brutal dominator regime that in some respects lingers on into the twenty-first century.

World War II also gave rise to the violent rivalry of the two superpowers, and the many large and little hot wars of the Cold War era, over 100 with 25 million dead. These included two major wars, Korea (1950–1953) and Vietnam. Korea had been divided as a result of World War II with each superpower supporting its local dictator. The huge battles of the war resulted in 100,000 American casualties, a million Chinese and two million Koreans killed, the country permanently divided, and the South occupied by American troops. A military stand-off continues to this day and it was in this conflict that the U.S. and China became enemies. Some analysts are pointing to an "inevitable" future war with China. The war system goes on and on.

Another nation divided by the end of World War II and the rise of the Cold War was Vietnam, a French colony whose indigenous people were fighting for independence. The Vietnamese defeated France at Dien Bien Phu in 1954. The U.S. considered using nuclear weapons to aid the French but in the end did not. However, the U.S. supported a dictatorial regime in the South while the Soviets did the same in the North, and soon the U.S. was drawn into the fighting with results that were disastrous for American troops and for all of the Vietnamese. The U.S. lost over 50,000 while two million Vietnamese died. Spin-off chaos in Cambodia led to the killing fields of the Khmer Rouge and the subsequent Vietnamese invasion. World War II did not bring peace to Southeast Asia.

In the aftermath of World War II, both superpowers supported callous dictators in their spheres of influence. For the U.S., it was Guatemala in 1947, Chile in 1973 when the CIA participated in a coup that set up Augusto Pinochet, and Nicaragua in the 1980s when the Contras killed 30,000 people in an effort to overthrow the Sandinista government. In the case of both superpowers, populist movements were crushed either directly or indirectly so that the lethal dictators friendly to "our" regime could continue. The U.S. supported Saddam Hussein and, early on, even the Taliban. In the Soviets' Afghan war (1979–1989) the U.S. allied with the dictatorial regimes of fundamentalist Muslims such as Saudi Arabia and Pakistan, supporting the mujehadeen, including Osama bin Laden. He later became the leader of Al Qaeda, which took responsibility for 9/11 and for numerous suicide bombings.

Additionally, World War II gave rise to nuclear weapons and the long nuclear terror of mutual assured destruction, as well as the horrendous environmental pollution from the nuclear processing plants in both countries, and deaths from radiation resulting from atmospheric testing.

The exhaustion of the old colonial empires in both world wars gave rise to the wars of liberation in Africa and the ultimate emergence of many failed states and violent dictatorships, civil wars, and revolutions as ethnic groups challenged the arbitrary arrangements set up originally by the colonial powers.

The so-called victory in the Cold War led to the wars of devolution in former Yugoslavia, which the U.S. and the European powers entered and which broke across Christian-Muslim fault lines, a situation exacerbated by the developing general hostility worldwide arising out of the failure to establish a just peace in the Middle East. The collapse of the Soviet Union opened the way for the Americans, with Great Britain hanging on, to enter the Middle East unopposed by any great power, with disastrous consequences for all concerned.

In the Middle East, the old dominator society arrangements of the British and the French colonial regimes began to break apart in the 1970s and 1980s, as the Palestinians, having gained nothing in peace talks, formed the Palestine Liberation Organization (PLO) and carried out vicious guerilla war against Israel, eventually resulting in the Israeli invasion and destruction of Lebanon in 1982. That war included the massacre of civilians at the Palestinians' Sabra and Shatila refugee camps, similar to the U.S. massacre of civilians at My Lai in the Vietnam War.

Returning to the case of Iraq, their failure in the war against Iran led first to the Iraqis' invasion of Kuwait, with U.S. connivance, and then to the U.S.-led coalition to drive them out, culminating in the infamous "Turkey Shoot," in which the U.S. air force slaughtered the retreating Iraqis. While the U.S. did not invade Iraqi territory, its terror-bombing campaign destroyed all the infrastructure needed for healthy life in Iraq, including power plants, water and sewage treatment facilities, fertilizer factories, roads, bridges, hospitals, and so on. The Americans then imposed an embargo that blocked spare parts necessary to rebuild and even the entry of basic medicines. It is estimated that hundreds of thousands died as a result of the ensuing water-borne diseases.

A concomitant of all this hostility, East vs. West in the Middle East, was the rise of Islamic terrorism; many of the terrorists were educated in the madrasa schools set up during the Soviet-Afghan war. This culminated in 9/11, which gave the Bush administration the excuse it wanted to attack Iraq and, presumably, bring peace and democracy to the entire Middle East, a totally failed policy leading only to more hostility. War did not bring peace in the twentieth century nor has it in the first decade of the twenty-first.

Global Dominance: The Necessity of the System

In a war system, the rational thing to do is to strive for global dominance by means of overwhelming force. The history of the U.S. since World War II demonstrates this necessity of the system, as the following brief description demonstrates. Unfortunately, another necessity of the system is that all such efforts inevitably fail, but not before causing vast misery in the process.

Thus far I have presented war and peace in terms of social systems but, of course, these systems now operate in a concrete historical context: the beginning of the twenty-first century. At this point in history there are several salient facts that act as strengths for the war system by exacerbating conflict. First, the global population is expanding rapidly as the environment that supports it is shrinking in terms of arable land, potable water, and mineral resources. The economic development of the Pacific Rim nations, including China, is placing ever-greater pressure on the environment as per-capita consumption increases. Second, the ongoing industrial revolution is dependent on high quantities of fossil fuel, often used in highly inefficient ways. Third, the gap between rich and poor is growing rapidly and is now at its worst in history. Fourth, world trade is controlled by the rich nations through the instruments of the World Trade Organization, the International Monetary Fund and the World Bank, and is tilted in the interests of the rich countries. Hundreds of millions of people are fated to remain desperately poor while knowing all about the lifestyles of those in the rich nations. The net transfer of wealth is from the poor countries to the rich ones. And finally, in this milieu, the United States has been attempting to establish an uncontested empire over the world using both its preponderant economic influence and, more to the point, its vast military.

The U.S. had always thrown its power around wherever possible, especially in Latin America by virtue of the self-proclaimed Monroe Doctrine. U.S. Secretary of State Dean Rusk justified the 1961 invasion of Cuba by pointing out that the U.S. had intervened militarily in 127 nations between 1798 and 1945.[62] However, the American rise to great-power status began during World War I when the European great powers exhausted themselves in battle. The U.S. came out of that war as the most powerful economic entity, with the Europeans owing it money. In World War II the U.S. became a military superpower. But its dominance in the world was challenged and balanced by the other super power to come out of the war, the Soviet Union. With the collapse of the latter in 1989–1990, the U.S. stood alone and said so. But the drive to dominance using military force began right after the war and has intensified ever since, generating a great deal of hostility around the world.

In 1946, George F. Kennan, ambassador to the Soviet Union, sent what was known as the long telegram home, outlining the containment policy of the U.S. and its rationale. This was followed in 1948 by Policy Planning Study 23, a part of which read:

> We have about 50 percent of the world's wealth but only 6.3 percent of its population.... In this situation, we cannot fail to be the objective of envy and resentment. Our real task in the coming period is to devise a pattern of relationships which will permit us to maintain this policy of disparity.... We need not deceive ourselves that we can afford today the luxury of altruism and world benefaction.... We should cease to talk about vague and ... unreal objectives such as human rights, the raising of living standards, and democratization. The day is not far off when we are going to have to deal in straight power concepts.[63]

During the Cold War the U.S. supported whatever dictators seemed likely to be anti–Communist and to support us, and even overthrew democratically elected governments in Guatemala, Chile, and Nicaragua (by funding and arming the Contras), and supported death squads operating on behalf of the big landowners in El Salvador. The U.S. supported dictatorial governments in the Middle East including Saudi Arabia, Kuwait, Iran under the shah, and Saddam Hussein in Iraq, and, early on, the Taliban regime in Afghanistan. Additionally, the U.S. has long adopted a one-sided approach to the key problem in the Middle East, the Israeli-Palestinian conflict, thus alienating most of the Arab world. Israel is the chief recipient of U.S. foreign aid, mostly military, and the Saudi Arabian royal family is kept on a loose leash by allowing them to buy high-tech jet fighters.

The first President Bush started the Gulf War not only to liberate Kuwait but also to establish what he called a "New World Order," in which "What we say, goes."[64] After Bush, Bill Clinton failed to reduce the military budget in spite of the fact that the Soviet Union had disappeared as a threat and even "prepared to initiate nuclear war against North Korea."[65] He echoed Kennan, saying that "we have 4 percent of the world's population and we want to keep 22 percent of its wealth."[66] It was during these years that the doctrine of Full Spectrum Dominance was developed, meaning that the U.S. would control the world. With the George H. W. Bush presidency, Dick Cheney affirmed that "the arrangement [for] the twenty-first century is most assuredly being shaped right now" to ensure that "the United States will continue to be the dominant political, economic and military power in the world."[67] And if that was not clear enough, he went on: "America needs an aggressive and unilateral approach in foreign policy, one that would secure dominance of world affairs, by force if necessary."[68] The administration of President George W. Bush began by dismantling the Anti-Ballistic Missile Treaty,[69] ignoring the Kyoto Protocol and the UN's anti–land mine treaty, removing the U.S. signature from the treaty that established the International Criminal Court, and violating the Geneva Convention and other international laws regulating the treatment of prisoners. It continued the long policy of ignoring the provisions of the Nuclear Non-proliferation Treaty that required the existing nuclear powers to give up their weapons in exchange for the non–nuclear powers' restraint in developing such weapons themselves. In effect, it revoked democratic safeguards at home such as *habeas corpus* and allowed the government to spy on its own citizens. In addition, it began a new military build-up including new generations of nuclear weapons and, as everyone knows, it ignored the United Nations and unilaterally invaded Iraq. The point was and is, as Deputy Secretary of State Paul Wolfowitz said, "Other nations fear us."[70]

To indicate that this posture was not a passing phase of the 1990s, the most recent weapons development program, the Prompt Global Strike system mentioned earlier, has this outcome as its intent: This weapon would carry an enormous conventional warhead on an ICBM rocket that would deliver the equivalent of a nuclear strike without the radiation anywhere on the earth in one hour or less with pinpoint accuracy.[71] It is the perfect weapon for full spectrum dominance and it is both an effect and a symbol of the war system itself, revealing the fear in which we all live as a result of the insecurity we have created. Since we have made the threat global, or common, the ability to deliver violence must also be common, or so the reasoning goes and will continue to go until we realize that security is also common and one cannot be secure unless all are. Prompt Global Strike will not make the world safer. Just the opposite, but it reveals perfectly the failed logic of the war system.

Unfortunately, the costs of this posture are high, not only in monetary terms, but also in exacerbating the very problem of jihadists. The attacks have greatly multiplied the number of young, Muslim men, both the poor and uneducated and the well-off and highly educated, who are violently angry at the United States and Britain. The current wars are a fertile breeding ground for jihadists and, as Mohammed Fathi Osman has observed, they have "allowed the juristic heritage of jihad and military to be strongly revived, with inevitable tones and actions of violence."[72] And as Robert Wright noted in a recent *New York Times* article, the practice of attacking targets in Pakistan with drones is counterproductive. He also cites research by Jenna Jones, who has "studied 298 attempts, from 1945 through 2004, to weaken or eliminate terrorist groups through 'leadership decapitation'— eliminating people in senior positions. Her work suggests that decapitation doesn't lower the life expectancy of the decapitated groups — and, if anything, may have the opposite effect."[73] And he further observes in the same article, "one good way to stoke a sense of injustice is to fire missiles into cars, homes and offices in hopes of killing terrorists, while in fact killing no few innocent civilians. Estimates of the ratio of civilians to militants killed are all over the map … but the estimate of the Pakistani people, which is all that matters, tends toward the higher end. And the notion that these strikes are a kind of national humiliation long ago entered Pakistani culture. A popular song from a couple of years ago says Americans 'kill people like insects.'"

All of this makes the evolution toward peace more difficult than a systems analysis by itself would seem to suggest, but there is reason for optimism, as we shall see in the coming chapters. In the first place, all empires fall and the American empire will be no exception. It is already showing severe signs of stress, including a great difficulty in trying to stamp out a third-rate insurgency in the two Middle Eastern countries it occupies, thus putting great pressure on its military forces as well as foisting off the cost of the war onto future generations. The majority of citizens are opposed to the wars at this writing. As suggested earlier, empires are becoming more and more impossible.

The war system doctrine of "realism" is no longer functional, if it ever was. As J. Milburn Thompson points out:

> While the ethical shortcomings of realism have long troubled its critics, in the twenty-first century realism seems politically inadequate to address the spectrum of issues posed by the contemporary world. Realism is narrowly focused on issues of security and power, the military, and war…. Realism is too reductionist and too constricted to handle the complexity, chaos, interdependence, and divisions of the contemporary world. Human security depends on factors that go well beyond military strength and political power.[74]

The old way no longer works. It is plain to see that aggression produces retaliation and retaliation produces further aggression. What war produces is war.

A Final Note on Social Relations in a War System

It is axiomatic that the social relationships in a war system are different from those in a peace system. In a just and peaceful society people are treated as ends in themselves. Their good and the common good are the objects of a social interaction in which each person is valued for himself or herself. Each person is seen to have an inviolable right to live and to be happy, to be treated as a subject and not as an object. In the war system individuals are treated as means to ends. Their value is not self-contained, but only exists insofar as it serves someone else's purposes. This is self-evident in the military, where in training individuals are coerced into losing their particular identity so they can act literally *en masse*, and thus in battle their commanders can use them to attain an end. They are not valued for themselves, their lives are not a good except insofar as they can achieve an "objective," take a hill or storm a fort. While it is regrettable, they are expendable, like things. One needs so many soldiers, so many rifles, so many land mines. Of course, the military objective is taken at the expense of other humans who are likewise objectified. Soldiers are cogs in a machine that employs violence to achieve its end, which is to mass produce death. It may be argued that this regrettable sacrifice is for the common good and that may or may not be true. One must ask, however, whose common good and if the price is worth the result. And one must keep in mind that in wartime, self-delusion and compartmentalized thinking nearly always prevail over the truth.

In *Thoughts in Solitude*, Thomas Merton writes that "when men are merely submerged in a mass of impersonal human beings pushed around by automatic forces, they lose their true humanity, their integrity, their ability to love, their capacity for self-determination."[75] He goes on to observe that such a society "can no longer be held together by love: and consequently it is held together by a violent and abusive authority." This is the bald truth about all armies, about concentration camps and conquered countries. People are not treated as ends in themselves.

So far we have looked carefully and realistically at the war system. It is and has been the dominant system for dealing with conflict for several thousand years. It is overdetermined, redundant, and self-fueling. It is the iron cage we have made for ourselves. It is no wonder that many people believe there is no way out of it. But the surprising truth is that there is no lock on the door. We can reach through the bars anytime we want and lift the latch and let ourselves go free. Section II, "Peace," shows us how to do that.

SECTION II. PEACE

CHAPTER 5

Defining Peace

The question that always comes up when talking about putting an end to war is, "What if we had not fought the Nazis (or Japanese, or Italians, or Iraqis, or Al Qaeda, etc.)?" And the answer follows inevitably, "We had to fight them." Well, maybe we did. But this is the wrong question if we are to find our way into a future without war. The right question is "What if we had not had to fight them?" It opens up new doorways to new lines of thought and gets us off the old treadmill that was taking us nowhere.

It is true that today we live in a broken world, one badly fragmented along lines of hostility. Nations sometimes war against nations, ethnic and tribal groups generate hatred and genocide against one another, some religions preach the damnation of others, the rich oppress the poor, and the ecosystems upon which human well-being relies deteriorate. Direct violence and structural violence are pervasive. One nation spends $4.5 million on a robot killing machine[1] while multitudes in another try to live on a dollar a day and scrounge in burning garbage dumps for food. True peace would be an end to this situation, a healing across the fault lines and a restoration of justice so that all have enough to live healthy lives. A true peace would eliminate the overt and structural violence. True peace is a society that, rather than suppressing life, nurtures it. The good news is that the brokenness, the hostility, and the acquiescence in structural violence are not all pervasive. There is a great deal of peace across the world and it is growing even though the media generally fails to report it as news. These developments include such things as the UN peacekeeping missions, the programs of the UNHCR (United Nations High Commissioner for Refugees), UNICEF (United Nations Children's Fund), UNEP (United Nations Environment Program), and citizen-led projects such as the Nonviolent Peace Force, UNA/USA, peace education programs at several thousand colleges and universities, Peace Brigades International, Citizens for Global Solutions, the Rainforest Action Network, Sister City programs, and

UN PEACEKEEPERS IN HAITI. The "Blue Helmets" provide post-conflict stabilization, including monitoring cease-fires, assisting in disarmament as combatants stand down, implementing agreements, and peace building, including strengthening the rule of law, power sharing, and economic and social development. These multilateral forces are made up of both soldiers and civilian experts. Since 1948 they have deployed on 63 missions and are currently serving in 16 ongoing missions at a cost of about 0.5 percent of current global military spending. (UN Photo/Marco Domino. Providing security during food distribution in Port-au-Prince, January 2010 [#426408])

other non-governmental organizations such as Doctors Without Borders, the Heifer Project, and hundreds of smaller but crucial projects being undertaken by such organizations as the Blue Mountain Project, by individual churches supporting schools in Haiti, and on and on. The growth over the last 100 years in the numbers and impact of these endeavors has been just stunning. It is especially so in the non-government sector, where the number of such organizations grew from only a handful in 1900 to over 100,000 today. The world is struggling to move in the right direction despite the fact that many people find it hard to visualize or describe peace. People do find it easy to define war and to visualize it. They can draw pictures of war. They have a harder time drawing pictures of peace. It is extremely telling that when you Google "war," you get thousands of images of people in action. If you Google "peace," mostly what you get are a few pages of images of the peace symbol or people making the V for peace with their fingers.

Negative Peace, Peace Through Strength, Pax, Deterrence

Serious students of peace categorize it in two ways. The first and least satisfactory is "negative peace," which is merely the absence of war. It is the kind of peace that one gets most frequently in a war system. Peace is seen as the result of a successful war. As Aristotle saw it, "We make war in order to have peace."[2] And more recently, Mao Tse-tung repeated the contradiction: "We are advocates of the abolition of war, we do not want war; but war can only be abolished through war, and in order to get rid of the gun it is necessary to take up the gun."[3] But it is not only Communist dictators who subscribe to this view in the modern world. President Barack Obama expressed this very definition of peace in, of all places, his speech accepting the Nobel Peace Prize. Echoing the common confusion that war has always been with us ("War, in one form or another, appeared with the first man"), he immediately pointed out that he is "a head of state sworn to protect and defend my nation." And he went on to say, "So yes, the instruments of war do have a role to play in preserving the peace."[4] This belief is so pervasive in our war-oriented culture that you can even buy a T-shirt off the Internet with Aristotle's saying as a logo.[5] The best case this school of thought can come up with is that peace, defined as the absence of war, is the result of a threat of overwhelming violence as in nuclear deterrence. The Strategic Air Command, whose mission is the delivery of overwhelming nuclear destruction, has as its motto "Peace is our profession."

While the absence of war is certainly to be desired, this definition of peace is not very helpful. It tells what peace is not, but not what it is. As we have seen, this is due in part to the nature of education in a war system, wherein war is explained as inevitable and peace a lull in international violence brought about and maintained by superior force. It is no wonder that many people have little hope and only a small ability to see the way ahead to peace. Our culture is impoverished. In fact, the Roman word for peace, which as noted earlier comes from the root word meaning the kind of treaty a defeated and subjugated people must sign with the victor, has became the standard Western understanding of peace. Even when there is no large-scale overt violence, often there is a hidden or structural violence as the result of one party in a war defeating another or of one class dominating the others in a system of inequality of wealth and power within the nation. Structural violence is the glue of a dominator system. It is the mailed fist in the velvet glove. Threat, economic power, and ideology are used to hold some people down, often in poverty. The peace at the end of World War I, dictated by the Versailles Treaty, was an example: the Germans, who had lost the war, were simply handed the terms of the treaty and told to sign it or face military occupation. They were not allowed to have an effective military and had to pay the victors for the entire cost of the war. Negative peace is simply order imposed from above. All dictatorships in which there is no armed rebellion fit the definition of negative peace but democracies also suffer from it. Negative peace is often accompanied by huge armaments systems and actively prepared militaries. In the case of the *Pax Americana* in the years since the end of World War II, U.S. soldiers and sailors have been stationed at hundreds of bases all around the world. After World War II the Soviets set up dictatorships in Eastern Europe. Since negative peace always involves the repression of someone else, or the threat to fight those who would change the terms of the order, war often breaks out after an indeterminate period, as we saw in the last chapter.

Negative peace is always unstable because it does not result in equal justice or equal security for all. Nevertheless, for a time it works well for the nation that, through its ability to project military power, can dominate the world economy. In that case, a disproportionate share of the world's wealth, such as oil, strategic minerals, commodities, manufactured goods, and so forth, will flow to the dominator nation. Great Britain in the nineteenth century was such a power and in the twentieth century it was the United States. To say the least, this unequal distribution of the world's wealth produces envy and resentment. It is also unstable because it relies on an inevitably shifting balance of power. As a top dominator nation loses power, either through economic weakness or a change of heart with regard to its imperial position (security realists would call this a "failure of will"), or a new alliance of rivals, the next great powers will be willing to attack and defeat it, setting up yet another round of violent competition.

Another aspect of negative peace is the drain of resources into military systems, into the hardware or weapons, the research, the personnel, and the cost of caring for the veterans of the previous wars. Money invested in weapons is economically wasted, since it does not produce anything of use value for consumers and instead produces machines that destroy use value and the economic systems of other countries. Nor does it create as many jobs, dollar for dollar, as money spent in such fields as education and health care. And as a great power begins its inevitable decline, the resources it must pour into holding on to power accelerate its economic decline. At the end of a reign, great powers are often in deficit financing to maintain their militaries, which are stretched to the limit. As the Romans found out, in the end there were never enough soldiers to hold the boundaries of the empire.

Empire: On Its Way Out?

One of the encouraging trends that seems to show that we are moving out of the age of warfare, or at least are in the end stages of it, is the difficulty of establishing and maintaining empires. The great historic empires began to collapse in the First World War. By 1918, the Austro-Hungarian Empire, which had been around in one form or another since the Middle Ages, had disintegrated, as had the more recent German empire, a creation of but 48 years. The Ottoman Empire, founded in 1321, also went down in World War I. The second German empire, Hitler's so-called Thousand Year Reich, lasted 12 years. The Russian empire, which had morphed in 1917 into the Soviet empire and then in 1945 expanded to conquer all of Eastern Europe, came to pieces in 1989–1991. The short-lived Italian empire in North Africa, which Mussolini trumpeted as the start of the revival of the Roman Empire itself, also came to naught in the crucible of World War II. The British, Belgian and Dutch colonial empires were fatally weakened by 1945 and in the 1960s they had to give up all but a fraction of the territories they controlled, as did the French, whose dreams of world power came crashing down at Dien Bien Phu in 1954 and Algeria in 1962. The last gasp of the British empire was in 1956 with the Suez debacle, although they did fight a rather ridiculous little war against Argentina in 1982 in order to hold onto a rock in the south Atlantic. The attempt of the Serbs to hold the Yugoslav mini-empire together resulted in disaster for all concerned and failed miserably in the 1990s. By 2000 only the Americans continued to thrash against this historical tide, in spite of the fact that they had failed utterly in Southeast Asia in the 1970s. Their efforts to remake the Middle East in their image turned into a disaster in Afghanistan and Iraq, in spite of all their conventional military might. Even in peacetime the U.S. maintains 207 military bases in 130 countries around the world, in addition to 6,000 bases in the U.S.[6] The total is actually more since these numbers do not reflect bases in Iraq, Afghanistan, Uzbekistan, Israel and elsewhere. According to a Pentagon map of base locations, "The United States Military is currently deployed to more locations than it has been throughout history."[7] The cost of bearing this burden is enormous — according to the Pentagon's own estimates, $658 billion a year out of a national budget that is raised through deficit financing. Empire is simply too expensive.

All of these empires, or attempts at empire, were justified in high-sounding moral terms, such as the French *mission civilisatrice*, German *Kultur*, and the Americans' claim that they were bringing democracy and freedom to the world. But when looked at honestly, these high-sounding claims were just covers for the desire to dominate and control resources, labor and the terms of trade. They were about power over, and their failure shows the impossibility of a global or even regional dominator society in the twenty-first century. Some were brought down by coalitions, others by nonviolent opposition, others thwarted by armed insurrection, but all were brought down. It is not just that empires come and go, as they have indeed during the long darkness, the 6000 years of the historical war system. This trend is something different; it demonstrates that empire is no longer possible. Too much communication, too much world awareness by those the imperialists would like to subject, and the power of nonviolent resistance and asymmetric warfare have all combined to make empire obsolete. Of course, the fall of empires leaves behind chaos and does not necessarily make for peace. But it does suggest that large-scale dominator societies may be becoming an impossibility.

The reason that empires fail amid competitive wars is that people think in terms of security rather than in terms of peace. If we think in terms of security, then we let fear dominate our actions. We will think in terms of walls, armies, weapons, defense, massive overseas deployments, preponderant force, preemptive strikes and victory by might. We necessarily demonize others. We see conflict as a zero-sum game — all out victory or unacceptable defeat. Therefore one cannot have too much potential to do violence to any potential "enemy." One must match and outmatch not only the other's capability but also their potential capability in the worst scenario that can be imagined. When other groups see this behavior they imitate it out of fear or prudence. Conflict is quickly militarized. If the goal is security, war is the result and even victory leads all too often not to peace but to pacification. However, if we think in terms of genuine peace, then we are able to follow an entirely different path. We think in terms of courts, parliaments, reconciliation, cooperation, mediation, law, human rights, fairness, the common well-being, and getting to know the full humanity of the other. We think in terms of food, medicine, education, and community development. We think in terms of conflict resolution, peace education, and nonviolence training. When we think peace, we act out peace, thereby reducing the fears of others.

Positive Peace

Positive peace is based on the recognition of the reality of interdependence, that national borders are no longer capable of providing security, that peace must be a comprehensive, systemic culture with built-in redundancies for the control of aggression. All thinking about peace must now be global. "Everything is interconnected. This interconnection is the Net of Indra, in which everything contains everything else. It is 'dependent co-arising,'" according to the Buddhist teacher Roshi Robert Aitkin.[8] This is true because, as Mary Kaldor has pointed out, "It is no longer possible to contain violence or lawlessness territorially."[9] The emergence of global civil society is a functional response to this reality. "What has changed," she writes, "are the opportunities for linking up with other like-minded groups in different parts of the world, and for addressing demands not just to the state but to global institutions and other states."[10]

It is no longer sufficient to think or act in partial ways. A peace system must be global and comprehensive. Gene Sharp, founder of the Harvard Program on Nonviolent Sanctions, has harshly criticized the so-called peace movement for settling for, at best, partial victories, for working away piecemeal against a particular weapons system, a particular war, or against a particular nation, all the while claiming piously to be the saving remnant, the only pure ones. All this, he believes, is futile.

> Peace groups have been willing to settle for things far short of abolishing war.... Where is there a peace organization that really expects that ... war is going to be removed from society? ... There is no fresh thinking among peace groups. There is no effective challenging of the political assumptions that underline the war system itself.[11]

As Arun Gandhi, the Mahatma's grandson, puts it, "It is almost as impossible to find a patchwork solution as it is to stay dry in a swimming pool."[12] But it is not enough to theorize while millions of people are struggling to meet the barest minimum of human needs. Thai professor and long-time peace activist Sulak Sivaraksa reminds us that "realistically speaking, you cannot expect the hungry and the oppressed whose basic human rights are violated to sit still while intellectuals and technocrats debate the vagaries of peace. Peace to these people means being free to attain their potential in life, to raise a family, find a place in their community, and to be able to have control of at least the most crucial aspects of their destiny."[13]

But while we create global institutions and networks, it is still the individual who must do the work, and for that we need a change in how we think about conflict and peacemaking. The first thing we have to jettison is anger. An angry peacemaker is an oxymoron. Many of us in the peace movement have marched in anti-war demonstrations chanting harsh slogans that simply alienated the majority of our fellow citizens. "If we work for peace out of anger we will never succeed," writes Buddhist monk Thich Nhat Hanh.[14] Commitment, yes; violent emotions, no. So how do we conceive of and work for peace? John Paul Lederach has the key; we use our moral imagination.

The question he poses is "How do we transcend the cycles of violence that bewitch our community while still living in them?"[15] Technical competence is not enough. What is required is "the capacity to imagine something rooted in the challenges of the real world yet capable of giving birth to that which does not yet exist."[16] There could be no better description of the aims of this book than this. Such imagining requires four things: "(1) the capacity to imagine ourselves in a web of relationships that includes our enemies, (2) the ability to sustain a paradoxical curiosity that embraces complexity without reliance on dualistic polarity, (3) the fundamental belief in and pursuit of the creative act, and (4) the acceptance of the inherent risk of stepping into the mystery of the unknown that lies beyond the far too familiar landscape of violence."[17] The opposite of moral imagination is dogma and dualistic thinking, unquestioned axioms and a posture of us versus them, of pure good versus pure evil. It is critical to look honestly at our relationships with our enemies and to acknowledge our role in perpetuating the enmity. This is simply taking ownership of our own acts, "acknowledging relational mutuality," and leaving blame behind in the search for a way out of the spiral of violence.[18] As Michael Nagler says, "We don't need to find out who is to blame for all the violence, we just need to find out how to make it stop."[19] In this regard, his recasting of conflict in a medical metaphor is helpful. Violence is a diseased community, and peace is a healthy one. Or, as he also reminds us, violence is a kind of ignorance, the response people give when they don't know of any alternative. The solution then becomes not counter-violence, but wisdom. One no longer fears learning about how the "enemy" perceives the conflict, or rejects his views out of hand, in the same way that the medical researcher does not fear learning more about bacteria. This opens us up to curiosity, to seeing the complexity in the conflict situation. Lederach writes that this curiosity "is excited by those things that are not immediately understood."[20] As in "Why do they hate us?" asked as a serious question and not a dismissive head shake, and then listening seriously to their answer. Only then can we initiate dialogue. And peacemaking requires us to believe in the creative act, that amid the barren landscape of violence we will be able to create something new. If we do not believe this, we are doomed to failure from the start. And so making peace is to take a risk, "to step into the unknown without any guarantee of success or even safety ... violence is known, peace is the mystery."[21] Peacemaking is an art, and, like all art, must often rely mainly on intuitive invention. Fortunately, there is plenty of it.

Creating peace means creating a whole culture. It requires that we give attention not only to international conflicts, international law and institutions, but also — at the opposite end of the spectrum — to our own mindsets and everything in between. This means attention to justice and fairness, to conflict resolution, to governance at all levels down to the very local, to the way in which our media need educating, to issues of ecological justice and human rights, to gross economic inequalities that distort the body politic, to the behavioral outcomes of religious belief, to the way in which we structure our families, to our educational system and so forth. In a culture of peace the news media will highlight these issues far more than they do now, and they will not seek to push the simple-minded dualisms that we currently see every night but rather report on their true complexity.

To summarize: positive peace is a social system that at all levels produces abundant life and justice, a system in which conflict continues to exist but is managed by non-military, nonviolent means at all levels, from the personal to the international. It is structured as a partnership society, that is, one based on shared power and consultation. In a peace system, war itself is the enemy, as is the injustice that often causes it. Institutions for creating and maintaining justice, such as laws, parliaments, and courts, deal with conflict nonviolently. And where these are not enough, active nonviolent resistance confronts those who are unjust, arbitrary, and violent. Education includes peace education. In a peace system basic human needs are met, including the right to life, to food and clean water, health care, education and worship. Human rights and diversity are respected. People know how to defend themselves against tyranny without using violence. In short, a many-layered, redundant system of institutions, values and ideas all work to perpetuate peace in the same way that their opposites perpetuate war. In a peace system people are nurtured and respected rather than exploited. In a peace system children bury their parents. Parents do not have to bury their children as they do in a war system. In short, a peace system would be a global social system for governing international and intrastate conflict by means of laws, courts, conflict resolution, nonviolence, and peace education. Many readers will be surprised to learn that this is the direction in which we have actually started to head over the last couple of hundred years. In spite of the overwhelming violence of the last century, the wheel of the ship has been turned and slowly, slowly, like a huge ocean vessel, it is responding to the helm.

The following chapters describe a peace system in detail, beginning with the assertion that peace exists in abundance in history and is, therefore, as real as war.

CHAPTER 6

The History of Peace in Ancient and Medieval Times

It may come as a surprise to many people that there is a long history of peace. Only a few years ago, the program director at the United States Institute of Peace replied to a request for funding to research the history of peace, "There is no such thing."[1] Women and African Americans ran up against this same reaction when they began the serious recovery of their histories.

Unfortunately, it is all too true that when we think of history we tend to think of war. In school we learned American history as a series of wars, beginning with the French and Indian War and going on to the War for Independence, the War of 1812, the Mexican War, the Civil War, the Indian wars, the Spanish-American War, World War I, World War II, the Korean War, the Vietnam War and the Gulf Wars, leaving out such little incidents as Grenada, Panama, and supporting the Contras. My own introduction to the study of history came as a high school boy reading Caesar's *Gallic Wars* in Latin class, and Winston Churchill's *The Gathering Storm,* his account of the run-up to World War II. The history channel on television is dedicated almost wholly to programs about war. And the proverbial man on the street, when he hears that I am a history professor, inevitably starts to talk to me about the Civil War or World War II. And when people learn that my current project is to be a book about peace, I invariably get the joke "That'll be a short book!" followed by "Ha ha!"

In fact, there is a lot of peace in history and one must ask the question "Why don't we all know that as a result of our common education?" Is it because, until very recently, history was written almost exclusively by men? The writing of history for a long time has been a patriarchal domain and, as we have seen in chapter 1, there is a school of thought in peace history that believes that war and patriarchy were invented together as part and parcel of a particular kind of civilization. War certainly does fascinate men. Is it because war is more interesting than peace? Why do we think that? Is it because our own nation was founded in and preserved by war, as we are led by historians to believe? Take, for example, Geoffrey Perret's 1989 history of America, titled *A Country Made by War: From the Revolution to Vietnam—The Story of America's Rise to Power*. The jacket blurb, written by the then dean of American historians, Stephen E. Ambrose, whose Civil War and World War II books are national best-sellers, reads:

> Since 1775 no nation has had as much experience of war as the United States — nine major wars in nine generations. And in between the wars have come other armed conflicts such as the Philippine insurgency and clashes in the Persian Gulf. America's wars have been like the rungs on a ladder by which it rose to greatness.... This book places the nation's military history as a constant factor in the evolution of American life. It is as important as geography, immigration, the growth of business, the separation of powers, the inventiveness of the people, or anything else that contributes strongly to America's unique identity among the nations of the earth.[2]

This is a distortion of history. Elise Boulding writes that "The missing element in social awareness of the nature of the human experience through history is an image of the dailiness of life ... that sustains human existence. The fact that most human activity revolves around raising and feeding families, interspersed with times of feasting and celebration of human creativity ... rarely shows through in history books."[3] Matthew Melko, who has researched historic peaces, concludes that "peace is a fact, not a vision. It is ubiquitous, incessant, normal. Peace prevails in most places at most times."[4] Kenneth Boulding concurs: "In the mass, war has probably always constituted a relatively small fraction of human activity."[5]

This bias in favor of war is not confined to American history education. A 1985 German publication titled *Peace—A Topic in European History Textbooks?* concluded that

> in history books — not just in the Federal Republic but in neighboring countries as well — the presentation of political conflicts and armed confrontation, despotic claims and acts of submission, veiled and open aggression leading to barbaric atrocities, is what by far predominates. Peace, understanding, tolerance, and respect for others regardless of political, cultural, or religious differences are paid far less attention, if they are given consideration at all.[6]

And so the writing of history has for a long time now had a war-ist bias. Like women's history and African American history, the history of peace got lost. A humble but telling example is a mural of Carrie Chapman Catt in her native town of Ripon, Wisconsin. The picture story includes her contributions to the women's suffrage movement but makes no mention of her prominent role in the international peace movement. Somehow, it got left out. And so goes our national story. It's no wonder that people think that war is normal and inevitable and that peace has a scant history, if any at all.

In spite of this overwhelmingly dominant trend, and countering it, a small group of historians has been at work recovering the lost history of peace. Beginning in 1964 they founded the Council on Peace Research in History, now expanding its work under a new name, the Peace History Society. They have produced articles and monographs that are beginning to show that a richly textured and varied peace has existed in the past in a meaningful and profound way.

Even the most cursory analysis reveals that there has been a great deal of peace in history. Looking at U.S. relations with Germany, the two countries were at war for six years in the twentieth century and at peace for 94. The U.S. has not fought Spain in over a century or been at war with Mexico since 1848 or Canada and England since 1815. The U.S. has never fought France, Poland, Hungary, Brazil, and so on. In short, if we add up all the nation-years of peace, they far outnumber the nation-years of war. And even during periods of major war, most of the nations are not involved. Costa Rica and Panama have no standing armies.

Even in the heart of darkness, in the midst of war, one can find some peace history taking place — for example, in the resistance to war movements and in the actions of the conscientious objectors. None of this information cancels out the fact that there have been many wars and that war is endemic in the nation-state system, but neither do those facts cancel out our very practical and abundant experience with peaceful relations. Unfortunately, our view of history and our educational system, especially at the secondary level, focus only on one part of reality and, by ignoring the other part, distort the past, give the lie to peace, and help to perpetuate the war system.

The history of peace includes an array of phenomena across a wide spectrum of activities from truces among the warlike nations to cultures that are truly peaceful, to opposition to particular wars, dedicated nonviolence as a way of life, peace with nature, the development of world-order models, literary works on peace, activists who organize for an end to war, philosophies of peace, environmental protection, human rights, conflict resolution, peace as a theme in the arts, and, at long last, the work of peace historians.

The new and growing interest in peace history is the result of the fact that the costs of war are becoming ever greater relative to the gains. Today war is so acute as to be seen by many as a major social problem. Veteran naval officer, military historian, and internationally syndicated columnist Gwynne Dyer observes, "The logical end point of living in ever larger groups is the evolution of a politically united world society in which every human being is regarded as 'one of us,' but the penultimate stage in which we live, with the world divided into about three dozen powerful states and over a hundred weak ones, is probably the most violent, and certainly the most dangerous phase of human history."[7]

Perhaps this new field of peace history study can enlighten us some. We know that we cannot do something we cannot think of, and if we cannot think of peace in any positive way because we mistakenly believe there to be very little of it in our cultural experience, then we are doomed to soldier on until we are all dead in some not-too-distant Armageddon made more dramatic by the newly invented weapons of mass destruction. And so the project that some historians now have under way to recover the lost history of peace might be not only interesting but also crucial to our survival.

Peace historians are looking for peaces, for long periods without armed hostilities, either prior to the invention of the war system or within the war system. They are also looking for the causes of these and of their failures, as people returned to war as a means of managing conflict. An example of a long peace would be the nearly 200-year-long peace between Canada and the U.S. Absolutely no one expects to see tank battles along the border in northern Minnesota. Another example is the long peace that has existed for the last two centuries in Scandinavia. Peace historians are looking for techniques of peacemaking and peacekeeping, including the history of diplomacy, instances of conciliation and conflict resolution, nonviolent campaigns, peace education, published theories about peace, and proposals and plans for a just world order. Another example is the teachings of various religions on peace. In more modern times one would be looking for the histories of peace institutions such as the Carnegie Endowment for Peace, the United States Institute of Peace, and the United Nations, as well as for the stories of citizen-based movements for peace, disarmament, human rights, and so forth. These are all examples of peace history with a small "p." Historians are looking for the overall pattern of peace throughout history, its ebb and flow, causes and conditions, and instances of more-or-less peaceful cultures for comparative study. Then there is peace with a capital "P"—that is, with the full sweep of history to see how peace has changed and evolved over the last hundred centuries or so and to assess the state of peace at this point in history. The marvelous work done by peace history specialists over the last 30 years has made it possible at last to take an overview.

The history of peace falls into three broad periods. The first era, lasting until approximately 4000 BC, we can call the Long Peace of Prehistory, the historical peace in the period after the development of agriculture but before writing. This period, it is hypothesized, was a time before the invention of war as we know it. The second era, from roughly 4000 BC to the present, I shall call Peace in the Long Darkness, that period of endemic warfare when fighting was considered glorious and honorable, or at least normal and inevitable, and when states attacked each other continuously. The latter part of this era has seen war become even more savagely destructive based on mass armies and technologically enhanced slaughter.

The third period appears to be an incipient historical break. I am proposing to call the last 200 years the Dark Light of Dawn, because in this time period more and more people have begun to take positive steps to de-legitimate and control war. These include the rise of organized peace societies beginning in the early nineteenth century, whose efforts came at last to their first fruition with the holding of the Hague Peace Conference in 1899, which resulted in the establishment of the World Court. The end of that century also included the early experiments with nonviolent resistance as a massive social technique undertaken by Mohandas Gandhi and, in the next century, its further evolution by Gandhi and such well-known individuals as Dr. King, Diane Nash, Cesar Chavez, Gene Sharp, and organizations such as the Fellowship of Reconciliation, Women Against Military Madness, and countless others. It also includes the first efforts of world-level bodies to control war, the two collective security organizations — the League of Nations and the UN — and a second court, the newly created International Criminal Court. And it includes the development of peace education and promising new techniques in the field of conflict resolution. In the twentieth century, and especially in its latter half, the number and scope of non-government organizations (NGOs) have multiplied dramatically. Even more importantly, they are interacting on a planetary basis. The new communications technology has allowed citizens to become much more influential in the development of war-limitation treaties such as the international convention banning land mines, recently ratified by the 133rd state and thus going into effect. But to begin at the beginning, what do historians know, or at least suspect, about the history of peace in the very ancient past?

The Long Peace of Prehistory

Historians and anthropologists tend to argue that ancient hunting and gathering peoples did not make war on one another. Gwynne Dyer states, "War is part of our history, but it is not in at all the same sense part of our prehistory," and he goes on to say that "the important point about precivilized societies is that people did not kill people much."[8] An earlier researcher, Quincy Wright, concluded in his study of war that "the collectors, lower hunters and lower agriculturalists are the least warlike. The higher hunters and higher agriculturalists are more warlike, while the highest agriculturalists and the pastoral peoples are the most warlike of all."[9] While there is very little hard evidence for prehistoric hunting and gathering bands, it would not have been worthwhile for small bands to risk losing the food-providing function of even a few hunters in a fight. Furthermore, there was plenty of room and game to go around. Still, such assertions must remain almost entirely based in speculative logic. With the invention of agriculture and settled village life a great deal more evidence becomes available to the researchers, even though written evidence was still 5000 to 6000 years in the future.

Archeological evidence is beginning to reveal a time after the invention of agriculture and before the invention of warfare, at least in the ancient Middle East, the cradle of Western culture. Riane Eisler's book, *The Chalice and the Blade,* summarizes the arguments for this interpretation of history. They are based in "Cultural Transformation theory."[10] Underlying the great cultural diversity of the world, it appears that there are two fundamental models of human society, the dominator societies and the partnership societies. The former are hierarchical — ranking people into gradations. They are patriarchal, worship vengeful male deities, and are warlike. Power is something that is held over others. The latter societies are more egalitarian, allow men and women equal roles and respect, tend to worship goddesses, and are peaceful. Power is something that is shared. Prior to the fifth millennium BC, the evidence shows partnership societies existing in the ancient Middle East. Villages were built out in the open with no fortifications, no caches of weapons are found, burials show no discrimination against women or major social class rankings, the deities were goddesses and the people worshipped Mother Earth. Religions stressed peace between humans and nature co-existing in a harmonious, productive and prosperous relationship. The art shows no scenes of wars or warriors. It is important to note that while these societies were not patriarchal, they were not matriarchal either. Eisler writes that a partnership society was "basically a cooperative social organization. Both men and women — even sometimes, as in Catal Huyuk, people of different racial stocks — worked cooperatively for the common good."[11] And further, she writes, "One of the most remarkable features of Old European society revealed by the archeological spade is its essentially *peaceful* character."[12]

Thomas Gregor argues in *A Natural History of Peace,* "Peace, where and when it occurs, is *over-determined.* We find no single basis for peaceful relationships, but a variety of overlapping institutions, values, and attitudes that run the scale from *agape,* or selfless love, to skill at reconciliation, to fear of deterrence and avoidance of others. It could hardly be otherwise. Violence is so contagious and politics so volatile that only a wide range of institutions, values, and inner motives can maintain peace."[13] The same is true of war — it too is over determined.

Peace in the Long Darkness

Beginning around the fifth millennium BC, a profound change began to occur. Volatile, contagious violence began to overwhelm the peaceful societies of Old Europe and the Middle East. It was brought into the region by invading nomads, identified by archeologist Maria Gimbutas as the Kurgans, who penetrated the region in three waves around 4300, 3400 and 3000 BC. Gimbutas points out that burials now show a ranked hierarchy of social order as well as the bodies of women sacrificed at the time of the leaders' deaths. Graves are replete with weapons. The art shows warriors and warfare. They tended to build on acropolises — hilltop forts with cyclopean stone walls. Their gods tended to be male deities and they were gods of war. The beginning of slavery also seems to be closely linked to the takeover by dominator societies. In some Kurgan camps findings indicate that "the bulk of the female population was not Kurgan, but rather of the Neolithic Old European population. What this suggests is that the Kurgans massacred most of the local men and children but spared some of the women, whom they took for themselves as concubines, wives, or slaves."[14]

By 3500 BC this model was dominant in Mesopotamia, where there was increasingly rigidly stratified society, slavery, endemic warfare and a declining status for women. Another male-dominated, warrior society carried this model into the land of Canaan, destroying the cities and villages of the local inhabitants, and, as we read in Deuteronomy 3: 3–6, "utterly destroying the men, women and children of every city." Yahweh was indeed a "man of war."

This pattern of violent warfare was carried westward to ancient Crete, a society whose art convinces us that they were successful and joyous. Crete was the last major partnership society to fall under the axe, sometime around 1000 BC. Warfare was established and became the dominant pattern. Humanity had entered the iron cage of endemic warfare.

A new, aggressive psychology came into being with the war-group. According to historian Gwynne Dyer, "The invention of armies required more than just working out ways of drilling large numbers of people to act together, although that was certainly part of the formula. A formation of drilled men has a different psychology — a controlled form of mob psychology — that tends to overpower the personal identity and fears of the individuals who make it up," and then Dyer quotes World War II veteran William Manchester: "You're dealing here with complicated psychological states. No man in battle is really sane. The mindset of the soldier on the battlefield is a highly disturbed mind, and this is an epidemic of insanity which affects everybody there, and those not afflicted by it die very quickly."[15] This must have been the kind of insane fury with which Joshua's warriors slaughtered the men, women and children of the Palestinian villages that they overran. It happened elsewhere, too. We do know that the Aryan conquest of the Dravidians in India brought in a violent, hierarchical patriarchy; we know that the Aztec civilization of Central America was a similar structure and that China evolved a war system as well. By the end of the era of cultural transformation the change was complete. Eisler writes, "Everywhere society was now becoming male dominant, hierarchic, and warlike."[16] The Long Darkness had begun in Western civilization.

Every literate person familiar with the history of Western civilization can recite the litany of famous wars that made history, from the Persian Wars of the Greeks to their Peloponnesian wars, to the wars of the Roman conquest and the wars of the barbarians who destroyed their empire, to the incessant warfare of the Middle Ages (including the Hundred Years War), to the Thirty Years' War that began modern history, to the wars of French expansion under Louis XIV, to the eighteenth-century wars of independence and the Napoleonic Wars, to the American Civil War, to the wars of Italian and German unification, and on into the twentieth century, which is renowned for its slaughter. What is surprising is that the peace historian can find material even here, although much of it is of a negative peace.

During the long epoch of patriarchal violence, or the institutionalized war system, there were many truces and there were other developments, including literary and other statements about the desirability of peace, even some anti-war literature, and the rise of religions that emphasized peace, especially Buddhism and early Christianity. These were definitely counter-currents to the main stream, but they were there and it is fair to say that peace, in its richly textured variety, did not wholly disappear from Western civilization either as a desired goal or as, in some instances, a social reality. War and peace existed in "an uneasy and constant tension," in the words of historian Ben Low, author of *Imagining Peace: A History of Early English Pacifist Ideas.*[17]

Still, like modern Americans, the ancients were so embedded in a war system as to be unable to believe that genuine, positive and lasting peace was possible, but they longed for it and so they often placed it in a mythic realm. Charles Chatfield and Ruzannah Ilukhina write in the introduction to their anthology of peace history, "Early Greek poets and dramatists, and Roman ones later, contrasted the painful discord of war with the harmony of peace. Sometimes this theme was expressed as the myth of a Golden Age, a myth that was widespread in the Ancient Middle East: humanity had fallen from an ideal state of peace to a worldly condition of interminable struggle. Greek philosophers also developed the notion of natural harmony into a vision of universal, peaceful civilization in the distant future."[18] Perhaps the Greek myth of a peaceful golden age in the dim past was, in fact, a cultural memory of the long peace of prehistory, so ancient as to be too vague to have details that would give it reality. Also, the Greeks placed peace above the human realm where Eirene was the Goddess of Peace, to whom the lyric poet, Pindar prayed, saying, "Kindly Goddess of Peace, daughter of Justice," and asking for her to give the favor of peace, since it seemed beyond the power of men to create it.[19]

And it will be obvious that even the ancient Hebrews, the patriarchal scourges of the lands of Canaan, had a similar myth in their Garden of Eden story. And similar longings, as in the prophecy in Isaiah: "He shall judge between the nations and decide for many people: and they shall beat their swords into plowshares, and their spears into pruning hooks, nation shall not lift up sword against nation, neither shall they learn war anymore" (2: 3–4). Unfortunately, such sentiments are in a minority among the verses of the Old Testament, as were the longings for peace expressed in Greek philosophy and literature. Nonetheless, they were there. The dramatist Aristophanes wrote three plays appealing for an end to the long Peloponnesian war: *The Archanians* (426 BC), *The Peace* (421 BC), and the most famous of them, *Lysistrata* (411 BC), in which the women withhold sex from the men until they agree to make peace and give them a place in the decision-making of the state. This play may be a clear echo of the partnership societies that existed during the long prehistory of peace. In the fourth century, Isocrates argued for a universal peace: "I maintain that we should make peace not only with the Chians, the Rhodians, the Byzantines and the Coans, but with all mankind."[20]

The Romans had a vision of universal peace that amounted simply to universal conquest, as the historian Florus indicated:

> Now that all the races of the west and south were subjugated, and also the races of the north ... the other nations too, who were not under the rule of the empire, yet felt the greatness of Rome and revered its people as the conquerors of the world.... Thus everywhere throughout the inhabited world there was firmly-established an uninterrupted peace or truce....[21]

Truce is the more accurate term. Another Roman, Tacitus, viewed this *Pax Romana* a bit differently: "*Ubi solitudinem faciunt, pacem appellant!*" — everywhere they create a desolation, and they call it peace![22] The Stoic philosophers, including their emperor follower Marcus Aurelius, did sometimes think of themselves not as Romans but as citizens of the world, planting the seeds of an idea whose fruition would only come in the twentieth century AD. And of course, the Roman poet, Terrence, gave us the best statement of tolerance ever written: *Homo sum, nihil humani alienum a me puto,*" I am a human, therefore nothing human is alien to me.[23] But Tacitus and Terrence were voices crying in a wilderness of war. As a civilization, Roman society was the archetypical dominator society. It wasn't that some of them did not want peace. Witness the philosopher and consul Cicero: "Most people think that the achievements of war are more important than those of peace; but this opinion needs to be corrected. If we face the facts, we shall find that there have been many instances of achievement in peace more important and no less renowned than in war."[24] And Silius Italicus, a Roman poet, wrote, "Peace is the best thing that man may know: peace is better than a thousand triumphs."[25] The problem was, like modern men, they thought that war was the way to get it. And there is another point to be made about the *Pax Romana*— it was based on slavery, on structural violence. Vincent Kavaloski's summation of the great Roman peace contrasts it with true peace: "At bottom, it is a vision, not of the free flourishing of human life in a state of security and abundance, but of an imperialized world, a world governed by fear and pacified by the shadow of the sword."[26] It was, as Mark Sommer has pointed out, an example of "false peace systems."[27]

There was one genuine peace movement in late antiquity; it was the Christians. Jesus of Nazareth had taught a thorough-going pacifism and had said, among other things "Blessed are the peacemakers" (Matt. 5: 9), "For all who take the sword will perish by the sword" (Matt. 26: 52), and "Love your enemies, do good to those who hate you, bless those who curse you, pray for those who abuse you" (Matt. 5: 38–44). Several scholars, including Kenneth Leach and Robert Nolan,[28] now understand Jesus and his movement to have been a protest against the dominator society imposed by the Romans on the Jews, in which the Jewish elites participated as enablers. Jewish society itself was stratified and the laws enforced by the Pharisees created hardship against the poor. What the early Christians preached was a different set of values, described by them as "foolishness to the Greeks," Greeks here meaning the ruler class of the dominant social system in which the elites spoke Greek, the *lingua franca* of the Roman Empire.

Leach writes of Jesus, "He was born into a double system of exploitation in Palestine. While the Roman Empire imposed economic control through taxes and political control through its officials, the Palestinian state operated through the Temple which demanded economic contributions in the form of tithes and other funds."[29] In contrast, Jesus was preaching and modeling a society in which there was no hierarchy — a partnership society. He ate with the poor and the outcast and even women were welcome in his presence, a shocking thing in the ancient Middle East. When he said, "My kingdom is not of this world" (John 18: 36), he was not saying that it lay in heaven in an afterlife, but rather that the values of worldly kingdoms — power over, greed for material wealth, and so on — were not the values of love and inclusiveness that he preached as being necessary to a society that would avoid violent disaster. Leach writes that Jesus' powerful critique of contemporary Jewish society was based on its truce with the Roman Empire and he then points out that "religion goes powerfully astray when it ceases to be a sign of con-

tradiction and becomes the cement for social conformity. The foolishness of
God [e.g., loving one's enemies] is then replaced by capitulation to the values
of the world.... Conformity to 'the world' of greed, materialism and power
over is the betrayal of its foundation in folly and contradiction, and of its
necessary role as a community of contrast and dissent."[30] Rita Brock and
Rebecca Parker write, in their groundbreaking book *Saving Paradise: How
Christianity Traded Love of This World for Crucifixion and Empire*, that John
the Baptist and Jesus "came from groups that were critical of the ruling aristocracy in Jerusalem. The baptizing sects offered a path by which people sep-
arated and purified themselves from the corruptions of the Roman occupation
and its client-king. To be baptized was to renounce allegiance o the polluting
and false powers of Rome"[31] Christ rejected authoritarian thinking.[32] Paul,
writing to the little group in Rome, exhorted the faithful to

> bless those who persecute you.... Live in harmony with one another .... Repay
> no one evil for evil.... If possible, so far as it depends upon you, live peaceably
> with all. Beloved, never avenge yourselves.... No, if your enemy is hungry, feed
> him; if he is thirsty, give him drink.... Do not be overcome by evil, but over-
> come evil with good [Rom. 12: 14–21].

His famous words on love in the letter to the Corinthians end with "So
faith, hope and love abide, these three; but the greatest of these is love" (I
Cor. 13: 13). And by love, the early Christians meant *agape*, not romantic
love, but the selfless love that manifests itself in acts of kindness. This message
is reiterated again and again in the New Testament. Excerpts from the first
letter of John include "He who says he is in the light and hates his brother is
in the darkness still. He who loves his brother abides in the light" (1: 9–10),
"For this is the message we have heard from the beginning, that we should
love one another, and not be like Cain" (3: 11–12) and "he who loves is born
of God and knows God. He who does not love does not know God; for God
is love" (4: 7–8). It is easy to see why the early Christians believed that war
was a violation of God's way and will. Christ's early followers refused military
service.

The early Church understood the message as God's direction to build
an earthly paradise — that is, communities of caring, partnership societies
characterized by abundant life where the poor would be healed and fed and
women would play an important role, in short, by peace and justice and the
fruits they yield.[33] The art of the early church always showed an empty cross
and pictures of an earthly garden as paradise. The first depictions of the crucified Christ did not appear for a thousand years.[34] The original church
emphasized life, not death.

The amazing thing is how, in the fourth century, the official church was
able to abandon that view as Christianity became the official religion of the

patriarchal, war-based state of Byzantium, the heir to the old Roman Empire in the East. This provided a profound dilemma that the official church weaseled out of by developing the Christian doctrine of the just war — a betrayal of the values preached by Christ. Augustine was left in the absurd position of saying, "For the true worshipers of God even wars are peaceful, not waged out of greed or cruelty, but from the zeal for peace, to restrain evil or to assist the good," a statement quoted some 800 years later by the greatest of the medieval scholar-theologians, St. Thomas Aquinas.[35] The medieval church had sold out to the state. Christ was turned on his head. Warfare, at least under certain conditions, became lawful for Christians. And some 700 years afterwards, that same confusion of means and ends would lure Woodrow Wilson into justifying a slaughter of ten million people as the "war to end wars." Finally it was satirized in chapter 1 of George Orwell's 1949 dystopian novel *1984* as "war is peace."[36]

But while the church accepted the principle of just war, it did seriously try to limit warfare through the institutions of the Peace of God and the Truce of God. The former provided that it was a sin to harm non-combatants in war and the latter that warfare could not occur on Holy Days. By the ninth century AD, the division of Charlemagne's empire in three and then into many warring parts had occasioned an increase in localized violence, including attacks on churches. This, as we might have expected, gave rise to a response on the part of the church. In 975, Bishop Le Puy called the local warriors to a great peace council. He shrewdly attracted the masses as witnesses by bringing relics of saints, and then persuaded the nobles under pain of excommunication to swear an oath to preserve the peace — namely, to refrain from robbing churches, attacking clerics, and stealing the peasants' cattle.[37]

The movement spread and many such councils were held, usually in an open field in front of masses of peasants who watched while the churchmen made the warriors take oaths of peace.[38] This began the more general movement to establish the Truce of God, which sought to outlaw war on holy days — a more severe restriction than most moderns realize, since war was only fought in the summertime and about one-quarter of the calendar was made up of holy days. But not all the saints agreed with every provision of war limitation the church devised. St. Thomas Aquinas argued that it was lawful to fight on holy days.

Unfortunately, the Germanic barbarians who took over in the West from the Roman Empire were just as patriarchal and violent as the old Romans, and as a result, these two war-limiting prohibitions were often observed in the breach. In the fourteenth century Honore Bonet appealed to God himself as the author of war, writing in his *Code of Chivalry,* "Where did wars first exist and why? ... It was in Heaven, when our Lord God drove out the

angels.... Hence it is no great marvel if in this world there arise wars and battles, since they existed first in Heaven."[39] If warfare was cosmic in origin,
there was little men could do to eliminate it from society. A not-so-brilliant
piece of logic, but this kind of thinking made it easy to underwrite holy wars,
the Christian equivalent of the Muslim jihad. Pope Urban II preached peace
and unity to Europe in 1095 and proposed it be achieved by turning the military forces against the Muslims, thus starting the era of the Crusades.

Since warfare was endemic in medieval Europe, there was plenty of
opportunity to develop the skills necessary to negotiate a reconciliation of
differences using third-party mediators. This was called "the resigning of
quarrels" and was frequently employed, sometimes with success. Historian
Roscoe Balch concludes his essay on this process by saying, "Medieval people
did not achieve perfect peace but they did peacefully resolve many disputes
and thus help their society to survive most dangerous conditions and, ulti-
mately, to prosper."[40]

The Renaissance was also a period of endemic warfare, especially among
the city states of Italy. One clarion call for peace in that time was the "*Querela
Pacis*," or "Complaint of Peace," authored by the great Dutch scholar, Erasmus
of Rotterdam, in which he ridicules and debunks the various Christian justifications for war. The Spanish humanist, Juan Luis Vives, also wrote on the
desirability of peace in his 1529 work, "Concerning Concord and Discord in
the Human Race." In it, he prefigures modern war-systems analysis by saying,
"war is born of war."[41]

The sixteenth century, clearly an age of religious slaughters, also saw the
rise of the historic Protestant peace churches. When Meno Simons established
the Mennonite sect in 1525, he set in motion a movement of Christian-based
passive nonresistance that has lasted almost six centuries and spread into sixty
countries as the Mennonites emigrated out of central Europe and into the
wider world. The Protestant Reformation also saw the emergence of the Society of Friends, popularly known as the Quakers. The Quaker movement grew
out of English Puritanism, which had been all bound up with the Cavalier
side in the English Civil War. It is not surprising, then, that the Quakers
were not at first thorough-going pacifists, but they quickly became so and by
1660 had adopted pacifism as "an official tenet of the sect," according to Peter
Brock's history, *The Quaker Peace Testimony: 1660–1914*.[42] Quakers have been
instrumental in staffing and promoting anti-war and peace movements ever
since. The most famous of these men was, of course, William Penn, whose
letter to the Indians in Pennsylvania would have changed American history
if only it had become the norm. In it he wrote, "This great God hath written
His law in our hearts, by which we are taught and commanded to love one
another and not to do harm and mischief to one another [and] ... that we

ST. FRANCIS AND THE WOLF. In a square in Gubbio, Italy, a bronze Francis kneels with the wolf, which, according to legend, had been ravaging the town. Francis was a reconciler of quarrels and the tamed wolf is probably symbolic of his role as a peacemaker. It is also important that Francis is the patron saint of ecology, that is, he understood that we must live in peace with and revere the natural world as well as each other. Symbolically, someone has placed two large sunflowers in his upraised hand. (Author's photograph)

may always live together as neighbors and friends.[43] Penn's observations on the lack of peace in Europe led him to conclude that only a general government over the nation states could bring peace, making him one of the early modern advocates of what we would today call world government. Another of these advocates was the famous philosopher, Immanuel Kant, whose tract "The Project of Perpetual Peace" (1795) also argued for a common European Parliament, prefiguring the European Union and the United Nations. His arguments were elaborations of earlier ideas by the Enlightenment *philosophes* the Abbe de Saint-Pierre and Jean-Jacques Rousseau. But the world had a long, bloody way to go before actually experimenting with such institutions. First the world had to go through the large-scale violence and slaughter of the Napoleonic Wars, which gave rise to the organized peace movement at the beginning of the nineteenth century.

CHAPTER 7

The History of Peace,
1800 to the Present

In spite of and in the midst of the slaughter of the last two hundred years, the last two centuries have been the most creative years for the development of peace in the 6000-year history of the war system. Certainly further research will clarify the causes of this sea change in Western civilization, but it seems that one of the more important sources was the democratization of society. In a democratic society, citizens believe they have not only a stake in public policy but also a rightful voice in framing it, and as a result a rich civic life develops. And growing revulsion for the escalating violence of war itself, brought on in part by democratization and by the industrialization of warfare, also played a role. As a result, organized peace movements came into being. Chatfield and Ilukhina write:

> Between the wars of the French Revolution and the outbreak of the Great War of 1914, the idea of peace advocacy was transformed into its modern forms of pacifism and liberal internationalism. From religious and philosophical foundations, peace thinking became a secular ideology that argued for a lawful international order and respect for the rights of peoples. Citizens organized for that cause. By the early twentieth century there were perhaps three hundred thousand European and North American peace activists from over a hundred peace societies that together formed a transnational movement and shared a common ideology they called "pacifism."[1]

Between 1815 and 1816, at least four peace societies were formed, three in the U.S. and one in England. On August 16, 1815, twenty men under the leadership of David Low Dodge founded the New York Peace Society to discourage war and promote peace.[2] The second society was formed as a result of a little book, which no publisher would take — it had to be privately printed by Pastor Noah Worcester of Brighton, Massachusetts, and was titled "A Solemn Review of the Custom of War." Picked up in Ohio by some Quakers, it was the stimulus for the founding of the Society for Promoting Peace in Warren County on December 2, 1815. Worcester himself founded the Massachusetts Peace Society on January 11, 1816. None of the three societies was aware of the others. In 1820, women in Cincinnati formed the Female Peace Society and by 1828 there were fifty peace societies in America alone. The movement was not confined to the leveling democracy of the United States. In 1816, a group of London men had formed the Society for the Promotion of Permanent and Universal Peace to oppose all wars and to do what we would today call public education on the subject throughout England and the continent By 1826 there were 40 branch societies in England alone.[3] A society was also formed in France in 1821 and in Geneva in 1830.

Back in the U.S. the movement was growing stronger and it was at this time that the Methodist Church began its long association with peace work. The various peace societies that had been founded were more or less active and the time had come to form a national society. The man who was the main agent behind the effort was a sea captain and successful merchant, William Ladd. He organized the various societies into one and on May 8, 1828, the American Peace Society was founded. The movement was populated largely by religious people: Congregationalists, Unitarians, Quakers, Baptists and Presbyterians. The society immediately opened correspondence with its counterparts in London, Paris, and Geneva. A transnational peace movement was under way for the first time in history. Yearly gatherings called Annual Peace Congresses led in 1892 to the founding of an umbrella organization, the International Peace Bureau (IPB), which, after reorganization in 1964, has continued to function successfully. IPB was instrumental in organizing the 1899 Hague Conference. Today they have 20 international member organizations and 262 national member organizations, as well as individual members.

> Since the 1960s the IPB's primary concerns have largely reflected those of the movement as a whole in Western countries. These include the struggle against the Vietnam war, the right to conscientious objection, the UN Special Sessions on Disarmament, the Freeze and Euromissile campaigns and the European Nuclear Disarmament movement, foreign military bases, the illegality (and abolition) of nuclear weapons (World Court Project, Abolition 2000 etc), the Gulf War, the arms trade, militarism and the environment, the Non-Proliferation Treaty, women and peace, and the prevention and resolution of conflicts.[4]

In the United States the movement for peace grew slowly during the nineteenth century. In what is now an historical curiosity of some note, Julia Ward Howe, who wrote the words to the Civil War song, "Battle Hymn of the Republic," worked hard after the carnage, to establish a Mothers Day of Peace.

In 1870, Julia Ward Howe took on a new issue and a new cause. Distressed by
her experience of the realities of war, determined that peace was one of the two
most important causes of the world (the other being equality in its many forms)
and seeing war arise again in the world in the Franco-Prussian War, she called
in 1870 for women to rise up and oppose war in all its forms. She wanted
women to come together across national lines, to recognize what we hold in
common above what divides us, and commit to finding peaceful resolutions
to conflicts. She issued a *Declaration*, hoping to gather together women in a
congress of action.[5]

Her proclamation was a robust feminist call for peace.

Arise, then, women of this day!
Arise, all women who have hearts,
Whether our baptism be of water or of tears.

Our husbands will not come to us, reeking with carnage, for caresses and
  applause.
Our sons shall not be taken from us to unlearn
All that we have been able to teach them of charity, mercy and patience.
We, the women of one country, will be too tender of those of another country
To allow our sons to be trained to injure theirs.

From the bosom of the devastated Earth a voice goes up with our own.
It says: "Disarm! Disarm! The sword of murder is not the balance of justice."
Blood does not wipe out dishonor, nor violence indicate possession.

Let them meet first, as women, to bewail and commemorate the dead.
Let them solemnly take counsel with each other as to the means
Whereby the great human family can live in peace,
Each bearing after his own time the sacred impress, not of Caesar,
But of God.

In the name of womanhood and humanity, I earnestly ask
That a general congress of women without limit of nationality
May be appointed and held at someplace deemed most convenient

And at the earliest period consistent with its objects,
To promote the alliance of the different nationalities,
The amicable settlement of international questions,
The great and general interests of peace.[6]

It is a testament to the power of patriarchy, the war system, and rampant
commercialism that Mothers Day eventually became a pale, sentimental echo
of her vision, promoted primarily for florists to make money.

    The peace movement eventually split into two factions: the pacifists who
opposed all war on moral principles, and the internationalists who hated war
perhaps as much but sought to create international institutions to limit and
replace war. This latter movement became the more influential and at the end
of the century was, in conjunction with the IPB, a major force behind the

establishment of the Permanent Court of Arbitration, the forerunner of what is popularly known as the World Court, established at the first-ever world peace conference, held in the Netherlands at The Hague in 1899. The correct title of its current incarnation is the International Court of Justice. The latter part of the century saw the establishment of other important institutions, including the Carnegie Endowment for International Peace, the World Peace Union, the Intercollegiate Peace Association, and many others. A second Hague Conference was held in 1907 to discuss the new idea of a congress that would meet regularly to deal with international conflict, to be named the "League of Nations," a term coined by Andrew Carnegie.

At the same time a considerable movement was under way, led by lawyers, to develop international treaty law. Treaties not only end wars but cover many other issues such as boundary delineation, fishing rights, and so forth. While some treaties have been notoriously broken, the great majority of them have been kept. To become known as a treaty breaker entails greater difficulty in obtaining the cooperation of other nations in the future. There are four sources of treaty law, which regulates the affairs between states. The first is classical writings such as Grotius' *On the Law of War and Peace* (1625), which argued that there is a natural law that transcends that of nations. David Barash writes, "As Grotius saw it (and subsequently international law has confirmed), international 'society' exists, which requires certain norms of conduct among states, including rules governing what is acceptable during war itself."[7] International law is established in treaties to which nation states are the signatories. The term itself first appeared in Jeremy Bentham's *Principles of International Law* in 1843. The second source is custom, such as the principle that foreign diplomats have immunity and can communicate freely with their home country, and the more recent development of the concept of the Common Heritage of Mankind (CHOM), the assertion that even though a resource is under the control of a particular sovereign nation, it nonetheless belongs to all of humanity, such as the United Nations World Heritage Sites. Certain areas are considered to belong to no nation, such as the sea bed, the ozone layer, and Antarctica, and are protected by treaty.

The last hundred years have seen impressive developments in international law, which now governs the use of the airwaves, air traffic control, banking, passports, international policing, disease control, satellite communications systems, mail delivery, weather forecasting, a variety of environmental concerns such as endangered species, the Geneva Conventions regarding prisoners, and many other areas.[8] An example is the United Nations Convention on Law of the Sea, which defines the rights and responsibilities of nations in their use of the oceans. It has been signed by 155 countries including the U.S., which has, however, failed to ratify it. It went into force in 1982. The Kyoto

Accord on climate change is another example of international law, as is the Convention on the Prohibition of the Use, Stockpiling, Production and Transfer of Anti-Personnel Mines and Their Destruction. It is notable that the United States has refused to ratify these treaties as of this writing.

The treaty banning the use of child soldiers, or the United Nations Convention on the Rights of the Child, includes provisions that all countries "take all feasible measures to ensure that persons who have not attained the age of fifteen years do not take a direct part in hostilities" and do not recruit anyone under the age of 15. In 1999 it was ratified by 191 out of 193 nations in the world. While the U.S. has not ratified the full convention, it is party to the provisions on child soldiers.

The third source is binational and multilateral treaties. An example is the Anti-Ballistic Missile (ABM) Treaty, which prohibited the development of missiles that would shoot down ICBMs. While an ABM defense system initially seemed to be good idea, it became quickly clear that should one side be able to achieve such technology, it would make possible a nuclear first strike, thus ending the balance of power and making nuclear war more likely. During the second administration of George W. Bush, the United States repudiated the treaty. Other treaties cover such things as the neutrality of the Great Lakes, established by the Treaty of Paris of 1815 and maintained ever since. Another example of international law, the Geneva Conventions, is a set of four treaties that set the standards of international law for humanitarian concerns. They chiefly concern the treatment of non-combatants and prisoners of war, including the prohibition of torture. They do not affect the use of weapons in war, which are covered by the Hague Conventions of 1899 and 1907 and the Geneva Protocol on the use of gas and biological weapons of 1925.

And finally, the rulings of international courts, such as the International Court of Justice, the Central American Court of Justice, and others, provide a means for resolving disputes between nations. The latest development has been the creation by treaty of the International Criminal Court, which is empowered to adjudicate charges of war crimes and crimes against humanity, such as genocide, when individual nations fail to act. The ICC is founded upon the principles set forth at the Nuremburg trials of the Nazi war criminals, trials in turn based on the Kellogg-Briand Pact of 1928. While there is always a tension between international law and state sovereignty, nonetheless, when they want to be considered legitimate by the international community, or even just by their own allies, states tend to conform to international law, a practice unknown in the pre-modern world. While hardly perfect, the ongoing development of international law constitutes a system strength for a peace system.[9]

Students of peace history differentiate between three types of peace activity: peacemaking, peacekeeping, and peace-building. The first is the ending of wars; the second, monitoring and intervening to keep the conflicting parties adhering to the peace. The UN Blue Helmets' presence in Cyprus and in many other places is a shining example of the latter. And the third type is the more complex and multifaceted work of people-to-people cooperation on economic and social development, international aid, environmental justice and protection, human rights, peace education, and spreading the techniques of nonviolent struggle to end both overt and structural violence.

In the history of peace, the twentieth century was actually a turning point. When looked at from the point of view of war and injustice, it was indeed the Dark Century. But when looked at in terms of the long history of peace, it was a time of tremendous innovation that saw several major trends emerge. These included the development of multinational governance institutions for managing conflict at the global and regional levels, such as the League of Nations and its successor, the United Nations; the Organization of American States the Organization of African Unity, now the African Union; and the European Parliament. The latter is the most surprising of all, representing a genuine burying of the national differences that had resulted in dozens of wars over the past five centuries, including World Wars I and II. No one now thinks that another major European war is a possibility.

In addition, the development of nonviolence as a powerful and effective social technique for regime change, developed by Gandhi, King, the Fellowship of Reconciliation, and others, brought down dictatorial regimes in India and the Philippines, and played a major role in a peaceful end to the Cold War in Eastern Europe and Russia. The following chapter is devoted to this development. Another major development has been the rise of a human rights movement powered by various organizations and based on international agreements, treaties and more informal norms.

A surprising innovation has been the rise of peace studies as a recognized academic program, now providing peace education from the primary grades through doctoral programs in many institutions around the world. Originally found at only a few religious institutions, such as the Mennonites' Goshen College, peace studies took off during the decade of the 1980s and has continued to spread to such prestigious institutions as Colombia University, Notre Dame, Colgate and hundreds of others. There is now a strong body of literature chronicling both the rise of peace education and pedagogy. Typical of these is Ian Harris's and Mary Lee Morrison's pioneering work, *Peace Education*. The jacket blurb indicates the wide range of topics covered in this academic field.

The present volume begins with a discussion of the concepts of peace and peace education. It then considers religious and historical concepts of war, peace and peace education, describes how peace education can move people to work for social change and look for alternatives to violence, and discusses ways to begin implementing peace education in schools, churches and other community settings such as youth groups. It goes on to address sensitive issues in peace education, key concepts and topics, important biological and cultural factors, and barriers facing those who teach peace. It provides the "how" of peace education by examining optimal pedagogy and practices.[10]

In several states there are state-wide organizations in higher education. Exemplary of these is the Wisconsin Institute for Peace and Conflict Studies, a consortium of 21 public and private colleges and universities. The institute provides a speakers program, an annual faculty conference, a student conference, the *Journal for the Study of Peace and Conflict*, faculty and student awards, opportunities for cooperative research, faculty development, and curriculum consulting for the member institutions.[11] The Central New York Peace Studies Consortium was established in 1985. At the national and international level the Peace and Justice Studies Association (PJSA) provides an umbrella for these programs, promoting peace studies at all grade levels from kindergarten through graduate programs, forging alliances between scholars, students, and activists, and creating and nurturing alternatives to war and structural violence through education, research and action. PJSA publishes the *Peace Chronicle* and a vehicle for scholars, *Peace and Change: A Journal of Peace Research*.[12] Scientific research into peace is carried out by the International Peace Research Institute at Oslo, Sweden, founded in 1959, which publishes the *Journal of Peace Research*. And within narrow limits, the United States Institute of Peace, established by an act of Congress in 1984, also sponsors research into international conflict. In Europe, graduate-level study is offered at the European Peace University, established in 1988. Its mission includes "spreading the idea of peace in the spirit of the UNESCO, giving scientific and educational support to global peace, promoting a 'world domestic policy' based on sustainable development, cooperative responsibility and ecological security, contributing to the development of a global peace culture, and training and improving individual capabilities in peace-making and conflict resolution."[13] The peace studies department at the University of Bradford in England offers graduate programs in the field.[14] The United Nations has established a graduate school, the University for Peace, located in San Jose, Costa Rica.[15]

Also new in the twentieth century has been the development of the techniques of non-adversarial conflict resolution, sometimes known as "win–win negotiation," principally by Roger Fisher and Richard Ury at Harvard Law School.[16] Their work has spawned a huge field of study and application — for example, the National Center for Conflict Resolution, which "provides training and technical assistance nationwide to advance the development of conflict resolution education programs in schools, juvenile justice settings and youth service organizations and community partnership programs."[17]

Also, the twentieth-century movement to include women in major social decisions and in the benefits of society, especially in developing countries, has been another "innovation" for establishing a culture of peace and justice, kindling hopes for a revival of the partnership societies of the ancient world. The degree of change in the last hundred years in the West has been remarkable: women are now commonplace in government, the law, business, and even in the military.

Additionally, perhaps most visible and impressive of all has been the emergence of a global civil society populated by tens of thousands of non-government organizations working within and across borders to further peace, social justice, environmental protection, human rights, disarmament, and development, as well as bringing international aid in times of famine and natural disaster.[18] These are all examples of peace-building activities that are going on all over the world. Finally, many of these trends have begun to merge as it becomes obvious that what is needed is a major shift to a culture of peace.

It is impossible to chronicle all of these twentieth-century developments in detail, or provide anything near a complete record in the space of half a chapter. We will review only some of the highlights. The era can be divided into two periods: early developments first, 1899–1939, and second, 1945 to the present. The new century opened with a burst of optimism, which, of course, broke down with the slaughter of World War I. As the tensions leading up to the war were building, a group of Christians gathered in Switzerland to see what they could do to prevent the outbreak, but before their conference ended, World War I had begun and they were required to return to their own countries. At the railroad station, Friedrich Sigmund-Schultze, a German Lutheran, and an English Quaker, Henry Hodgkin, pledged to continue their efforts for peace. Out of that pledge came the Fellowship of Reconciliation (FOR), founded at Cambridge, England, in 1914. The URLs for this, and the other organizations mentioned subsequently can be found in the appendix, or simply by Googling them directly. During the war FOR supported conscientious objectors; some governments wanted to shoot them and many COs were jailed for treason. FOR also helped to organize the American Civil Liberties Union. Throughout the century they have worked for labor rights, nonviolent resistance to wars, African independence, and civil rights. They have opposed nuclear weapons, taken a leading role in founding the nuclear freeze campaign, led nonviolence training seminars around the world, and carried out many other peacemaking and peace-building activities. It is the flagship peace organization of the world. Today FOR is an international, interfaith movement working for peace in over 40 countries and includes Jews, Christians, Muslims, Buddhists and others.

Also founded during the war (1916) was the Women's International League for Peace and Freedom (WILPF). It began as a gathering of 1,300 women from belligerent and neutral countries to protest the slaughter of World War I and demand an immediate end to hostilities, issuing 20 resolutions to that end, calling on belligerent governments to publish their grievances and war aims and on neutral governments to pressure them to end the fighting. Jane Addams and Emily Greene Balch took leadership positions. Both were eventually awarded the Nobel Peace Prize. They also put forward ideas for a just peace, some of which were adopted by President Wilson for his Fourteen Points. They established a conference of women to monitor the 1919 peace process at Versailles and correctly recognized the final treaty as a vengeful and dictated settlement. WILPF continues in existence as one of the two oldest international peace organizations, working for total and universal disarmament, human rights, the peaceful resolution of conflicts, recognition of the right of conscientious objection, reforms that would make the United Nations a more effective peacemaking institution and so on. The year 1921 saw the initiation of War Resisters International, whose symbol, two arms holding up a rifle broken in the middle, has become a widespread symbol used in anti-war demonstrations.

A major non-government organization that developed between the wars was the Peace Pledge Union in Great Britain. In 1933 the Rev. Dick Sheppard, the canon of St. Paul's Cathedral, posted a letter in the *Times* asking men, but not women, to send him postcards pledging never to support war again. The card read, "War is a crime against humanity. I renounce war, and am therefore determined not to support any kind of war. I am also determined to work for the removal of all causes of war." He wanted to counter the popular opinion that peace was a women-only issue. Women were later admitted to membership. He received 135,000 responses. PPU continues to campaign for a warless world.

The most important governmental organization to come out of the end of World War I was, of course, the League of Nations. Established by the Treaty of Versailles, it came into existence in 1919. It was based on an important, even revolutionary concept: the doctrine of collective security as a replacement for the failed system of the balance of power. Members pledged to refrain from the use of force against other members and to submit disputes to the League Council. The Covenant read, "Should any member resort to war ... it shall *ipso facto* be deemed to have committed an act of war against all other Members." The Covenant provided for sanctions and, if necessary, recommended that member states raise military force against the aggressor. The League did have some notable successes. It ended wars between Bulgaria and Greece and between Lithuania and Poland. It employed an arms embargo against Bolivia and Paraguay when they went to war. The social and economic successes of the League were ground-breaking and set the pattern for future international cooperation in these areas.

But the League was unable to prevent major wars in the 1930s, including the Japanese invasion of Manchuria and the Italian invasion of Ethiopia. Japan withdrew from the League, as did Germany in 1934 when the League refused to lift the arms restrictions placed on it in 1919. And by 1939 Europe had descended into World War II. The League's failures were the result of three things. The first was structural deficiencies. Its powers were far too limited to effectively limit sovereign nation states that wanted to make war. Second was the fact that the most important nations in terms of power and potential power — the United States and the Soviet Union — were not in it at the beginning and the U.S. never joined. Germany and Japan withdrew when faced with criticism. Third was the failure of the leading parties, Britain and France, to show the resolution necessary to make it work. At the same time, they also failed to use the old balance of power system as a deterrent to Japan and Germany. It seems that the great powers believed in collective security as long it did not require any real-world obligations on their part. Still, the League was a bold experiment and after World War II it was revived as the United Nations, a considerably strengthened body with the two leading powers at the time, the U.S. and the Soviet Union, as members. The League's social and economic agencies were passed over to it virtually intact. However, the old idea that security could be assured by an alliance system that had ended with its disastrous failure in World War I was also revived in the NATO and Warsaw Pact alliances. Still, the new idea — that security could be collective, administered by a "government of governments" — was a sea change in world history, marking out a course we are still on.

The United Nations was established in 1945 and is composed of the General Assembly, which is open to all states; the Security Council, staffed by the five great powers of the day — United States, Soviet Union, Great Britain, France and China — as permanent members with other states elected to serve temporary terms, and having the main responsibility for preventing war; the Secretariat, which houses the administration; the Economic and Social Council, which houses all the social service agencies, such as UNICEF, UNESCO, the World Health Organization, and many others; and the Trusteeship Council, whose mission is to oversee the eventual liberation of colonies.

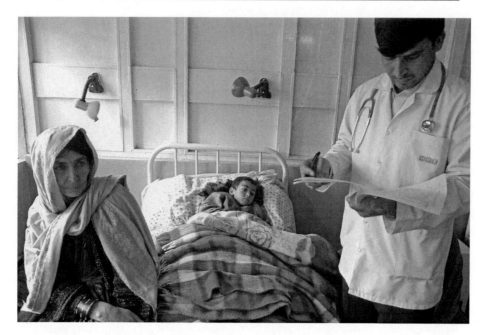

**UN HEALTH OFFICER IN AFGHANISTAN. Here is a man doing peace. Caring for the
health and well-being of children defines peace just as killing them defines war. This,
and the myriad other social and humanitarian functions of the United Nations are
proof on the ground of a global peace system that has been gradually emerging over
the past hundred years. (UN Photograph/ Fardin Waez [#398290])**

The Charter outlawed aggression and the Security Council can impose
sanctions on violators and even call on member states to raise military forces
against the aggressor. It is not a world government in any sense of the word,
but rather a reflection of the system of sovereign states. If they choose to
cooperate, it can be very effective. If not, then it will not be effective.[19] Nevertheless, the social service agencies of the UN have been astonishingly successful in combating disease and diminishing poverty around the world, and
the peacekeeping force (the "Blue Helmets") has made important contributions
to keeping the peace in the Middle East and many other places.

The immediate post-war period saw large-scale support for institutions
of international governance, three worthy of significant mention. First, the
citizen-based United Nations Association of the United States, whose efforts
are primarily to educate Americans about the UN and the issues that come
before it. Second, the World Federalists, whose slogan "World Peace Through
World Law" underlay their pressure for an international governance institution
more effective than the existing UN. Founded in 1947 in Switzerland, it is a
global movement bringing together individuals and organizations dedicated

to strengthening the United Nations so that it will evolve into a democratic, constitutional, federal government, similar to the pattern established in the United States. There is a very strong U.S. branch, which recently changed its name to Citizens for Global Solutions. They propose, among other measures, a more democratic Security Council with an end to the veto, a democratically elected General Assembly (members are now appointed by their respective governments), and a standing UN police force. The Federalists were instrumental in the creation of the International Criminal Court. Another global non-government institution to emerge in the twentieth century is the World Parliament. It was initiated in 1958 with a call for a World Constitutional Convention, which, after suitable preparation, was held in 1968. They have developed a Strategy for Reclaiming the Earth for Humanity and issued a Decree for the Protection of Life outlawing nuclear weapons.

The invention and use of nuclear weapons in World War II brought forth an ongoing anti-nuclear movement opposed both to the weapons and to nuclear power. The complete history of anti-nuclear protests is too rich and manifold to be fully recounted here.[20] Some of the nuclear scientists who had worked on the atomic bomb project rather quickly repudiated these weapons when they saw what they had done, including some famous names such as J. Robert Oppenheimer. In 1945, they established the *Bulletin of Atomic Scientists*, with its doomsday clock originally set at seven minutes to midnight. It is currently set at five minutes to midnight.[21]

Thousands of other scientists protested nuclear weapons after Albert Schweitzer alerted the world to their danger. Nobel laureate Linus Pauling gathered 2000 signatures from scientists and sent them to the White House in June 1957. In the same year the Committee for a Sane Nuclear Policy (SANE) was founded by, among others, members from the American Friends Service Committee and the World Federalists. Within a year they had 25,000 members. They published full-page ads in the *New York Times* and many local papers. Twenty thousand supporters turned out for a rally at Madison Square Garden in May of 1958. In July of that year Bertrand Russell founded the Pugwash Conference, bringing together in Canada scientists from both sides of the Cold War. In 1958 Pauling gave a petition signed by 9,235 scientists to UN Secretary General Dag Hammarskjold, urging an international agreement to stop testing.

It was at this time that the universal peace symbol came into being. It is a representation of the semaphore letters N and D (for Nuclear Disarmament) surrounded by a circle. Designed in Britain in 1958 by Gerald Holtom, it became the symbol for the British Direct Action Committee Against Nuclear War. It was brought to the U.S. by a student at the University of Chicago in 1960 and became the symbol of the Student Peace Union and afterward its use spread throughout the world.

Another important and effective organization was the Women's Strike for Peace, an activist group that lobbied and demonstrated for an end to nuclear testing as well as the abolition of the McCarthy-era House Un-American Activities Committee, and who were among the early opponents of the Vietnam War. Composed primarily of middle-class, married mothers, their early tactics included street demonstrations and marches when these were mainly unknown in the U.S. They argued their cause from a woman's perspective, pointing out that radioactive fallout had been found in mother's milk. They have been credited with a major role in bringing about the Limited Test Ban Treaty,[22] which bans nuclear explosions in the atmosphere. In 1963 the Partial Test Ban Treaty was signed and President Kennedy cited their work as being crucial. However, France was not party to it and continued to test aboveground in the Pacific until pressure by the New Zealand government and public protests by Greenpeace led them to move tests underground in 1974, where they continued to test until 1995. Finally they signed on to the 1985 South Pacific Nuclear Free Zone Treaty.[23]

In 1978 the UN held its first major conference on disarmament and 20,000 people, organized by Mobilization for Survival, rallied in support. In 1979, 15,000 people demonstrated at Rocky Flats Arsenal where the triggers for the H-bombs were made. And in 1980, the Berrigan brothers (both Catholic priests), Molly Rush and five others carried out the first of the Plowshares direct actions, entering a General Electric plant and hammering on nuclear warheads in order to provoke court appearances to bring the issue further to the public's attention. They received prison sentences. Plowshares actions of civil disobedience against nuclear installations have continued, including those against the navy's ELF (extremely low frequency) facility in Wisconsin, led by Tom Hastings, Donna Howard and others who have gone to jail to witness for nuclear disarmament. ELF was an aboveground, earth-return communications system that purportedly allowed the nuclear submarines to receive the attack order without surfacing. Its critics argued plausibly that it was a first-strike weapon, since it was not a hardened site and if the Soviets had decided to strike first, they would have easily eliminated it. Demonstrations against the site continued for fifteen years, organized by Stop Project ELF. The facility was closed down in 2004, the navy claiming technological obsolescence.

Many other peace organizations have flourished in the aftermath of World War II. The Union of Concerned Scientists was founded in 1969 by faculty and students from MIT and has concentrated on an end to nuclear weapons testing and a halt to the development of space-based weapons. More recently it has become involved in global climate change issues. In Great Britain several anti-nuclear organizations were founded right after World War II, but the most prominent and long lasting has been the Campaign for Nuclear Disarmament. Founded in 1958, the organization has brought out tens of thousands of protesters for its Easter Sunday marches and lobbied Parliament against nuclear weapons. In Holland, the Dutch Interchurch Peace Council gained ground, as did various groups in East and West Germany. In the 1980s there were major citizen protests against the Pershing, cruise and SS-20 missiles the U.S. and Soviet Union were installing in Europe. These weapons would have destabilized the balance of terror (or MAD, Mutual Assured Destruction) and threatened to trigger launch on warning by either side, hence an "accidental" nuclear war. Hundreds of thousands demonstrated on weekends. In England a famous women's peace camp was set up at Greenham Common Air Base, where the U.S. had installed cruise missiles. They established a permanent presence and at one time 30,000 women linked hands and surrounded the base.[24] In the Netherlands, 3.75 million people signed petitions against the cruise missiles. Many acts of civil disobedience prompted mass arrests. Other women's peace camps were established in Sicily, the U.S., Australia and Holland. This pressure resulted in the INF (Intermediate-range Nuclear Missiles) Treaty, signed by the U.S. and the Soviet Union in 1987, resulting in the elimination of an entire class of nuclear missiles. Following the reforms and then collapse of the Soviet Union, the anti-nuclear movement turned to Asia, out of concern for Pakistan and India, which had by then acquired the bomb. The Movement in India for Nuclear Disarmament (MIND), Pakistan's Action Committee Against Arms Race and Japan's Congress Against Atomic and Hydrogen Bombs keep the threat of nuclear devastation in the public eye in those regions.

In the United States the protests against nuclear weapons began early and have proved surprisingly strong and long lasting. In 1956 the Committee for Non-violent Action held vigils at the headquarters of the Atomic Energy Commission, where many people were arrested for civil disobedience, and in 1959 they carried out civil disobedience at Strategic Air Command Headquarters in Omaha. Demonstrations continued throughout the century. There were 536 demonstrations at the Nevada Test Site with a total of 37,488 participants and over 15,000 arrests for civil disobedience. In 1975, Jim and Shelley Douglas organized Ground Zero, which protested at the Trident nuclear submarine base in Washington and carried out civil disobedience against the so-called white train, which transports nuclear warheads across the country.

In 1979 the American Friends Service Committee proposed a nuclear moratorium, and arms-control expert Randall Forsberg wrote an essay suggesting a freeze on the production of nuclear weapons, including a resolution for other groups to endorse. The idea of a freeze spread like wildfire. Endorsements came in quickly from Clergy and Laity Concerned, Pax Christi, Physicians for Social Responsibility, FOR, WILPF, and other groups. At the same time many towns and cities passed freeze resolutions, as did a number of state legislatures. Pro-freeze candidates were winning elections to the House of Representatives. Resolutions introduced to Congress were barely defeated even though the most popular president in history, Ronald Reagan, was opposed to the measure.

Dr. Helen Caldicott, who had worked against nuclear testing in Australia, spearheaded a public education/mobilization effort that included a short film titled *The Last Epidemic* that was shown worldwide. In 1980 she started the Women's Action for Nuclear Disarmament (WAND), and formed the International Physicians for the Prevention of Nuclear War, which won the Nobel Peace Prize in 1985. During the decade of the 1980s many major religious denominations and professional organizations joined in the condemnation of nuclear weapons. In July of 1996 the World Court ruled that the threat or use of nuclear weapons violated international law. A petition for abolition organized by Abolition 2000 garnered 13.4 million signatures. In the same year 120 world leaders, including Mikhail Gorbachev, former head of the Soviet Union, and Jimmy Carter, a former nuclear submarine commander as well as president of the United States, issued an appeal for abolition.

Monitoring nuclear weapons issues is Nukewatch.

> Nukewatch brings critical attention to the locations, movements, dangers, and the politics of nuclear weapons and radioactive wastes. Staff and volunteers advocate Gandhian nonviolence in education and action, and report on nuclear issues in a quarterly newsletter, *Nukewatch Quarterly*. Nukewatch began in 1979 in response to the cold war buildup of nuclear weapons and the secrecy surrounding the nuclear industry. Nukewatch conducted TrackWatch; a program to monitor and expose secret shipments of radioactive waste on U.S. rails; TruckWatch, the transportation of H-bombs and component parts in unmarked trucks by the DOE; Nukewatch mapped all 1,000 land-based nuclear missile silos for educational and organizing purposes.[25]

Their publication, *Nukewatch Quarterly*, is a publication of the Progressive Foundation and is available online.[26]

The development of serious concern for human rights occurred as a result of World War II and was enshrined in the United Nations Universal Declaration of Human Rights promulgated in 1948. Since that time there has been a growing acceptance of the norms that it offers as a fact of natural law that ought to be observed in international law. Two major organizations, Human Rights Watch and Amnesty International, have emerged to monitor human rights worldwide and apply citizen pressure against those states that persist in violations.

These citizen-based organizations have not been without success. Many millions of citizens all over the world have demonstrated and signed petitions and some have committed civil disobedience to protest the testing, stockpiling, threat to use and actual use of nuclear weapons. These protests have made progress, resulting in the Nuclear Non-proliferation Treaty, the Limited Test Ban Treaty and the Anti-ballistic Missile Treaty, and in the near-passage of a Comprehensive Test Ban Treaty.[27] These disparate campaigns and organizations are known collectively as the peace movement, and while there is little long-term coherence or unified strategy, they have achieved notable successes, not the least of which was pressuring the hard-line Cold Warrior, Ronald Reagan, to negotiate a serious nuclear weapons limitation treaty with the Soviet Union, a development that contributed to the ending of the Cold War.

David Walls writes that the four major accomplishments of the American peace movement are as follows: (1) pushing the Kennedy administration to negotiate arms control agreements with the Soviet Union, including the Limited Test Ban treaty, (2) turning public opinion against the Vietnam War, (3) preventing a massive and direct intervention by the U.S. in the Third World, primarily in Central America and South Africa, and (4) swinging popular opinion so strongly behind nuclear arms control that even Ronald Reagan was forced to work with Gorbachev to dramatically lower nuclear stockpiles.[28]

In this brief space I have been able to merely highlight a few of the peace organizations and movements that have characterized the last half of the twentieth century and the

DR. HELEN CALDICOTT. This peacemaker (b. 1938) played a major role in alerting the world to the dangers of nuclear war in the 1970s and 1980s, spearheading the fight against French nuclear testing in the atmosphere, and co-founding the Physicians for Social Responsibility, whose film *The Last Epidemic* was seen by millions. The International umbrella of PSR, the international Physicians for the Prevention of Nuclear War, won the Nobel Peace Prize in 1985. Dr. Caldicott also founded the Women's Action for Nuclear Disarmament (WAND) in 1980. (Photograph provided by Dr. Caldicott)

opening decade of the twenty-first. Most of them are operating underneath the radar of the nightly news or the *New York Times*. Nevertheless, they are there — a myriad of dedicated peace activists. But the movement, if it can even be called that, is still lacking a comprehensive vision and organization and has yet to develop a systemic approach to the problem of war and global injustice. But such an approach is developing. The United Nations' call for the development of a "Culture of Peace" has been a major step in the right direction. In 2000 the United Nations General Assembly proclaimed an International Year for the Culture of Peace. The declaration recognizes that peace requires much more than simply controlling war-like states. Peace is an enduring commitment to global cooperation based on values, attitudes, and modes of behavior that reject violence and prevent conflicts by solving its root causes. Its manifesto has been signed by over 75 million people worldwide. Hundreds of its peace education projects are under way.

In sum, there has been more progress in the past 100 or so years for the cause of peace than in all the centuries together since we sank into the dominator society with its inherent war system. We are living in a new story. The old one — which teaches us that war is inevitable, that it is rooted in human nature, that it is even sanctified by God, and that the only real power is violent power over others — is still around, still very much embedded in our everyday culture. But no longer is it the only story. The new story tells us that we have been working behind the scenes on peace for two centuries now and that we have created new ideas, values, institutions and techniques that are capable of controlling war in the future. We need to stop telling the old story as if it were the only one. The new story needs to be told widely to journalists, to teachers, to preachers, and to our neighbors. We can now break the old pattern. As Harry Meserve has written, "For telling ourselves and others that evil is inevitable while good is impossible, may we stand corrected."[29]

The twentieth-century history of peace gives us hope that *Homo sapiens* will yet be able to break out of the war system and establish a genuine peace for the world. The recapture of our common heritage, the history of peace, provides us not only the models and examples we need, but also the realization that peace is as real as war. It is unlikely today that a program director at the United States Institute of Peace would say there is no such thing as peace history. Humanity now has a great deal of experience with peacemaking, peacekeeping, and peace-building as well as a solid basis of scientific research on the causes of war and the conditions of peace. The problem that remains is how to spread this knowledge, how to get it into the teacher training programs, college history courses, the secondary school curriculum, and the consciousness of the media. A key component in this story of the developing culture of peace is the practice of nonviolence, to which we now turn.

CHAPTER 8

The Successes of Nonviolent Struggle

People try nonviolence for a week and when it doesn't work they go back to violence which hasn't worked for thousands of years.
— Anonymous

the security of individuals varies inversely with the destructive force embodied in the systems meant to ensure that security ... we have misidentified power with the capacity to cause destruction.
— Robert Holmes[1]

Anything that exists, is possible.
— Kenneth Boulding [Boulding's Law][2]

While nonviolent struggle grew out of pacifism, they are not identical. Pacifism is a non-response to evil, to injustice and oppression. It is based on the refusal to return evil for evil. It accepts the suffering imposed without malice, perhaps even with forgiveness for the oppressor. It is a largely individual phenomenon. In contrast, nonviolent action, or struggle, is something more. It is a proactive, collective, and often ingenious confrontation with the oppressive powers. It works, whether against armed bands of terrorists like the KKK or the armies of the Soviet Union in Eastern Europe. It has even worked against the Nazi regime during World War II. Nonviolent struggle changes the power relationship between oppressed and oppressor. It reverses seemingly unequal relationships, as, for example, in the case of the "mere" shipyard workers and the Red Army in Poland in the 1980s, and in many other cases. Speaking more accurately, it reveals the true power relationship, which is that *all* government rests on the consent of the governed, which can always be withdrawn. As we shall see, it changes the social psychology of the conflict situation and thus erodes the will of the oppressor to continue injustice and exploitation. It renders oppressive governments helpless and makes the people ungovernable. Robert Holmes points out that "people who have sought security in arms alone are defenseless once their military forces have been defeated. They are a conquered people. A people committed to nonviolence may be deprived of their government, their liberties, their material wealth, but they cannot be conquered."[3]

Properly organized nonviolent resistance or defense, based on prior planning, professional training, strategy and tactics, and the necessary material support (though only a fraction of what we spend on military defense), can have a deterrent effect because if a people cannot be governed there is no reason to conquer them. Any attempt would bring only costs without gains.

Nonviolence is a practical alternative. It is nonviolence that now allows us to escape from the iron cage of warfare into which we trapped ourselves six thousand years ago, but most people know very little about it, especially our leaders, whose wisdom runs in very narrow circles. Henry David Thoreau knew this over a hundred years ago:

> Statesmen and legislators, standing so completely within the institution, never distinctly and nakedly behold it. They speak of moving society but have no resting-place without it. They may be men of a certain experience and determination ... but all their wit and usefulness lie within certain, not very wide limits.[4]

Our teachers and the media are uninformed and so the history and efficacy of nonviolence remain invisible to most of us. Canadian scholar George Crowell writes that

> schoolchildren are constantly exposed to the military history of their nations. They are bombarded with television images of violent villains, and of heroes who use violent means to overcome them. They learn hardly anything of the history of nonviolent action. We all grow up taking for granted the necessity for violence as the ultimate sanction.[5]

Overview of the History of Pacifism and Nonviolence

Nonviolence has a surprisingly long and a surprisingly short history. It is both venerable and novel. Twenty-five hundred years ago some of the great religious teachers began to preach nonviolent pacifism. The earliest known of these was the Jain sage, Mahavira, who preceded the Buddha in India and taught the doctrine of *ahimsa*, or nonviolence. For the Jains, who continue the tradition today, nonviolence was the means to Moksa, or liberation. The three great principles, or Guptis, included mental nonviolence, verbal nonviolence, and physical nonviolence. A little later, in the sixth century BC, the Buddha Shakyamuni, who also lived in India, taught nonviolence and reverence for all life. And farther to the east, a couple of centuries later, the Chinese sage Lao Tse was experimenting with ideas of nonviolence. He wrote:

> This world has no need for weapons,
> Which soon turn on themselves.
> Where armies camp, nettles grow;
> After each war, years of famine.
> The most fruitful outcome
> Does not depend on force,
> But succeeds without arrogance
> Without hostility
> Without pride
> Without resistance
> Without violence[6]

But the best known to us of the ancient teachers was, of course, Jesus of Nazareth. His way of compassion for all people, he said, was the way to the truth that leads to life. His message continued to inspire individuals down through the centuries, causing the early Christians to refuse military service until, as we have seen, the state finally overwhelmed the Church by co-opting it in the fourth century. Even then, it continued to inspire. In the thirteenth century St. Francis composed his beautiful prayer of peace that still rings down the ages with the ethic of nonviolence. (See chapter 10.)

Biblical nonviolence informed the great peace churches that developed during the Protestant Reformation: the Mennonites and the Brethren, and later the Society of Friends. These churches continue their witness and many of their young men have been imprisoned as conscientious objectors in this age of dominance by the national security state. Christian teachings on nonviolence inspired the great Russian pacifist, Leo Tolstoy. He was well aware that the state is the source of war, and wrote, "In all history there is no war which was not hatched by the governments, the governments alone, independent of the interests of the people, to whom war is always pernicious even when successful." He was fully aware that men must sedate their psyches in order to wage it—"War is so unjust and ugly that all who wage it must try to stifle the voice of conscience within themselves"—and that war violated all Christian standards, of which he said, "War on the other hand is such a terrible thing, that no man, especially a Christian man, has the right to assume the responsibility of starting it."[7] Tolstoy was one of the sources of inspiration for Mohandas Gandhi.

But up until Gandhi, the witness for nonviolence was primarily individualistic and based simply on non-resistance to evil, on turning the other cheek. It was primarily passive, although there were small-scale efforts to change local conditions, as in the Quaker "nonviolent invasion of Massachusetts Bay Colony in 1756."[8] In this respect, Gandhi was a revolutionary. Yogesh Chandha writes in his biography of the Mahatma that "Gandhi's greatness — nay uniqueness — lies in his role as an innovator in politics…. He was the first in human history to extend the principle of nonviolence from the individual to the social and political plane."[9] It evolved from being a matter of individual conscience to a pragmatic tool for positive social and political change. It is in this sense that the history of nonviolence is novel, and for such a recent development, it has been spectacularly successful. It is also in this sense that nonviolence is, in spite of the names that cling to it such as "passive resistance," anything but passive. As formulated by Gandhi and others in this century, it is a highly activist form of struggle useful for creatively confronting violence and oppression.

Kinds and Degrees of Nonviolence

There are several forms and degrees of nonviolence. The oldest, as mentioned, is non-resistance to the powers of evil while totally renouncing the use of violence for oneself. The second kind is passive resistance, or noncompliance with the directives of government and other powers that would coerce one to do or to be a part of something evil, such as the structural violence of segregation. When Rosa Parks refused to get up and yield her seat to a white person on that city bus in Montgomery, Alabama, on December 1, 1955, she was committing an act of passive resistance. She refused to go along with the injustice of the system and her act initiated the beginnings of the nonviolent struggles of the civil rights movement, the Montgomery bus boycott. The third kind is nonviolent direct action. When four students from the North Carolina Agricultural and Technical College sat in at the lunch counter in Greensboro, North Carolina, in 1960, they had sought out the system to confront it, albeit nonviolently. This was a pure form of nonviolent struggle or nonviolent direct action and, as is often the case, it sparked similar actions over a wide area. Nonviolent struggle is inspirational and catching. Gandhi's was also of this third kind — he carried the struggle to the apartheid regime in South Africa and then to the British Raj in India.

Then there are degrees of commitment to nonviolence. What Robert Holmes calls, in his book *Nonviolence in Theory and Practice*, "unqualified nonviolentists" are people whose commitment is based in religious principle and who will carry through no matter the consequences and regardless of whether it achieves some goal or not.[10] The Jains are examples of unqualified nonviolentists. It is a way of life for them and they can lead no other. Others are committed in lesser degrees. Gandhi, for example, was himself thoroughly committed to nonviolence as the most effective way of combating evil, but he knew it took great courage and he counseled those who could not muster such courage that the worst sin of all was submitting to evil and if they could not combat it nonviolently they should take up arms. Still others, such as the American expert Gene Sharp, whose Program on Nonviolent Sanctions in Conflict and Defense at Harvard University produced the definitive research on nonviolence, see it only as a tactic. For them, it is not about changing people's hearts and minds, but is simply an effective tool in power politics.

Does Nonviolence Work?

Whenever someone is asked to think about nonviolence they want to know, "Does it work?" As with most important questions, the answer is complex. Holmes writes "Considered simply as a tactic, nonviolence sometimes works and sometimes does not."[11] For those for whom nonviolence is a way of life, a spiritual commitment, if they have practiced it in a conflict situation, it worked. They remained true to their convictions, showed respect for their opponent, and they did not add any violence to the world, even if the cause they advocated did not prevail. Father Philip Berrigan's life provides a good example of conversion to this kind of religiously based nonviolence. He tells the story in his autobiography:

> In my own case, I remember May 1945, when I came close to shooting two German prisoners of war who happened to be Waffen SS, Hitler's elite body-guard troops. They stared at us arrogantly and hatefully and cursed us Americans in German as we slowly passed them at a railroad siding, a few days after the German surrender in May 1945. They were unarmed, I was armed, an officer of the victorious American Army — and I could hardly stomach their hatred and hostility. I very nearly shot them, knowing at the time that if I had, a mere tap on the wrist would result as punishment. They were SS scum, unworthy to live. And I was a victor, with the right to shoot them or let them live.
>
> I have come from that level of brutalization as a young infantry officer to today and the certainty that my relationship to an enemy is precisely my relationship to God. It makes no difference if the enemy has truly harmed me or attempted to kill me — or if the government has picked my enemy — a Communist, Arab, Cuban, North Korean, Libyan. No difference whatsoever. My enemy might be artificial or real — he or she still bears the image of God and what I do to them I do to God.[12]

Father Berrigan provided a relentless witness against nuclear weapons with numerous direct actions against nuclear facilities as part of the Plowshares movement, for which he has repeatedly been imprisoned by the U.S. national security state.

Of success or failure with regard to this kind of principled nonviolence, Holmes writes, "In short, if one thinks of nonviolence as a way of life, then it works to the extent that one lives nonviolently and infuses everyday conduct with a nonviolent spirit. Effectiveness of this sort is not measurable in the same way as social and political changes."[13] But this is an unsatisfactory answer for most people who want to know about the efficacy of nonviolence as a tool for dealing with social and political repression and invasion by an armed enemy. Still, the question is not as simple as it appears. We are not asking if nonviolence works in some utopian sense, so that in a nonviolent struggle against Fascism or Communism or terrorism we prevail quickly and no one gets hurt. What we are asking, to be fair, is this — does nonviolence work better than violence? That changes the picture considerably and requires us to first examine the question of how well violence works. Part of the answer to that is that it only works half the time. In every war there is one winner and one loser. But there is more to this consideration because even the victors lose, and as the destructiveness of modern weapons has escalated, they lose horribly. In their victory against the Nazis in World War II, the Russians lost 20 million people. What is more, the violent adversarial conflict that our society has taught us is the only workable response to oppression can actually create and magnify resistance. Then one must use even more force to smash it down. Violence escalates counter-violence, as we witnessed in Vietnam and are now witnessing in Iraq and Afghanistan. What the United States government had expected to be short-term violence turned into long-term chaos.

There are other flaws in the military option as well. Canadian scholar George Crowell has listed some of these:

(1) A capacity for defense by military means can all too easily be employed for aggression. (2) When democratic societies rely on military systems which, hierarchically organized, are the antithesis of democracy, their democratic institutions are subverted. (3) Military systems require defining some outsider as the enemy, and therefore promote enmity. (4) Allies are seldom sought in genuine friendship, but are often exploited and manipulated by the more powerful partner. (5) Consistent international cooperation is generally thought to be unrealistic and impossible. (6) Military systems develop symbiotic relationships with the industries which devise and produce expensive weapons, and divert vast economic resources away from meeting human and environmental needs.[14]

Thus violence does not work anywhere near as well as we would like to think. In fact, the violent struggle against Fascism in World War II cost somewhere between 50 million and a hundred million lives. To make a point *reductio ad absurdum* here, if a nonviolent campaign had been waged instead, and had also succeeded and had cost only one life less, it would have been preferable. Wars and terrorism simply create further violence. World War I led inexorably to World War II, which led to the violent struggles of the Cold War in which 25 million people lost their lives. The terrorist attack on the World Trade Center, itself a violent response to perceived oppression, has led to escalating violence in the Middle East and to the U.S. attacks on Afghanistan and Iraq, which lead to further terrorism. The point is that while nonviolent struggle can be costly, it must be measured not against some utopian situation, but against its real-world alternative, violence. But is there any evidence that nonviolence works?

There is. Crowell writes, "The history of nonviolent action is full of startling discoveries of effective nonviolent response to highly volatile conflict situations."[15] One can go back to ancient Rome for the first well-known case of effective nonviolence. In the year 494 BC the plebian class, who did all the physical work in Rome, petitioned for representation and participation in the government, which was the exclusive club of the aristocracy. They were turned down flat. They considered armed rebellion. Instead, rather than murdering the chief magistrates, they just walked out of the city to a hill, later known as the "sacred mount," and sat down. After a number of days when the wood did not get hewn and the water did not get drawn and nothing in the city worked, the aristocrats gave in and admitted them to meaningful participation in the government. It is important to remember that the Roman government was in the habit of crucifying armed rebels *en masse*— ten thousand at once in the Spartacus rebellion.

Of course, such a remote event can easily be dismissed. One wants to know, can nonviolence work in modern society? And once again, we are confronted with Boulding's tongue-in-cheek law: "Anything that exists is possible."

Successful Nonviolence in the Twentieth Century

There are many modern instances of the successful use of nonviolence. Gene Sharp writes, "A vast history exists of people who, refusing to be convinced that the apparent 'powers that be' were omnipotent, defied and resisted powerful rulers, foreign conquerors, domestic tyrants, oppressive systems, internal usurpers and economic masters. Contrary to usual perceptions, these means of struggle by protest, noncooperation and disruptive intervention have played major historical roles in all parts of the world."[16]

The suffragette movement, which persuaded men to acknowledge women's right to vote after centuries of denial, was the outcome of a nonviolent campaign in both Britain and the U.S. In Washington, DC, women demonstrators were imprisoned without cause and brutally treated, including painful force-feeding when they went on hunger strikes in prison. Feeding tubes were shoved down their throats. But they prevailed and women won the vote. Nonviolence was also used in the labor movement. In Lawrence, Massachusetts, in 1912, thousands of striking textile workers were marching to demonstrate their solidarity when they were confronted by a line of the militia with fixed bayonets. The commanding officer gave the order to disperse the crowd and the solders advanced. The marchers at the front were being forced forward by those at the rear who did not know what was happening ahead. As the gap narrowed and a tragedy was moments away, a young woman in the lead line wrapped herself in the American flag she was carrying and walked resolutely toward the advancing soldiers. Shamed and embarrassed, they fell back and the march continued unopposed.[17] This story demonstrates the ingenuity and spontaneous creativity that nonviolence often brings out. Young American men were not going to bayonet a girl wrapped in the American flag. Nonviolence proved more powerful, in this case, than a line of rifle-toting soldiers. Even though the police used a great deal of violence during this strike, and even threatened the workers with machine guns, the workers prevailed in their nonviolence and won their demands for a decent wage and union representation. The strike was led by the young American minister, A.J. Muste, a firm "pacifist," as they were called in those days.[18]

In another labor case, this time in the city of Windsor, Ontario, in 1945, Ford Motor Company workers were striking because the company refused to talk with them about wages even though they had endured a wage freeze through the entire war. As the company made plans to bring in scabs, the workers made plans to resist. A detachment of Royal Canadian Mounted Police was moved to the outskirts of the city. Knowing that the Mounties had been used before to charge crowds of strikers and beat them into submission, the strike leaders planned to ask those who owned cars to bring them to the plant so that a barricade of autos could be placed between the picketers and the horses. Word came through the grapevine to the workers that the Mounties were saddling up. Word went out to the car owners to go home and get their vehicles, but they were slow in arriving, and then someone had an inspiration. The first few cars to arrive were used to block the entire street next to the plant, causing a giant, immovable traffic jam. Strikers even directed traffic from other streets into the area, including loaded buses. When the RCMP arrived on horseback, the commander took one look, said there was nothing he could do, and ordered his detachment to leave town. Crowell writes, "With the attention of the whole city and much of the nation focused on the blockade, the intransigence of Ford became blatantly clear. Bargaining in good faith quickly ensued."[19] This story underlines a key element of nonviolent

NONVIOLENT PROTESTERS FACING THE BAYONETS. Striking workers in Lawrence, Massachusetts, in 1912. Eventually, the use of nonviolent struggle led finally to the legalization of labor unions and their right to organize under the leadership of Frances Perkins, secretary of labor during the first Franklin Roosevelt administration. (Lawrence History Center, Lawrence, Massachusetts)

resistance, the creative spontaneity that citizens find within themselves in times of resistance. But labor disputes are one thing; civil and international war is something else. Has it ever worked in these cases?

One famous case was the 1905 revolution in czarist Russia. For decades the czars had been besieged by dissidents, most of them armed, and many assassinations had occurred, including the killing of Czar Alexander II in 1831. But in the 1905 revolution the masses were at first nonviolent. At a great demonstration outside of the palace in St. Petersburg, soldiers who were given the order to fire on the demonstrators refused and, instead, joined them. It was only when the revolution turned violent that soldiers, with their lives threatened, obeyed orders and defeated the uprising. Still, this partially nonviolent revolution produced the first significant reforms in the Russian government in centuries, including an elected legislature.[20] One of the most remarkable acts of nonviolent resistance occurred in the trenches of Eastern Europe in 1917, when the Russian infantry just got up, dropped their guns, and walked home in spite of the fact that their officers threatened to shoot them as deserters. The real source of power in the situation was revealed. Even in this most hierarchical institution, the czarist army, real power came from below.

In 1920 in the new democratic Weimar Republic of Germany, a private, right-wing army under the command of General Lüttwitz and a Captain Kapp marched into the capital and declared a *coup d'état*, ousting the elected government, which fled to Dresden. It appeared that the democratic experiment in Germany was over, but Kapp, the ringleader, had not consulted the citizens, who simply refused to operate the city. No lights would go on, no water flowed, no garbage was picked up, no public transport ran. A total, general strike was set in motion. Kapp's army occupied the city, but they could not govern it. After a week, they marched out and the legitimate government of Germany returned.[21]

Three years later in the western part of Germany nonviolence was used to frustrate an armed invasion. French and Belgian forces invaded the Ruhr coal-and steel-producing area with the intention of collecting by force the reparations that had been imposed by the Versailles Treaty. The resistance was improvised and spread quickly, creating great difficulty for the invaders. Mine owners and miners cooperated in refusing to operate the mines. Railway workers refused to run the trains and when the French military tried to take them over, workers removed key operating parts from engines and even whole sections of track. Electric workers would not provide electricity to the train system. Shopkeepers would not sell food to occupying forces. Tram operators stopped the trams if a foreign soldier got on. Journalists circumvented the rules against publishing. There were protest demonstrations involving huge crowds. There was some sabotage, which in fact weakened the effectiveness of the resistance. France and Belgium lost the support of their World War I allies, the U.S. and the British. Many of the occupying soldiers returned home advocating the justice of the German cause. The nonviolent resistance was kept up for seven months. Crowell writes in summary, "Maintaining the occupation had become so burdensome that the French and Belgians abandoned it even after their apparent victory of inducing the German government ... to call off the nonviolent resistance."[22]

The two case histories of successful nonviolent resistance that almost everyone knows about are those associated with Gandhi and Martin Luther King, Jr. It was in South Africa and India that the historical shift from pacifism to nonviolent struggle took place, largely invented by Gandhi through a process of trial and error against brutal repression. Gandhi believed that both kinds of nonviolent struggle — that which transforms the hearts and minds of the oppressor (the moral-religiously based), and that which affects his political and economic power base (the strategic) — were necessary for success.[23] For Gandhi himself, nonviolence was an expression of religious truth and he disparaged quietist religions, writing "A religion that takes no account of practical affairs and does not help to solve them is no religion."[24] He also voiced the pragmatically obvious: "An eye for eye only ends up making the whole world blind." He knew that sometimes violence can appear to be temporarily effective, but observed that "when it appears to do good, the good is only temporary; the evil it does is permanent."

He was well acquainted with the Russian revolution of 1905 and the works of Tolstoy and also found his inspiration in the Bhagavad-Gita and the Sermon on the Mount. He was a relentless experimenter, beginning in South Africa in 1906 when the government passed discriminatory legislation regarding rights to travel and requiring Indians to carry registration cards. He was aware of what we now call structural violence, writing, "An unjust law is itself a species of violence. Arrest for its breach is more so." Gandhi organized a mass meeting where everyone swore not to obey these unjust laws. They held mass burnings of the registration cards, traveled illegally into forbidden areas, and organized a miner's strike. Thousands were jailed, including Gandhi (three times), but eventually the government gave in and withdrew the discriminatory legislation. He took these lessons to India in 1914. There, the national liberation movement was

already working in two diametrically opposed ways, one by seeking moderate reforms of British rule through the British legal system, and the other by terrorism. Gandhi saw that neither way would work and invented a third alternative: popular defiance of the unjust laws that discriminated against Indians

GANDHI AND SAROJINI NAIDU. The Mahatma, or Great Soul, transformed nonviolence from an individual act of pacifism to a mass movement of political power able to overthrow dictatorial military regimes, perhaps the greatest single invention on the road to a culture of peace. Sarojini Naidu, seen here with him, was an important feminist and political activist who became the first woman president of the Indian National Congress, exemplifying the crucial role played by women in the long struggle to achieve a culture of peace. (Gandhi Foundation)

in their own land. His first experiment was a violation of the laws against selling prohibited literature. The protest turned violent and was repressed with even greater violence. General Reginald Dyer's troops opened fire on an unarmed demonstration where thousands were trapped inside a large square. In ten minutes over a thousand were killed. Following the Amritsar Massacre the government imposed curfews, summary trials and public executions, even bombing and machine gunning Indians from the air. Gandhi was appalled at the violence and fasted for three days. Other campaigns of noncooperation were planned, including the great salt march, a protest against the British government's monopoly on the manufacture of salt, a staple commodity needed by everyone. During that campaign nonviolent activists led by Gandhi marched to the sea and, in open defiance of the law, made salt. Others marched on a government salt factory and were severely and repeatedly beaten, but they kept coming. What Gandhi did here was much more important than getting the salt law repealed (as he did). He showed all India and the world the lie that British rule was humane and in the interests of the Indian people. By exposing the government's willingness to use brutality he undermined its legitimacy. There were many more campaigns, and a whole other dimension to Gandhi's work — the movement toward self-sufficiency. It was a complex and evolving movement and it took 28 years to force the British to leave, but it was successful and by 1947 India was sovereign and free. As Gandhi said, "First they ignore you, then they laugh at you, then they fight you, then you win."[25] Later liberation movements, using Gandhi's methods, worked far more quickly. In El Salvador and Guatemala, brutal dictatorships were overthrown using nonviolent resistance in 1944.

In the southern United States, a brutal Jim Crow regime of discrimination against African Americans, enshrined in state and local law and supported by lynchings that induced terror in would-be protestors, was overcome in less than ten years. Among other forms of discrimination, African Americans had to ride in the back of the buses and in special railroad cars, could not eat at lunch counters, sit with whites at the theater, drink from the same water fountains as whites, go to the better-funded public white schools or universities, or vote. Perhaps most poignant, African Americans could not use the bathrooms designated for whites in public places, and in many cases there

Opposite: LYNDON JOHNSON SIGNING THE CIVIL RIGHTS ACT. Proving the efficacy of nonviolence, African-Americans struggled against and overturned the racist Jim Crow laws that prevailed in the United States. Here President Johnson, a southerner in the White House, is seen signing the act that outlawed segregation based on race in public places, schools, and voting registration. "We Shall Overcome" was more than just a song title, it was a peaceful power that changed our world. (Library of Congress, LC-USZ62-95480)

simply was no bathroom for them in a downtown area. Even the armed forces were segregated up until the Truman administration. African Americans could die for their country, but they had to do it in black-only units; one of these, the Tuskegee Airmen, was the most decorated fighter escort unit in the United States Air Force and the one the white bomber crews called for first for the long raids over Germany in World War II.

A key effort was getting the United States Supreme Court to declare school segregation illegal in *Brown vs. Board of Education* in 1954. This was the result of a long campaign by Thurgood Marshall, later a justice of the United States Supreme Court, and other legal scholars of the National Association for the Advancement of Colored People. In a brief effort by the federal government to enforce the law in Little Rock, Arkansas, President Eisenhower sent in federal marshals to accompany high school children to the all-white schools. However, for the most part, the state and local governments of the South ignored the decision and the federal government turned a blind eye. The Democrats came to power in 1960; their party was based on a compromise between northern liberals and segregationist southerners to keep Jim Crow in place. It would take direct, nonviolent action to overthrow Jim Crow.

Black ministers had previously traveled to India to visit Gandhi, and the Fellowship of Reconciliation was conducting teaching and training in the techniques of nonviolent struggle. Leadership training in nonviolence was being provided by the Highlander Folk School in Tennessee, which Rosa Parks, Ralph Abernathy, and Martin Luther King, Jr., among others, had attended. The state of Tennessee saw fit to close it down. It later reorganized and reopened. The Montgomery bus boycott, transportation boycotts in other cities in the South, the sit-ins in North Carolina and Tennessee, and the Freedom Rides through the Old South, succeeded in toppling the system. Blacks in Montgomery and elsewhere organized and refused to ride the buses. They carpooled, they walked, they rode bikes, and they were arrested. Dr. King, who became the leader of the movement, was bombed out of his home. In Nashville, black college students sat in at lunch counters and suffered beatings as the police looked on. And black and white men and women chartered buses and rode through the South, suffering beatings and a fire-bombing of one of the buses. Fire hoses, police charges and attack dogs were loosed on the marchers. Freedom Riders were murdered. Black leaders were assassinated, including Medgar Evers and, of course, Dr. King in 1968. But they prevailed. Eventually, the willingness to brave violence and endure suffering in a just cause showed the nation the lie that was the Old South and revealed its moral illegitimacy. And the sit-ins and boycotts hurt the merchants economically. And finally the federal government moved to act under the leadership of Robert Kennedy, U.S. attorney general. School integration was upheld by federal marshals, as was integrated transportation. Commercial facilities were integrated. The separate black and white water fountains and toilets became a thing of the past, as did seating in theaters and other forms of segregation. Blacks were able to register and vote in public elections. Racism has hardly ended in America, but the legal structure supporting it has been replaced by a legal structure outlawing its institutional manifestations. The U.S. has changed dramatically since the 1950s.

Nonviolence was employed in 1968 in Czechoslovakia. Warsaw Pact troops had invaded with the intention of removing the reform-minded government of Alexander Dubček and replacing it with a hard-line regime subservient to Moscow. The invaders expected to overcome any military resistance in a few days' time. Instead, they found nonviolent resistance, which delayed their removal of the reform government for eight months. People stood or sat in front of the tanks. They removed or changed road signs. They organized mass blowing of horns and klaxons and ringing of church bells all over the country at designated times, which unnerved the soldiers. The civilian-based defense caused such morale problems among the Soviet troops that they had to be rotated out and sent, not to the European part of Russia where they could have reported what was happening, but to Siberia. The Czechs found ingenious ways to keep secret radio transmitters going and used police cars with flashing lights and sirens wailing to sneak resistance newspapers past military checkpoints. They organized massive demonstrations and strikes and held secret meetings. The president of the country, Ludvik Svoboda, refused to name a new government even though Dubček had been arrested. In the end, of course, a compromise was reached with Dubček and Svoboda, allowing them to remain in office and retaining some of the reforms they had initiated. While it was not a total victory, many valuable lessons were learned in the "Prague Spring" that would be put to use in the final victory of the nonviolent forces in the successful Velvet Revolution of 1989.[26] And one always has to compare what was achieved to what the devastating results would have been had they tried a violent revolution against the Soviet tanks. In 1989 Alexander Dubček was elected a member of Parliament in a free Czech Republic.

Another interesting case demonstrating the ingenuity of nonviolent resisters happened in Bolivia in 1977. The country was in the grip of the military dictatorship of General Hugo Banzer when the wives of four miners, with their fourteen children, arrived in La Paz and began a hunger strike to protest the brutal conditions in the mines and the firing of their husbands for union-organizing activities. They went to the archbishop and announced their intention to fast unto death, with their children, or until the government reinstated the unions and allowed imprisoned and exiled labor leaders to return. The archbishop welcomed them into his residence for the duration of the fast. Some people were shocked that the children were also fasting and the women said that they could be relieved if adult volunteers would take their place, which was promptly done. In fact, some 1,300 other people all over the country joined the fast. The Roman Catholic Church took up their cause and within 21 days the government caved in and acceded to all their demands.

In Iran, Shah Reza Pahlavi had set up a brutal dictatorship with U.S. support. His secret police regularly tortured dissidents and his military was massively armed with American weapons. In 1979 a popular and primarily nonviolent uprising overthrew the shah's government.[27] While the final result was an equally repressive regime, this outcome does not diminish the fact that the seemingly impregnable government of the shah was brought down in a matter of months by nonviolent people power. It underscored the fundamental truth that all governments govern by the consent of the governed and when that consent is withdrawn they will collapse like a house of cards.

This was the case in the Philippines in 1986 when a faith-inspired resistance movement tumbled the dictator Ferdinard Marcos. The corrupt dictatorship of General Marcos was supported by the might of the United States. Returning for the presidential elections, which were routinely rigged by Marcos, Benigno (Ninoy) Aquino was assassinated by government agents as he stepped out of the airplane in full view of the world. After a long day of prayer and contemplation with nuns, his widow, Corazon, decided to run in his place. This was a profoundly Christian nonviolent resistance, supported and encouraged by the Church. Bishop Francisco Claver wrote:

> We choose nonviolence not merely as a strategy for the attaining of the ends of justice, casting it aside if it does not work.... We chose it because we believe it is the way Christ himself struggled for justice. In short, we equate it with the very Gospel of Christ.[28]

Numerous workshops and seminars in nonviolence were held in 1984 and 1985. The plans of Marcos for stealing the election and the ruthless armed forces were no match for people power as the masses rose up. A small contingent of the army defected and the main body moved to assault their barracks. The cardinal called on the masses to place their unarmed bodies between the little band and the main force of the army, and tens of thousands of people turned out in the streets while the contemplative orders of nuns prayed. A young girl placed a little statue of the Virgin in front of a line of tanks and an old woman sat down and prayed next to it. Street corner masses were held. People sang hymns. The army tried to intimidate the people with flights of fighter planes and armed helicopters but they stood their ground. Soldiers were met with gifts and invited to join in the blockades. It took only 77 hours for the regime to collapse. Marcos was finished and had to be smuggled out of the country by the U.S. air force.

Perhaps the most striking examples of successful nonviolence came in 1989 as Solidarity in Poland, and other resistance movements in Estonia, Latvia and Lithuania, and the Velvet Revolution in Czechoslovakia brought the Communist empire in Eastern Europe crashing down after 40 years of repressive rule. It began with the Gdansk shipyard workers in Poland. They had formed a union that they named Solidarity.

> On Friday night in December 1981, Lech Walesa and other leaders of Solidarity were arrested.... For sixteen months, their free trade union movement had shaken the foundation of Communist power in Poland by occupying factories and staging strikes. Now martial law had been imposed, and Solidarity was looking down a gun barrel at defeat. But when he was taken away, Walesa challenged his captors. "At this moment, you lost," he told them. "We are arrested, but you have driven a nail into your communist coffin.... You'll come back to us on your knees."[29]

In 1990, Walesa was elected president of a free Poland and in 1993 he was subsequently awarded the Nobel Peace Prize.

After World War II, the Warsaw Pact nations had stationed in Eastern Europe the largest concentration of mechanized, armored forces in the history of the world. They had an enormous secret police apparatus in each country. The Berlin Wall and the Iron Curtain in general were rock solid. The Communists were so firmly in control that no one predicted their collapse. As Robert Gates, former director, said, the CIA "had no idea in January, 1989, that a tidal wave of history was about to break upon us."[30] But nonviolence training had been going on in Eastern Europe for some time, especially in the churches, carried out by the Fellowship of Reconciliation and others. The works of Gene Sharp were being circulated and discussed. And in the fall of 1989 over 500,000 people poured into the streets.

The movement began in the Leipzig churches and became a mass, national movement for ousting the Communist dictatorship. In the fall of 1989 in Leipzig (then part of East Germany), prayer meetings and demonstrations were being held every Monday night at Nikolaikirche, led by Lutheran Pastor Christian Fuhrer, who had been arrested in September and told to call off the prayer meetings and demonstrations. He did not. He later told the story to NPR in an interview:

> In September, the Stasi, the secret police, started beating people up and arresting them in large numbers in front of the church. So we started to make lists of the people arrested, and we put those lists on display in public right here by the church door. On Monday, the 9th of October, when we tried to leave the church after evening peace prayers, the square and the streets were completely

flooded with people; people everywhere. And ... this mass of 70,000 people
with their candles and flowers trying to move peacefully toward the city center.[31]

It wasn't at all clear that the Stasi and soldiers were not preparing to gun them
down. In fact, they were. But as Pastor Fuhrer said later,

> I felt immense gratitude because no one shot at them. I also felt that the GDR
> that evening was not the same GDR of the previous day. Something huge and
> completely different had happened.

That something was the power of nonviolence to change situations.

> As the crowd made its way towards the city's century-old train station — accom-
> panied by thousands of helmeted riot police — tension grew. But at the decisive
> moment, the police stood aside and let the protesters march by. "They didn't
> attack," Fuehrer says. "They had nothing to attack for." Organizers made sure
> the crowds gave the police no excuses. They carried nothing but candles and
> banners reading "We are the people." The Stasi planted plainclothes officers in
> the crowd to cause trouble, but they were all quickly surrounded and neutral-
> ized by protesters chanting "no violence."[32]

Birgit Scheffle was one of the demonstrators.

> "We all carried lighted candles," said Scheffle. "The candles had a pacifying
> impact on the soldiers," she said. "When you walk with a lighted candle you
> must use both hands. One hand holds the candle the other keeps the flame from
> going out. So, you cannot throw a stone at soldiers, and soldiers can see that
> you cannot throw a stone. That day marked the beginning of the end of East
> Germany."[33]

The police did not fire on the crowds. They parted and let them pass. As one
Communist official said later, "We were prepared for everything except the
prayers and the candles."[34] The October 9 mass demonstration was the beginning of the end. The Communist dictatorship in Eastern Europe was shortly
to be history. The peaceful revolution rapidly spread to the rest of the country
and then into the rest of Eastern Europe. In East Germany, after some weeks
of demonstrations, the dictator Erich Honecker, ordered the army to end it,
to fire on the crowds, but local party leaders, aware of the international condemnation of the Chinese government's response to Tiananmen Square,
refused to give the order to the security police.[35] On October 18, after only
a few weeks of demonstrations, Honecker resigned and on November 9, after
28 years, the Berlin Wall was opened. Honecker was charged with treason. If
NATO, with all its conventional and nuclear firepower, had tried to use armed
force to liberate Eastern Europe from the Communists, we would all be dead.
Nonviolence, however, was successful, was more powerful than NATO or the
Warsaw Pact. The historical epoch of Eurocommunism was over.

Two years later, in Russia, where Soviet President Michael Gorbachev was conducting his liberalizing experiment with *perestroika*, the Communists organized an armed *coup d'état*. Gorbachev was held under house arrest in the Crimea where he was vacationing while tanks surrounded the government buildings in Moscow. What the coup planners did not plan for, however, was a massive, spontaneous uprising of the citizens who surrounded the tanks and clogged the streets, and talked the soldiers out of it. The coup attempt failed in one night, going down before the power of the people. Again, the historical record of successful nonviolence demonstrates the truth of Boulding's Law.

The final objection that skeptics raise about nonviolence often goes like this: "Well, you could use it against the British, who [it is said without much evidence] were basically humane, but what about the Nazis?" In fact, the British were not humane. When confronted with violent rebellion in the nineteenth century, they tied native prisoners over the mouths of cannon and executed them by firing. But the answer to the Nazi question is that nonviolence was used successfully against the Nazi regime, both in the conquered countries and even in Berlin itself. The Nazi-dominated Danes refused to go along with the deportation of Jews. The Danes successfully smuggled 7,500 of Denmark's 8,000 Jews to safety across the Baltic Sea to neutral Sweden, in some instances hiding them in secret compartments built in little fishing boats and even crossing in kayaks.[36] When the Nazi government cracked down and arrested all the Danish police, they also came to the palace and arrested the king's own police and announced that the Nazi flag would be hoisted over the palace. The king replied to the German officer, "Then a Danish soldier will take it down." The officer replied, "That Danish soldier will be shot." And the king answered, "That Danish soldier will be myself."[37] The flag was never raised.

In Norway the Germans ordered that the school curriculum be Nazified and all teachers were required to join a Nazi teachers' union. Ninety-eight percent refused. Three hundred teachers were rounded up and taken to a concentration camp in the far north, above the Arctic Circle. A nonviolent resistance campaign was carried out for several months and it resulted in the release of the teachers and the withdrawal of the Nazi curriculum. The Nazis also tried to crack down on the Church and required all pastors to join a Nazi "unity movement." Only 20 of 1,139 did and they were boycotted by their congregations. All the Norwegian bishops resigned their offices. The campaign to Nazify the Church failed utterly.

There were other resistance movements in the occupied countries. In Holland resistance movements sprang up among doctors and artists and other professions. The general strike of the railway workers paralyzed the country and the Dutch people held out all through the winter of 1945 without heat and had to do with dwindling supplies of food.[38]

In Bulgaria, which was allied with the Nazis in World War II, the perse-

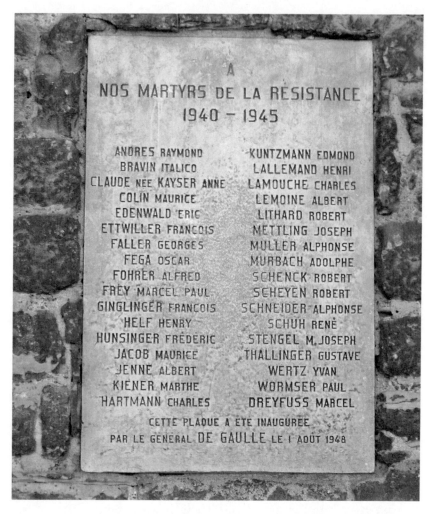

A

NOS MARTYRS DE LA RÉSISTANCE
1940 – 1945

ANDRES RAYMOND	KUNTZMANN EDMOND
BRAVIN ITALICO	LALLEMAND HENRI
CLAUDE NÉE KAYSER ANNE	LAMOUCHE CHARLES
COLIN MAURICE	LEMOINE ALBERT
EDENWALD ERIC	LITHARD ROBERT
ETTWILLER FRANCOIS	METTLING JOSEPH
FALLER GEORGES	MULLER ALPHONSE
FEGA OSCAR	MURBACH ADOLPHE
FOHRER ALFRED	SCHENCK ROBERT
FREY MARCEL PAUL	SCHEYEN ROBERT
GINGLINGER FRANCOIS	SCHNEIDER ALPHONSE
HELF HENRY	SCHUH RENÉ
HUNSINGER FRÉDERIC	STENGEL M. JOSEPH
JACOB MAURICE	THALLINGER GUSTAVE
JENNE ALBERT	WERTZ YVAN
KIENER MARTHE	WORMSER PAUL
HARTMANN CHARLES	DREYFUSS MARCEL

CETTE PLAQUE A ÉTÉ INAUGURÉE
PAR LE GÉNÉRAL DE GAULLE LE I AOÛT 1948

To the Martyrs of the Resistance. This plaque is one of thousands seen all over France, dedicated to those who lost their lives fighting in the French resistance movement against the Nazi occupation in World War II. What might have been the outcome if all of France had been trained in nonviolent resistance? (Author's photograph)

cution of the Jews began with the usual denial of civil rights and anti–Semitic graffiti on homes and synagogues. Rabbi Avraham Bachar reports, "By morning, people had already cleaned it. They risked their lives to do this. This risked death! They — the Christians." Then the deportation orders went out to round up the Jews for transport to the death camps. Stephan, the metropolitan bishop of the Greek Orthodox Church, and Kiril, head of the Church in Sofia, took active steps to oppose the deportation. Leaflets circulated by the Bulgarian Fascist party called for the murder of Stephan. When the first 800 Jews were rounded up Stephan went to the king, who had been complicit in the Nazi orders, and threatened to open all the churches in Bulgaria for the Jews to take refuge. He sent a telegram to the king saying, "Do not persecute so that you yourself will not be persecuted. Your measures shall be returned to you,"[39] and reminded the king that God was watching him. In the city of Plovdiv, where Kiril was bishop, 1,500 Jews were held in a schoolyard awaiting deportation. He threatened to lie across the railway tracks to prevent the trains from moving away. He quoted to the Jews from the Book of Ruth: "Where you go, I will go; and where you lodge, I will lodge; your people shall be my people, and your God my God; where you die, I will die; and there I will be buried."[40] The Jews were allowed to go home. All of Bulgaria's 50,000 Jews were saved. On the Greek island of Zakynthos, occupied by the Nazis, Bishop Chrysostomos was ordered to give the commandant a list of all the Jews so they could be rounded up. He did. He provided them with a list that had two names on it: non–Jews, his own and the mayor's. The Jews were left alone.[41]

There was successful nonviolent resistance in Germany itself. In 1943 a number of Jewish men married to non–Jewish women were rounded up throughout Germany and taken to the Gestapo prison in Berlin to await deportation to the death camps. Their wives organized, came to Berlin, surrounded the Gestapo jail, and screamed for three days. The men were freed.[42] Another example comes from Le Chambon, a village in southern France, where Pastor Andre Trocmé and his French Protestant congregation carried out an operation in which 5,000 Jewish children smuggled in from all over Europe were hidden from the Nazis and thus saved from the death camps. Toward the end of the war it appears that the Nazi officials knew of the operation, but did not in any serious way seek to stop it. They arrested Pastor Trocmé but then let him go, even though the regime was executing Jews in the death camps right up to the end of the war.[43]

The historical record demonstrates that nonviolent resistance has worked against all degrees of regimes, from segregationist states in the American South to colonial regimes, to right-wing military dictatorships, to totalitarian regimes of Fascism and communism.

How Nonviolence Works

Nonviolence works by a sort of "moral jiu-jitsu.... The non-violence and good will of the victim act like the lack of physical opposition by the user of physical jiu-jitsu, to cause the attacker to lose his moral balance. He suddenly and unexpectedly loses the moral support which the usual violent resistance of most victims would render him."[44] As we have seen earlier, violent conflict relies on dehumanizing the opponent — making him into a thing, the "enemy," and treating him as outside the pale, as a subhuman. The Nazis actually used the word *Untermenschen,* or subhumans, to describe the Jews. Its effect is obvious: "One thing violence can be counted on to do is bring forth the antagonist in battle dress."[45] For the average person who has grown up in this dominator culture and who has been inducted into the military, if you point a gun at him, he will shoot you. Not only does he know no other response and is ordered to shoot; but he also is afraid for his life.

Nonviolence reverses this process. It re-humanizes the opponent's soldiers and functionaries and re-includes them in the common humanity. This is especially true of the kind of nonviolence that is more than just making trouble by noncooperation and sabotage, as was the case in the Ruhr in the 1920s, which was the kind of nonviolent struggle that Gene Sharp advocates. Rather, this kind of nonviolence seeks to liberate not only the victim but the oppressor as well. It was most effectively practiced by King and Gandhi. A Midrash based on the Talmud teaches, "it is insufficient to have been freed from hate; one must seek to free one's opponent from it."[46] And it greatly reduces the need for a fear response on the part of the soldier or the opponent. At the end of Gandhi's successful campaign in South Africa, one of General Jan Smuts' secretaries said to him, "I often wish you took to violence ... and then we would know at once how to dispose of you. But you will not injure even the enemy. You desire victory by self-suffering alone and never transgress your self-imposed limits of courtesy and chivalry. And that is what reduces us to sheer helplessness."[47]

Barbara Demming explains in detail:

> In violent battle the effort is to demoralize the enemy, to so frighten him that he will surrender. The risk is that desperation and resentment will make him go on resisting when it is no longer even in his own interest. He has been driven beyond reason. In nonviolent struggle the effort is of quite a different nature. One doesn't try to frighten the other. One tries to undo him ... only in the sense that one tries to shake him out of former attitudes and force him to appraise the situation now in a way that takes into consideration your needs as well as his. One is able to do this — able in a real sense to change his mind (rather than try to drive him out of it) — precisely because one reassures him about his personal safety all the time one keeps disrupting the order of things he has known to date.[48]

Nonviolence is based on the fundamental premise that the means determine the ends. Adopt violent struggle and the end will be violent, even for the victor whose character and society will be changed.

Nevertheless, one would be wrong to think that Gandhian nonviolence, which seeks to protect and care for the oppressor while fighting the oppression, is some kind of agapic love feast. Oppressors can remain violent for a long time and the nonviolent struggle is nonetheless a kind of battle. In his now famous three-volume work, *The Politics of Nonviolent Action*, Sharp emphasizes that

> nonviolent action is designed to operate against opponents who are able and willing to use violent sanctions. There is no assumption in this technique that such opponents will ... suddenly renounce their violence.... However, the use of nonviolent means against violent repression creates a special, asymmetrical, conflict situation in which the two groups rely on contrasting techniques of struggle.... The [nonviolent] actionists will then be able to apply something like *jiu-jitsu* to their opponent, throwing him off balance politically, causing his repression to rebound against his position, and weakening his power.[49]

The secret of success lies in the counterintuitive fact that power in a state comes from below. Even in repressive, dictatorial regimes, the state apparatus requires an enormous amount of cooperation from the people in order to function on a daily basis. If they accept the regime as legitimate, or fear it, then they will cooperate with it, providing the base of power on which it rests. Sharp writes:

> If the withdrawal of acceptance, submission and help can be maintained in the face of the ruler's punishments, then the end of the regime is in sight. Thus, all rulers are dependent ... on the cooperation of their subjects. This applies not only internally, but also ... in cases of attempted foreign invasion and occupation. The theory that power derives from violence and that victory goes to the side with the greater capacity for violence, is false.[50]

As ought to be obvious, he writes, "The means one chooses to respond to an assailant will largely determine his reaction." Sharp has outlined hundreds of methods by which citizens have withdrawn support from and undermined oppressive powers. He organizes these methods under five headings. The first is "Methods of Nonviolent Protest and Persuasion" and includes the following

> Public speeches; letters of opposition; declarations by organizations and institutions; signed public statements; declarations of indictment; group or mass petitions; slogans, caricatures, and symbols; Banners and posters, Leaflets, pamphlets, and books; underground newspapers and journals; recordings, radio and TV; skywriting and earthwriting; deputations; mock awards; group lobbying; picketing; mock elections, displays of flags and colors; wearing of symbols; delivering of symbolic objects; prayer and worship; protest disrobings; destruction of own property; paint as protest; new signs and names; haunting land; taunting officials; fraternization; vigils; singing and processions, pilgrimages,

motorcades; political mourning; mock funerals, homage at burial places; assemblies of protest; performance of musicals; marches and parades; camouflaged meetings of protest, Teach-ins; Walk-outs; silence; renouncing honors; turning one's back.

Second are "Methods of Social Noncooperation":

Social boycott; excommunication; interdict; suspension of social and sports activities; boycotts of social affairs; student strike; social disobedience; withdrawal from social institutions; staying at home; sanctuary; collective disappearance. [The latter was used, interestingly enough, by some members of the Texas Legislature to avoid a vote on what they perceived to be an unjust redistricting bill. They hid out in Oklahoma.]

The third category he lists in *The Politics of Nonviolent Struggle, Part Two* is "Methods of Economic Noncooperation":

Economic boycotts including consumers' boycotts at the national and international levels; withholding of rent; producer's boycotts; workmen's boycotts; traders and middlemen's boycotts; refusal to rent or sell property; refusal to provide industrial assistance; refusal to pay debts or taxes; refusal of a government's money; and embargoes. A special case is the strike, including quickie walkouts or the lightening strike; the protest strike, strikes by peasants, farm workers, prisoners; refusal of forced labor; craft and professional strikes; slowdowns; sick-ins; the general strike, and the general hartal or total economic shutdown.

Fourth are "Methods of Political Noncooperation":

Withdrawing allegiance and public support; publication of literature advocating resistance; boycotting legislative bodies and government positions; boycotting government departments & agencies; withdrawal from government agencies and educational institutions; refusal to assist government agents; removal of signs and placemarks; refusal to dissolve existing institutions; slow compliance with government orders; nonobedience; disguised disobedience; hiding; escape; false identities; civil disobedience of illegitimate laws; blocking lines of command and information; judicial noncooperation; mutiny; non-cooperation by constituent government bodies; withholding diplomatic recognition; and the severance of diplomatic relations.

And finally, "Methods of Nonviolent Intervention":

Fasting; reverse trials; nonviolent harassment; sit-ins (stand-ins, ride-ins, wade-ins, etc.); nonviolent raids, invasions, interjections, obstructions, occupations; overloading facilities; guerilla theater; alternative social institutions; alternative communication system; nonviolent land seizure; blockades; defiance of blockades; alternative markets; transportation systems; overloading of administrative systems; disclosing identities of secret agents; dual sovereignty and parallel government.

What Gene Sharp is underscoring in *The Politics of Nonviolent Struggle* is the incredible ingenuity of those who have practiced it. These struggles are replete with spontaneous invention. Spontaneous nonviolent struggle has been surprisingly successful over the past century.

For most practitioners of nonviolence, and certainly for the great ones like Gandhi and King, it was crucial to understand the correct relationship between means and ends. Violent means seldom produce peaceful ends and never in any genuine sense do they produce peace. While they may end a particular war, they perpetuate the war system itself. Victory, or even a mere cessation of hostilities, does not break the cycle of violence. As Gandhi was fond of saying, "There is no way to peace. Peace is the way." Nonviolence is a tried, demonstrated, and proven alternative to violence, one that does not perpetuate conflict but rather dissolves it. In an age of increasingly horrific weapons of mass destruction, Dr. Martin Luther King was prophetic when he said, on the night before he was assassinated, "For years now, we have been talking about war and peace. But now, no longer can we just talk about it. It is no longer a choice between violence and nonviolence; it's nonviolence or nonexistence."[51]

If, and when, states realize the utility of nonviolent defense, they may begin to experiment with training their citizens. But given that citizens so trained can overthrow regimes, they may fear it, which is why this training may have to come from nongovernment organizations such as the Nonviolent Peaceforce, the Fellowship of Reconciliation, and so forth. Widespread nonviolent training can help to render armies a thing of the past. Nonviolent training is being carried out today by many groups. Over the next 100 years such training could become part of a complex peace system, one layer in a heavily redundant culture of peace that will make war obsolete. We turn to this system in the next chapter.

CHAPTER 9

Abolishing War and Building a Comprehensive Peace System

"We are what we think. All that we are arises with our thoughts. With our thoughts we make the world."
—Gautama Buddha, opening lines
of the Dhammapada

"The future is not a result of choices among alternative paths offered by the present, but a place that is created—created first in the mind and will, created next in activity. The future is not some place we are going to but one we are creating. The paths are not to be found, but made, and the activity of making them changes both the maker and the destination."
—John Schaar[1]

Thinking Constructively and Holistically about a Peace System

When we have succeeded in abolishing war it will be because we have rooted peace in institutions, values, and beliefs that penetrate all aspects of culture. No single treaty, no single institution, however global, can create it. Toward the end of the twentieth century many people were realizing that any single-dimensional approach to peace would not suffice to replace the complex war system under which the world has suffered for several thousand years. Individuals and the United Nations began to talk about a "culture of peace." In 1989 the term "culture of peace" was first used at a UN conference. In 1997 the General Assembly declared the year 2000 to be the "International Year for the Culture of Peace" and in 1998 announced the International Decade for a Culture of Peace and Non-Violence for the Children of the World, to

168

last from 2001 to 2010.[2] UN documents are quick to point out that establishing a culture of peace does not imply cultural homogenization; in fact, just the opposite — it requires a healthy respect for cultural diversity. Recognizing that peace is more than the mere absence of war, the UN documents assert that it is not an absence of conflict either, but a way of dealing with conflict that results in justice and satisfaction without resorting to violence. UNESCO has promulgated the "Manifesto 2000 Pledge," now signed by hundreds of thousands of people from around the world. The pledge, drafted by Nobel Peace Prize laureates, includes "Respect all life; Reject violence; Share with others; Listen to understand; Preserve the planet; and Rediscover solidarity."[3] The UNESCO movement aims to establish a culture of peace primarily via education on the following principles: "Promote sustainable economic and social development; promote respect for human rights; ensure equality between men and women; foster democratic participation; advance understanding, tolerance and solidarity; support participatory communication and the free flow of information and knowledge; and promote international peace and security."[4]

These manifestos and education programs are a piece of the puzzle, but by no means the whole picture. Their authors are, of course, aware that governments need to play a role. In fact, it is not surprising that, the UN being an organization of sovereign states, they argue that governments must take the lead. But this could mislead our thinking. The evolution of a peace system must come from both top down and bottom up — these are not opposites, they are complementary and form a continuum with influences running in all directions, creating a synergy so that the whole is more than the sum of its parts. Furthermore, action must be both local and global.

The structural changes must be much more far-reaching in order to ensure stable peace for the whole world. While in terms of Boulding's paradigm, stable peace has been achieved in certain areas of the world, it is not so in others. Different regions are in different phases. At this writing the United States is engaged in the Stable War phase in Iraq, Afghanistan, and the border areas of Pakistan, and is threatening Iran. And even where a phase of Stable Peace has been achieved, the war system has not been replaced with a peace system, so a region could, at least theoretically, revert to unstable or even stable war. Nevertheless, while the UN declaration and manifesto remain frustratingly vague, especially as to structural changes needed in international law, the UN itself, education, national defense and other areas, it is encouraging that the principle of a holistic and systematic approach to eliminating war is becoming widespread. We are beginning to understand the nature of a comprehensive peace system.

According to Robert Johansen, a well-known peace studies scholar, in a peace system "conflict is resolved through nonviolent, political, social, and judicial processes. There are no expectations of war and no national military arsenals. There is a widespread sense of solidarity with the rest of the human species."[5] But the control and abolition of war is only one part of a peace system. Peace requires justice, that is, a global economic system in which no one goes without the necessities while others fatten on the resources of the poor nations. Only when all peoples have enough food, shelter, water, medical care and educational opportunities will the sources of anger and rage that help fuel the war system be eliminated. In "The Tangled Web: The Poverty-Insecurity Nexus," authors Lael Brainard, Derek Chollet, and Vince LaFleur write, "The fight against global poverty has become a fight of necessity, not simply because personal morality demands it, but because global security does as well."[6] They point out that even the national security planners of the U.S. seem to be aware of this reality. The 2006 National Security Strategy plan of the U.S. says, "Development reinforces diplomacy and defense, reducing long-term threats to our national security by helping build stable, prosperous and peaceful societies."[7] If they could only see that "defense," as they manage it, reinforces poverty and insecurity! The problem here is, of course, real commitment. The defense planners pour the overwhelming majority of resources into militarized approaches to national security rather than into the development measures that would lead instead toward peace.

So what is to be done? Brainard, Chollet and LaFleur argue for a three-fold effort: (1) "help policymakers to better understand the issue's significance and urgency," (2) "understand the specific conditions that heighten the risk of conflict" in the regions, and (3) "require building long-term, local capacity."[8] The first step is a job for NGOs and their citizen members to instruct, first of all, the press and to encourage responsible journalists. This includes copying and forwarding their articles to lawmakers, other journalists and citizens in general. It is also important to reward politicians and bureaucrats for carrying through on commitments. All too often, peace movement people are quick to point out the crises and the wrongs, but fail to acknowledge and thus empower those leaders who are making the right decisions. Peace workers need to be positive as well as to speak truth to power. It is encouraging that much positive work is already going into these conversations about the relationship between security and development.

Achieving the justice that strengthens peace will require a major shift in the way the global economy is managed because most "development" now taking place under the rubric of globalization is really de-development. Sharon Delgado writes:

> The current form of corporate-dominated globalization is escalating the plunder of the earth's riches, increasing the exploitation of workers, expanding policy and military repression and leaving poverty in its wake.[9]

By measuring progress in terms of economic growth, we mask the destruction of natural capital, the growing divide between rich and poor, the immiseration of millions of humans, and the escalating anger in the global south. In a peace system we will use an alternative index, something like the Genuine Progress Indicator developed by Ted Halstead and Clifford Cobb, which includes such variables as income distribution, and such costs as resource depletion, pollution, and long-term environmental damage, and such value-added factors as housework and nonmarket transactions, investment in sustainability, life span of consumer durables, and so on.[10] Other obvious measures will be longevity, educational levels attained, health care, literacy, and housing conditions. In short, in a peace system the economy will be evaluated not in terms of some abstraction like the gross domestic product measure, but in terms of human well-being. One of the reforms on the way to peace will be a fundamental reform of the undemocratic and powerful World Trade Organization so that it cannot override national laws protecting the environment and workers' rights in the name of so-called free trade.[11]

It should be obvious that a well-functioning global economy that meets the basic needs of all requires a healthy global ecosystem. The looming specter of major climate shift, which may well result in a dramatic decline in agricultural production in some heavily populated regions, will severely test our ability to keep the peace, as large numbers of people will be on the move in search of food and water. This is where a United Nations forecasting agency and the office of the High Commissioner on Refugees will need serious upgrades in funding and staff. It will also require the more fortunate nations to give thought to producing food instead of biofuels, and opening their borders to the starving refugees. This situation is most clearly limned along the India-Bangladesh border. Already, prior to the most serious effects of climate change that are widely predicted, Bangladesh is subject to heavy flooding during storms — for example, storm surges of 78 inches. There are already refugee camps along the border and India is building a fence.[12] Combined with the melting of the Himalayan snowcaps that feed the rivers necessary for irrigated food production, we can conclude that Bangladesh is dangerously overpopulated. The United Nations Convention on Refugees legally obligates signatories to take in refugees. A great deal of work needs to be done in order to prepare the more affluent, or climatically fortunate, nations to be receptive to the coming challenges and to be prepared with necessary infrastructure and laws, lest a xenophobic response exacerbate the potential crisis. Here is where a major shift in attitude, discussed in the next chapter, must come into play if we are to avoid resource wars in the near future.

A systems approach allows us to see that the organizations working on the kind of international development aimed at the people and not the elites, and those working to maintain a healthy environment, are also working toward the establishment of a global peace system. This is not some utopian dream, but an on-the-ground reality that is new in just the last century. The *Directory of Development Organizations* lists 65,000 examples of both governmental and, mostly, non-governmental organizations working to achieve the goals of a just and environmentally sound development.[13]

These two things — the winding down of war and the winding up of global justice — are linked together in a direct feedback loop. For example, the amount the United States would need to contribute toward ending extreme poverty in the world is only three and a half weeks' worth of U.S. military spending.[14] Lester Brown calculates that it would require $187 billion annually to achieve both the basic social goals needed to end poverty, thus stabilizing the poorest societies, and global environmental restoration, whereas the U.S. spends $604 billion and the world's nation states together spend $1,464 billion annually on maintaining the war system.[15] We are clearly able to afford this.

As the war system winds down and there is less military spending, more money will be available for sustainable development, and as sustainable development occurs in the world's poorer regions, there will be less need for huge military budgets. It's a positive feedback loop. People who are working for peace must constantly explain to a wide audience the opportunity costs of a militarized security system. But it is not just the affluent nations whose resolve will need to be bolstered by world opinion. Many states in the global south are making similar mistakes. It was recently reported that Uganda, a nation where the AIDS epidemic is again on the rise due to lack of sufficient funds for drugs, has negotiated a deal with Russia for a $300 million purchase of a squadron of Sukhoi fighter bombers.[16] Venezuela is another state buying the Russian warplanes.

A peace system will be equally as complex as the war system and as deeply rooted in institutions, laws, values, and beliefs. No single treaty, no single pledge to remove a particular weapons system, no single technology or technique, no single belief or value can provide the assurance of security. Only a broad-based, general movement toward a social system that has peace as its outcome will suffice to get people to risk giving up old habits, however unworkable they have become. Also, we must be clear at the outset that a peace movement is not the same as an anti-war movement. While organizing opposition to a particular war can be a peaceful act, if it is done without righteous anger and moral arrogance, it can generate its own angry and violent opposition. An anti-war movement is a negative approach. Creating a peace system, by contrast, is a positive movement, a creation of something new.

Thinking about a peace system cannot be incremental. We need a radical vision of the whole. If we try to extrapolate from the present one step at a time, we will not get there. This is because a social system that results in peace must be layered, redundant, resilient, robust and proactive. Its various parts must feed back to each other so the system is strengthened and the failure of one part does not lead to systems failure. In this respect it is identical to a war system. Having said that we need a radical vision of the whole in advance, it will nevertheless inevitably be true that we will learn as we go and the final result will always be a continuously improving process rather than a static, absolute structure.

However, the progress toward creating the institutions and norms of peace can and already is occurring incrementally. We have many of the parts of a peace system; we just need to put them together. As we make the transition we will see movement toward the following: the peaceful resolution of disputes; observance of human rights; the establishment of economic justice and a global economy in which everyone's basic human needs for food, shelter, water, education, personal safety and health care are met and that is capable of being sustained by the earth's ecosystems; and finally, the emergence of a partnership society to replace the patriarchy of the last 6000 years. Of course, all of this sounds too good to be true. But two considerations are in order. First, there is scientific and historical evidence that when systems change phase, they change relatively quickly. An obvious example from the world of nature is the transition from water to ice. The water temperature of a lake declines gradually, a degree at a time, and no change is visible for many days. And then one morning the surface of the lake is hard. The sudden disintegration of Soviet Communism is a powerful example of this phenomenon from the world of international politics. And second, we are already moving in this direction, not as a result of some cosmic fate, but a result of the cumulative effect of millions of acts of will.

The acts of creating a peace system will occur — indeed, are occurring — at many levels and often simultaneously, often in overlapping ways, all of them feeding back into the others. The overall appearance may well be confusion, but like the water temperature dropping, the phase change will emerge. We look next at how the existing international and national structures need to be strengthened and who is working on them.

The Institutional/Governance Structure of a Peace System

There are four levels at which institutional change will move the world toward a comprehensive peace. These are international institutions, international law, the sovereign state, and local government. The key international institutions include the existing body of international law, the United Nations, the two world courts, and regional governance bodies. None of the ideas presented below for strengthening these institutions is new. They have been discussed by numerous organizations and individuals since the middle of the twentieth century.

First, war needs to be redefined in international law, abandoning the concept that a war between two nations or two groups within a nation is somehow their own business. It is not. Rather, war is "a crime against the international community."[17] War needs to be outlawed. A first and rather naïve run at this was the Kellogg-Briand Pact of 1928.[18] Currently, the United Nations Charter declares only aggression illegal, but all forms of military violence need to be outlawed.[19]

Achieving this should begin with a campaign to persuade the International Court of Justice, which has already outlawed the threat or use of nuclear weapons, to outlaw all forms of war, including civil war. In an example of feedback loops and systems synergy, other bodies such as municipalities, states or provinces, religious bodies, and citizen groups will need to pass resolutions supporting such a change in order to bring pressure on the Court and the General Assembly. Then the General Assembly of the United Nations should pass a similar declaration to bolster the Court's decision and plan for a convention to change the Charter, to be ratified finally by the member states. Some may object that it is useless to pass a law that cannot be immediately enforced, but the process has to start somewhere, as it did with the outlawing of slavery long before slavery was finally abolished. Outlawing war is the first step toward abolition. There appears to be legal precedent for this in the foundation for the International Criminal Court's jurisdiction over crimes against humanity. While the ICC deals only with individuals, war can easily be defined as a crime against humanity, especially since the majority of its victims are now non-combatants, thus giving jurisdiction to the International Court of Justice and providing the rationale for action by the General Assembly.

The international trade in arms by governments and by private arms merchants that work together in close cooperation also needs to be outlawed. The Campaign Against the Arms Trade has published an excellent briefing paper, "Private Gain, Public Pain: The Case for Ending the Government's Arms Selling," available online.[20] They point out that the trade aids governments with gross human rights abuses, deprives the economy of funds for creating green jobs, contributes to international instability, and perpetuates the belief that peace is a security issue and that security is a military issue. A treaty based on the concept that the trade in weapons is a crime "aiding and abetting manslaughter as a crime against humanity" could be enforced by the International Criminal Court and monitored by existing international policing agencies.

Outlawing war does not mean outlawing police power, especially at the international level. It only means outlawing war between and within nation states. The United Nations Charter does include a provision for a standing military force that, in a world where war is outlawed, could apprehend outlaws, whether terrorists or the leaders of nation states, and bring them before the appropriate world courts. The Charter provision has never been invoked, but it is a simple step to move from temporary UN peacekeeping units to a permanent police force. This would also solve the problem now faced by the peacekeeping process — namely, that assembling a force from national contingents takes months, during which conflicts sometimes escalate out of control. The additional problem of a chaos of incompatible training and armaments would also be eliminated. A rapid reaction force, now being called an "Emergency Peace Force," of 10,000 to 15,000 troops trained in diverse responses to crisis situations, deployable within 48 hours and under the control of the Security Council, could put out brush fires before they get out of control. The EPF would include soldiers, and also police, as well as judicial and civilian experts. They would then be followed, if necessary, by the standard UN Blue Helmets peacekeeping force for longer-term deployment.[21] This could also reduce the need for national armed forces, enforce the rule of international law, and base its military objectives on an impartial understanding of international law.[22] There is a robust conversation on this whole idea. The Global Policy Forum, which follows the work of the UN, has posted 24 papers on its website.[23] Such a force would, of course, be subject to the jurisdiction of the International Criminal Court and the General Assembly, as further checks against its misuse. Creating such a force needs to be paired with a general reduction in armaments and changes in force posture at the national level, a topic we will examine shortly.

Other changes need to occur at the United Nations. First, a United Nations truly capable of preventing war would have to make significant changes to the Security Council. Presently the permanent members are the victors in World War II, an absurd situation today. A more representative council adding permanent members from the global south and nations that have recovered from World War II — namely, Japan and Germany — would be far more effective. Second, even more important is the abolition of the single-member veto power, which basically castrates the council because unanimity is almost impossible to get. The Council could easily operate by a supermajority of 75 or 80 percent of the members voting.[24] Third, the UN needs to add a third body, a World Parliament elected by citizens of the various nation states, acting as an advisory board to the General Assembly and the Security Council. A citizen-based World Parliament movement has been in existence for some years. Their program is available on their website.[25] Such a body at the UN would allow for the expression of non-state views and for a greater expression of the will of the common people.

New or strengthened functions would also include a Conflict Management Agency (CMA) located in the Secretariat and taking on several critical functions. First, it would function as an early warning system that would continuously monitor the world, reporting to the General Assembly and the Security Council on general trends leading toward future conflicts based on such factors as the following:

- Demographic pressures: rapid changes in population, including refugee movements, insufficient food or access to safe water.
- Unresponsive regimes and lack of accountable government practices.
- Criminalization of the civil system or delegitimization of the state.
- Gross human rights violations.
- Significant differences of ethnic (or tribal) composition of a ruling elite from the population at large.
- A legacy of vengeance-seeking group grievances.
- Massive, chronic or sustained human flight.[26]

We want to add regional economic and environmental collapse to this list. Also, the CMA would maintain standing, multinational conflict mediation teams, made up of trained experts, which could be dispatched to areas where conflicts appeared to be imminent. These changes would prepare the UN to be proactive rather than reactive. They would also require a significant increase in funding for the United Nations. The UN needs the power to tax. A minuscule tax on one or a few types of international transactions such as telephone calls, or postage, or international air travel, or electronic mail, would provide the UN with a greatly expanded budget and relieve a few wealthy states from being its major funders.[27] The overall UN budget including the cost of peacekeeping is currently about $60 billion, or about 11 percent of the U.S. military budget. The U.S. currently pays about 25 percent, or some $12 billion. The overall result of a tax system would very likely be to reduce the U.S. portion of the UN budget.

Other governance structures include regional bodies such as the European Union, the Organization of American States, the African Union and various regional courts. These institutions are already well established on the ground and while they do work toward the control of conflicts, their ability to do so needs to be strengthened with, for example, regional conflict forecasting and mediation structures.

In addition, there is a large body of international treaty law governing conflict. Many critical treaties have been ratified and are in place; others have yet to be fully supported but are nevertheless partly operational. For example, by 2004, 144 nations had signed the treaty banning land mines and it is now in effect, although as of this writing, the U.S. has refused to sign. Treaties limiting nuclear weapons include the 1963 Partial Test Ban Treaty prohibiting tests above ground, in the water and in space; the Comprehensive Nuclear-Test-Ban Treaty, awaiting sufficient signatures to go into force; and various treaties that drastically reduced the stockpiles of nuclear weapons from absurd levels (50,000) down to about 10,000 each for the United States and Russia. These nations recently signed another treaty further reducing the number of strategic warheads from 2,200 to 1,550 for each side, with 800 launchers apiece. This will bring the total number of strategic weapons down from the 22,000 maintained at the height of the Cold War. The treaty is to be fully implemented in seven years.[28] While this level of weaponry is still enough to threaten the very existence of civilization, the treaties prove that difficult negotiations can succeed. Other proposals have been put forward to further reduce the stockpiles. A world enjoying a peace system will have no nuclear weapons. The ultimate goal is abolition.

Further change may be on the horizon in the U.S. where some former government elites have now called for a nuclear-free world. In January of 2007, former secretaries of state Henry Kissinger and George P. Shultz, William J. Perry, former secretary of defense, and Sam Nunn, former head of the Senate Armed Services Committee — all hawks — reported that they have received positive responses from a host of other former secretaries of state, and defense, national security advisors and others from six past administrations. Among these men and women there was "general agreement about the importance of a vision of a nuclear free world."[29] Leaders of other nations have already signed on to the proposal. President Obama has indicated his preference for a nuclear-free world as well. They offer seven concrete steps toward a nuclear-free world, including bringing the Comprehensive Test Ban treaty into effect. Ten years ago this proposal by these particular men would have been unthinkable.

Other treaties have also been proposed, including the ban on weapons in outer space, verification of the existing ban on biological weapons, and a permanent halt on the production of fissile materials. Unfortunately, the United States has blocked progress on these treaties while at the same time unilaterally abrogating the Anti-Ballistic Missile Treaty. Also, the U.S. has refused to be party to the treaty establishing the International Criminal Court for the prosecution of genocide and other crimes against humanity. However, the future holds an opportunity to make genuine progress on these efforts. And regardless of U.S. inaction, the rest of the world is moving in the direction of serious arms control and war limitation and it is expected by many that in the near future progress will begin anew on these treaties. Many of these reforms are advocated by a civil society organization called Global Action to Prevent War, which proposes a four-stage implementation of the several reforms suggested here and an additional one — namely, a General Assembly resolution for required reporting of non-compliance with the 80 existing human rights conventions and immediate access for human rights observers.[30]

What I have suggested here by a few examples is the historic movement toward international peace through international law. We have been trending in this direction for over a century and, although the changes that still need to be enacted in terms of international institutions and laws seem far-reaching at the moment, we need to remember that we have almost a hundred years to implement them if our goal is the abolition of war by AD 2100. Remarkable progress has already been made at the international level and we see where we need to go next.

At the national level there are many obvious steps to reduce the likelihood of war. The first of these is to withdraw the military to a non-threatening posture called "non-provocative defense." This means both withdrawing from military bases and ports around the world and transforming the military into a defensive posture, that is, placing the emphasis on defensive weapons (i.e., no long-range missiles and bombers, no long-range naval deployments). At the same time, global talks on military reductions should be convened. Arms transfers would be cut drastically during this time. Also suggested is a ten-year freeze[31] and then a gradual, multilateral disarmament by treaty, getting rid of classes of weapons and numbers of weapons within classes in order to reduce the likely outcome of what Alexander Nikitin calls "Chekhov's Law," stated as "if in the first act of a play there is a rifle hooked on the wall, it will be fired in the last act."[32] Some progress has been made, as in the Treaty on Conventional Forces in Europe and the ban on anti-personnel land mines. Making this happen will require a massive initiative on the part of global civil society to prod governments into multilateral action since each would be reluctant to take the first steps or even to move at all.

Third, at the national level, is the emplacement of a universal service requirement that would provide training for all able adults in nonviolent civil-ian-based defense. Putting 10 percent of the current military budget of the world into this training would make a huge difference. The training would include not only strategies and tactics but also education about the theory and history of successful nonviolent defense. Fourth is the creation of a cab-inet-level Department of Peace to assist the president in focusing on alterna-tives to military violence in potential conflict situations. Among other strategies, this could involve greater interaction with InterPol[33] and treating terrorist attacks as crimes rather than as acts of war. Fifth would be a program

of trans-armament. Nations would reinvest in training for those working in
the arms industries, training geared to new industries in such businesses as
sustainable energy, and would invest start-up capital in those industries, gradually weaning the economy away from its dependence on military contracts.
Incremental reductions would make a large amount of funds available for the
support of peace-building, peacekeeping and peacemaking. For example, a 5
percent annual reduction in the U.S. military budget (app. $540 billion) over
five years would free up a total $135 billion and still leave the U.S. with by
far the largest military budget in the world. If that reduction is considered
too destabilizing, it could occur over ten years. The positive impacts would
be enormous if the rest of the world did the same, giving a total of nearly
$240 billion for the further development of a peace system. In other words,
there is plenty of money in the world for peace.[34] The Bonn International
Center for Conversion is just one of many organizations showing the way to
detaching ourselves from a war economy while stimulating positive investment
in goods that create value (e.g., electric cars) versus those that destroy value
such as nuclear weapons.[35]

Below the national level, state and local governments can declare free
zones such as the many existing nuclear-free zones, as well as armaments-
free zones and peace zones, and can establish departments of peace. This
would be exceedingly helpful in our larger cities, where conflict resolution
and nonviolence training are badly needed to deal with civil violence and
crime. States and cities can also further pursue the sister institution program.
Sister cities have been around for over half a century, bringing knowledge of
each other and direct contacts between peoples from far parts of the world.
States and cities can also put on conferences, bringing citizens and experts
together to understand violence and plan strategies for diminishing it in their
locales.

Peace education is also better fostered at the local level. There is already
a thriving peace education movement at the college and university level and
many public schools are providing conflict resolution and peer mediation
training for their students. This also needs to spread and will spread over the
next century. NGOs such as the Peace and Justice Studies Association, Edu-
cators for Social Responsibility, the Wisconsin Institute for Peace and Conflict
Studies, the Harvard Program on Nonviolent Sanctions, the Kroc Institute
for International Peace Studies at Notre Dame, and others are already providing venues for research and discussion and curricula for classrooms at all
grade levels. A movement to remove the ROTC programs from schools and
universities and to ban the military from basically buying poor young men
and women with college scholarships in exchange for a commitment to join
would also move the world further toward a peace system.

The Rise of International Civil Society

Perhaps the most important development in the already-existing progress toward a comprehensive peace system has been the astonishing growth of international non-government organizations (INGOs). While the International Postal Union and the International Red Cross have been around for a long time, the rise of thousands of INGOs, large and small, has brought into existence for the first time in history a global civil society. Just listing them all would fill a book on its own. The Internet has been immeasurably valuable for bringing these organizations into view and for providing them the means of interacting. Thousands of non-government organizations working for development, international aid, peace and justice can be found online at Paul Hawken's website, *www.wiserearth.org*[36] and elsewhere. Associations include the NGO Global Network and the International Organization Websites, the UN NGOs Network, the World Association of Non-governmental Organizations and others. All of these provide easy venues for the cooperation of citizens across the old and increasingly non-functional borders of nation states. A citizen-based world is rapidly coming into being.

Nonviolent, Trained, Citizen Peacemaking

At the international level, some of the most crucial NGOs for peacekeeping and the control of violence have been the accompaniment organizations including Peace Brigades International, Witness for Peace, the Nonviolent Peaceforce, Christian Peacemaker Teams and Muslim Peacemaker Teams.[37] Liam Mahony and Luis Eguren write in their book, *Unarmed Bodyguards*:

> The accompaniment volunteer is literally an embodiment of international human rights concern, a compelling and visible reminder to those using violence that it will not go unnoticed [acting] essentially as unarmed bodyguards.... The premise of accompaniment is that there will be an international response to whatever violence the volunteer witnesses. Behind such a response lies the implied threat of diplomatic and economic pressure.[38]

Peace Brigades International was established in 1981. According to their website, "From women's groups in Colombia to indigenous groups in Papua, we accompany a wide variety of threatened activists worldwide."[39] Witness for Peace[40] was established in 1983 and maintains a permanent presence in Mexico, Nicaragua and Colombia. Like its sister organizations, its model is to provide "on-the-ground documentation, assertive media strategies, a dynamic delegations program, and stateside grassroots mobilization."[41]

Christian Peacemaker Teams "is an international organization set up to support teams of peace workers in conflict areas around the world. These teams believe that they can lower the levels of violence through nonviolent direct action, human rights documentation, and nonviolence training." CPT sums their work up as "committed to reducing violence by *getting in the way.*" CPT has a full-time corps of over 30 activists who currently work in Colombia, Iraq, the West Bank, the United States–Mexico border, and Kenora, Ontario, Canada. These teams are supported by over 150 reservists who spend two weeks to two months a year on location.[42] These organizations give witness to the power of moral commitment to peace and to one's fellow humans who are living in dangerous situations. They have provided a great deal of on-the-ground experience in dealing nonviolently with very hostile forces.

The most ambitious of these is the Nonviolent Peaceforce. NP was born out of conversations at the Hague Appeal for Peace citizen conference held in the Netherlands in 1999. Gandhi's dream of a Shanti Sana, a peace army, lay behind the plans of Mel Duncan and David Hartsough. Ten years later they have made it a developing reality with over 200 internationals protecting thousands of civilians in Sri Lanka and the Philippines and, as of this writing, they plan to bring teams into the South Caucasus, the Sudan, Honduras, and Burma. They have worked previously in Latin America. They have been recognized as an official part of the government peace talks in the Philippines and will take responsibility for monitoring cease-fires and protecting the security of non-combatants. NP works closely with the United Nations.

> The mission of Nonviolent Peaceforce is to build a large-scale trained, international civilian nonviolent peaceforce. Nonviolent Peaceforce is sent to conflict areas to prevent death and destruction and protect human rights, thus creating the space for local groups to enter into dialogue and to seek peaceful resolution to local conflicts. We envision a world in which large-scale unarmed civilian peacekeeping using proven nonviolent strategies is recognized as a viable alternative in preventing, addressing, and mitigating violent conflicts worldwide. Our primary strategy for achieving this vision is the creation of space to foster dialogue.[43]

It is a truly global organization, governed by a board from the global north and south.

Perhaps no other INGOs are as well known as Amnesty International and Human Rights Watch.[44] They are a response to the human rights movement that began with the 1948 UN Declaration of Human Rights, whose preamble begins, "Whereas recognition of the inherent dignity and of the equal and inalienable rights of all members of the human family is the foundation of freedom, justice, and peace in the world...."[45] At the time, this was a call in the wilderness and human rights were violated without any public awareness or pressure on the violators. Today human rights are still violated, but doing so is a violation of the norm and Amnesty International and HRW have been successful in focusing a strong light on violators and bringing pressure to bear on them. Again, the Internet makes it impossible for dictators to work their evil behind closed doors, and there are networks of people watching out for the well-being of their fellow humans in a way never before possible.

Another component of the developing culture of peace are think tanks focusing on peace research and peace policy, including the Stockholm International Peace Research Institute, the Center for International Policy, the Carnegie Endowment for International Peace, Worldwatch Institute, the Center for Nonproliferation Studies at the Monterey Institute, the Clingendael Conflict Information Unit in the Netherlands, the Conflict Research Consortium at the University of Colorado, and many, many others easily found by googling "peace research." Never has so much intellectual power been directed toward understanding the causes and conditions of peace in all of its dimensions.

In addition to scholars, religious leaders will be important players in creating a culture of peace. For a truly peaceful world, the great religions are going to have to emphasize the peace teachings within their traditions and cease to hallow the old teachings about violence. This means that certain scriptures will have to be, at the very least, ignored, or, if possible, understood anew as belonging to a very different time and serving needs that are no longer functional. The Christian churches will have an especially great challenge here, but if their shift in attitude toward the environmental crisis, from suspicion to concern for many, is any indicator, they will be up to it. They will need to walk away from both holy-war and just-war doctrine. After all, the core teachings of their founder are all aimed at peaceful relationships within a just community where all are cared for. In so doing, they will put themselves at odds with the larger, secular, post–Christian culture of materialism and nationalistic patriotism. It will take vision, leadership and courage. Muslims will likewise have a major challenge in dealing with their doctrine of jihad, placing all the emphasis on the inner struggle for righteousness and giving up, in their turn, just-war doctrine. In addition, all religious leaders will need to encourage respect for each other. It is encouraging to remind ourselves that there are more and more voices in the world of religion who are advocating for peace and against violence, terrorism and dogmatism. Of course, this has already begun. Pope John Paul II led the way toward inter-religious respect when he held a peace prayer conference in Assisi in 1986. He invited 160 representatives from over a dozen faiths that included Protestants, Greek Orthodox, Hindus, Sikhs, Muslims, Jews, Buddhists, and others. "At his invitation, leaders from the religions of the earth gathered under glowering skies in the

INTERNATIONAL PANEL ON CLIMATE CHANGE ADDRESSES ECOSOC. A major player in global peace building, the Economic and Social Council of the UN has responsibility for monitoring and coordinating efforts of 14 UN agencies working to preserve human rights and freedoms and to improve global health, the standard of living, and the global economy, functions it inherited from the old League of Nations. Now, with almost 100 years of experience, ECOSOC is living proof of the revolutionary development of global peace system institutions in the last century. (UN Photo/Mark Garten [#182223])

tranquil medieval Italian town of Assisi and, with quiet dignity, uttered prayers for world peace. The throng included rabbis wearing yarmulkes and Sikhs in turbans, Muslims praying on thick carpets and a Zoroastrian kindling a fire."[46] He held two other summits, one in 1993 and one in 2006.

In the past 30 years there have been a number of seminal gatherings at the global level aimed at creating a peaceful and just world. The Earth Summit, held in Rio de Janeiro in 1992, laid the foundations for the modern global conference movement. It was convened by the United Nations, attended by 100 heads of state, 30,000 citizens from around the world, and 10,000 journalists who disseminated its message with unprecedented coverage.[47] Focused on environment and development, it produced a dramatic shift in direction toward the elimination of toxins in industrial production, the development of alternative energy and public transportation, deforestation, endangered species, and a new realization of the scarcity of water. Five separate agreements were achieved, including the Convention on Biological Diversity, the Frame-

work Convention on Climate Change, the Principles of Forest Management and Agenda 21, a blueprint for sustainable development. The UN has held subsequent global conferences on human rights, including the right to a healthy environment, population, women, human settlements, and more.

In 1999, approximately 9,000 concerned citizens from all over the world gathered in the Netherlands for the Hague Appeal for Peace conference and its follow-up activities, which were organized under four interrelated strands.[48] They are "Disarmament and Human Security"; "Prevention, Resolution and Transformation of Violent Conflict"; "International Humanitarian and Human Rights Law and Institutions"; and "Root Causes of War/Cultures of Peace." The conference was sponsored by 1000 organizations from around the world. Coming out of the Hague Appeal have been many initiatives bringing together Nobel laureates, intellectuals, cultural figures and NGO activists to promote disarmament, demilitarization and a culture of peace.[49] The goal was and is to create an international movement for realizing the Hague Appeal's call for every nation to adopt a resolution prohibiting their government from going to war, as is the case in Article 9 of the Japanese constitution.

In sum, the number of people and organizations working for the welfare of the world, for the well-being of future generations — in particular, an end to war as well as human rights and ecologically sustainable economic development based on a healthy global ecosystem — is mind-boggling. One can simply google these terms for exhaustive lists of international and national non-government organizations. Enormous progress is being made toward a culture of peace in spite of the wars that continue

At this point in history we are at an in-between stage but moving toward a fundamental phase change, toward a comprehensive peace system that will take as its goal human security rather than national security. Trying to achieve peace by means of the national security approach has failed miserably over the last 100 years. It has not protected people from war or from the poverty and ecological destruction that accompany even just the preparation for war. The twentieth century was the bloodiest century in all history. What we have been doing is not working. What we can do is erect a peace system with built-in redundancy, one whose institutions would be designed to provide positive feedback to the system and thereby strengthen our defenses, not against each

Opposite: CLEAN WATER IN TANZANIA. Water-borne diseases kill 3.5 million people each year; 84 percent of them are children. 884 million people lack access to safe water. Yet a tiny fraction of the money wasted on wars past, present and future, would alleviate the suffering of millions. This small water project in Tanzania, funded by the United Nations, represents only a pitiful fraction of what is needed and what the world could easily afford. (UN Photo/B. Wolff [#149506])

other, but against war and the economic and social causes of violence. And we are doing it. A new story is being written in on-the-ground, real-world actions all over the globe. A new history is being created alongside the old one.

But it is not enough to think only in terms of institutions. Values and beliefs are also changing. What are the wellsprings of peace from which individuals can draw for beliefs and values that lead to peace-building in the public and civil sectors? Out of what worldviews does the knowledge and desire to abolish war and establish global justice arise? We will look briefly at these in the final chapter, "The Wellsprings of Peace."

CHAPTER 10

The Wellsprings of Peace

"First we need to decide what needs to be done. Then we do it. Then we ask if it is possible."[1]
— Lester Brown, president of Worldwatch Institute

A social system that sustains peace will arise — indeed, is arising — out of beliefs and values. People understand all too well that the world is broken across the fault lines of nationalism, ethnicity, class, skin color, and religion. What is also true is that many people realize this brokenness is not what ought to be and it does not have to be. A tremendous motivation for peace exists in the world. The desire for peace and the strength to pursue it through many vicissitudes and over many years wells up continually in people's hearts. It comes up out of the wellsprings of their spiritual beliefs. These may be theistic or not. We find their sources in the great religions, in humanism, and in ecology and earth spirituality. While religions have sometimes stimulated wars, they are also powerful reservoirs of motivation and strength for stimulating peace. Christianity, Judaism, Islam, Buddhism, Jainism, Hinduism and other traditions are replete with exhortations to do peace.[2]

Christianity is filled with scriptural exhortations for peace, with long-standing pacifist and peace traditions, great exemplars of peace, and, contemporaneously, peace organizations. All of this would and has filled whole books. The teachings of Christ alone, a mere few of which are excerpted here, make one wonder how any Christian leader could ever have advocated war.

> Blessed are the peacemakers, for they shall be called the children of God. [Matt. 5: 5]
> Blessed are the merciful, for they shall obtain mercy. [Matt. 5: 7]
> You have heard it said, "An eye for an eye and a tooth for a tooth." But I say do not resist him who is evil, but whoever slaps you on the right cheek, turn to him the other also. [Matt. 5: 38–39]

You have heard it said, "You shall love your neighbor and hate your enemy," but I say to you, love your enemies and pray for them who persecute you. [Matt. 5: 43–44]

Do not judge that you be not judged. For in the way you judge you will be judged. [Matt. 7: 1–2]

Then Peter came to him and said, "Lord, how often shall my brother sin against me and I forgive him, up to seven times?" And Jesus said to him, "I do not say to you seven times but up to seventy times seven." [Matt. 18: 21–22]

Then Jesus said to Peter, "Put your sword back in its place for all those who take up the sword shall perish by the sword." [Matt. 26: 52]

Therefore all things whatsoever ye would that men should do to you, do ye even so to them. [Matt. 7: 12]

In the very early history of this religion Christians were persecuted because they would not take an oath to the Roman emperor or fight in his armies. The standard reply to the imperial summons — "I am a Christian. I cannot fight" — comes from that time. Most monastics withdrew from the world in order not to take part in its ways, including war. In the thirteenth century St. Francis preached peace and several versions of his peace prayer are current today:

O Lord, make me an instrument of your peace.
Where there is hatred, let me sow love.
Where there is injury, pardon,
Where there is doubt, faith,
Where there is darkness, light,
Where there is despair, hope,
Where there is sadness, joy.
O divine master,
It is not so much that I would seek to be consoled,
As to console,
To be understood as to understand,
To be loved as to give love,
For it is in giving that we receive,
It is in pardoning that we are pardoned,
And it is in dying to self
That we are born into eternal life.

In the aftermath of the Reformation several peace churches were founded: the Brethren, the Mennonites, and the Society of Friends, better known as

Opposite: THE UN SECURITY COUNCIL. Charged by the Charter with maintaining international peace and security, including peacekeeping operations, sanctions, and military actions. Five permanent members (U.S., Great Britain, France, Russia, China) and ten others elected for two-year terms meet in continuous session. Critics would eliminate the veto and permanent membership and point out that the five are all nuclear powers and major dealers in arms. (UN Photo/Mark Garten [#435638])

Quakers. Christian Peacemaker Teams is an arm of the Mennonite and the Brethren Churches. In the twentieth century there have been notable advocates of peace within Christianity, including Dorothy Day and Peter Maurin, Thomas Merton, Pope John Paul II, the Fathers Berrigan, the Rev. Martin Luther King, Jr., Mother Teresa, and countless others less well known.

One of the pathways to peace in Christianity is through the doctrine of the Incarnation, the belief that God became human in Jesus Christ and thus linked all human beings together in what Christians call the "Mystical Body of Christ." Dorothy Day, who along with Peter Maurin founded the Catholic Worker Movement in the twentieth century, believed that "...in the Incarnation we are not only brought into a new unity with God, we are brought into radically deeper and more significant relationships with each other ... [and] if any part of the Body suffers we all suffer."[3] Or as the famous twentieth-century Trappist monk, Thomas Merton, put it:

> Hate in any form is self–destructive, and even when it triumphs physically it triumphs in its own spiritual ruin. [And] Hell is where no one has anything in common with anybody else except the fact that they all hate one another and cannot get away from one another and from themselves.[4]

And further, Merton wrote:

> It is absolutely clear to me that we are faced with the obligation, both as human beings and as Christians, of striving in every way possible to abolish war. The magnitude of the task cannot be allowed to deter us. Even if it seems impossible, we must still attempt it.[5]

Like Day and Maurin, Merton believed that the authentic self is rooted in the doctrine of the Incarnation — which he understood as God being incarnated in all humans, not just in Christ, and this understanding not only lets us slip the mask of individuality, but also lets us see that we are linked in loving brother- and sisterhood with everyone else. If only we could each see who the other truly is, as Merton did in a mystic moment standing on a street corner in Louisville, Kentucky.

> Then it was as if I suddenly saw the secret beauty of their hearts, the depths where neither sin nor desire can reach, the person that each one is in God's eyes. If only they could see themselves as they really are. If only we could see each other that way there would be no reason for war, for hatred, for cruelty ... we would fall down and worship each other.[6]

Merton's was a powerful voice in opposition to the Vietnam War, just-war doctrine, nuclear weapons and the use of violence in general, writing, "The Christian who has recourse to force and hatred in order to protect himself is, in fact, by that very action, denying Christ and showing that he has no real understanding of the Gospel."[7] Hence the American Catholic Bishops' statement:

> Every child murdered, every woman raped, every town "cleansed," every hatred uttered in the name of religion is a crime against God and a scandal for religious believers. Religious violence and nationalism deny what we profess in faith: We are all created in the image of the same God and destined for the same eternal salvation. No Christian can knowingly foster or support structures and attitudes that unjustly divide individuals or groups.[8]

Today there are many, many Christian peace organizations, including the Episcopal Peace Fellowship, Christian International Peace Service, Churches for Middle East Peace, and Christian Peace Witness. One of the better known is Pax Christi International, whose philosophy was expressed by Father John Dear, SJ: "As a member of Pax Christi, I share with you a dream rooted in the promise of the Resurrection. Together we dare to dream of a world that embraces nonviolence over violence, peacemaking over war making, love and justice over fear and vengeance. We practice the disarming of our own hearts so that it may lead to the disarming of nations," and further, it is "time once and for all to reject the culture's path of war and violence and follow Him anew on the Gospel path of peace and nonviolence."[9] Pax Christi was started in 1945 as a modality of reconciliation at the end of World War II. They see the interrelatedness of all major peace and justice issues, and work on human rights, disarmament, economic justice, and ecology. Their mission statement reads:

> As a faith-based network, Pax Christi International seeks to transform a world shaken by violence, terrorism, deepening inequalities and global insecurity. Pax Christi International works to create a culture of peace and believes that religion should be an unequivocal force for peace and social justice. Pax Christi International is committed to non-violence and to demilitarisation and disarmament, human security, human rights and the rule of law as the basis of peaceful societies. As a movement and a global network, Pax Christi International brings together people from many different backgrounds and cultures as they shape and act upon their shared vision of peace, reconciliation and justice for all. In all its work, Pax Christi International explores innovative approaches to peace building, identifying beforehand the "signs of the times" through a process of collaborative learning with all those associated to its work.[10]

Many churches are joining the peace church movement, whose literature states, "Following Jesus in nonviolent struggle for justice and peace, we love our neighbors and enemies as God loves us all, becoming a peace church to share in God's work to save the world," [as well as] "We support alternatives to war and violence such as Christian Peacemaker Teams and conscientious objection, making peace through nonviolent action for justice."[11]

Christian opposition to the dominator system of ancient Rome has carried through to inspire the present. Walter Wink, a Christian author, describes the current dominator system, of which war is a crucial element, and "eloquently challenges us to interpret the gospel in the light of that domination system and the web of violence it constructs and supports in all areas of life and human relationships across the globe."[12] This influence crosses religious boundaries. Gandhi was influenced by it. The Mahatma Gandhi Album[13] reports:

> John Newman's "Lead Kindly Light" was Gandhi's favorite prayer. Millie Graham Polak has given affectionate and intimate recollections of the Gandhi household and her conversations with Gandhi. "Is Mr. Gandhi a Christian?" a visitor asked. Ms. Millie asked for further clarification whether she meant one converted to Christianity or one who believed in the teachings of Christ. The visitor emphatically told she meant the former. She was talking about him with some friends and they were wondering that Gandhi knew Christian scriptures so well, and was fond of quoting words of Christ frequently and hence her friends thought he must be a Christian. Ms. Millie brooded over this. What the visitor said was true. Mr. Gandhi frequently quoted the sayings and teachings of Jesus. The lesson of the "Sermon on the Mount" seemed to be constantly in his mind, and was a source of guidance and inspiration to him. There was beautiful picture of Jesus Christ that adorned the wall over his desk.

Older religions, such as Hinduism, Jainism and Buddhism, are also steeped in peace. Gandhi was a follower of the Bhagavad-Gita, an ancient text wherein the god, Krishna, speaks in the Bhagavad-Gita of a unity of all beings:

> With spirit following the Rule, with equal vision toward all things, he beholds the Greater Self in all beings and all beings in the Greater Self. When a man sees Me in all things and all things in Me, I am not lost to him nor is he lost to Me. The man of the Rule, who, setting himself to union with Me, worships Me as dwelling in all beings, abides in Me, wheresoever he may abide.[14]

One of the most famous passages in the Hindu Upanishads reads, "May He protect us both. May he take pleasure in us both. May we show courage together. May spiritual light shine before us. May we never hate one another. May peace and peace and peace be everywhere."[15] A contemporary Indian spiritual leader, Yogi Bhagan, a master of Kundalini Yoga, was a founder of International Peace Prayer Day, joining people of all faiths to pray for and celebrate peace.[16]

The nonviolence of the Jain tradition is legendary. A Jainist peace prayer reads:

> Peace and Universal Love is the essence of the Gospel preached by all Enlightened Ones. The Lord has preached that equanimity is the Dharma. Forgive do

I creatures all, and let all creatures forgive me. Unto all have I amity, and unto none enmity. Know that violence is the root cause of all miseries in the world. Violence, in fact, is the knot of bondage. "Do not injure any living being." This is the eternal, perennial, and unalterable way of spiritual life. A weapon, howsoever powerful it may be, can always be superseded by a superior one; but no weapon can, however, be superior to non–violence and love.[17]

Another prayer rising out of the Jain tradition has become an all-faiths prayer said around the world every day at noon.

> Lead me from death to life,
> from falsehood to truth;
> lead me from despair to hope,
> from fear to trust;
> lead me from hate to love,
> from war to peace.
> Let peace fill our heart,
> our world, our universe.

This prayer is a well known adaptation of the famous mantra from the Hindu Upanishads by Satish Kumar. Satish Kumar is a former Jain monk.... His adaptation was designed to be able to be used by all people of all languages and beliefs. The prayer was first publicly used in July 1981 by Mother Teresa in the Anglican Church, St. James,' Piccadilly in London.... There is a world peace prayer society encouraging its use."[18]

In the Buddhist tradition, nonviolence is one of the most fundamental teachings. It is based on the belief in "dependent co–arising," which posits that there is no such thing as an isolated, individual self. What and who we are is dependent on others, without whom we could not live. This is self-evident: without the farmer and the trucker we would not eat. Without our parents, teachers, and the media, we would not have the ideas we have about reality. We are all essentially one body. It's not that I am my brother's keeper, but that my brother and I are inescapably related parts of a single whole. The Dalai Lama writes that the word self "does not denote an independent object. Rather it is a label for a complex web of interrelated phenomena."[19] Then it becomes obvious that what we do to others, we do to ourselves. Here we are face to face with Indra's Net, an ancient concept found in the Mahayana Buddhist "Flower Garland" Sutra.

> The sutra describes a vast net that reaches infinitely in all directions, and in the net are an infinite number of jewels. Each individual jewel reflects all of the other jewels, and the reflected jewels also reflect all of the other jewels. The metaphor illustrates the interpenetration of all phenomena. Everything contains everything else. At the same time, each individual thing is not hindered by or confused with all the other individual things.[20]

Peace is in everyone's self–interest. Therefore, to injure another is to injure one's self. The health and well-being of the individual is directly dependent on the health and well-being of the community. The suffering in the world is suffering we cause to one another. The liberation from suffering can only come from a change of mind in which we recognize dependent arising and practice Metta, or universal compassion, not only for other humans, but for all sentient beings since, according to karma, in their next lives they could be reincarnated as humans, and it is only humans who can obtain liberation from suffering. Hence the Theravaden Buddhist prayer on universal love:

> May all beings be happy and at their ease. May they be joyous and live in safety. All beings, whether weak or strong — omitting none — in high, middle or low realms of existence, small or great, near or far away, born or to be born — may all beings be happy and at their ease! Let none deceive another, or despise any being in any state; let none by anger or ill-will wish harm to another! Even as a mother watches over and protects her child ... so with boundless mind should one cherish all living beings, radiating friendliness over the entire world, above, below, all around without limits; so let him cultivate a boundless good will towards the entire world, uncramped, free from ill-will or enmity.[21]

Spiritual practice in Buddhism requires clearing the mind of the delusion of separate identities and acting for the well-being of others. It requires a "radical turn toward the wider community of beings with whom we are connected."[22] Thus the supreme human faculty is empathy, the ability to feel the pain and joy of others, leading then to restraint of one's own selfishness, to compassion, to honesty. "Without inner peace," according to the Dalai Lama, "it is not possible to have world peace," and as a result, he writes, "My religion is kindness." It is only on this kind of spiritual foundation that the institutions of a peace system can be erected.

The Jewish peace tradition is also older than Christianity. Perhaps there is no scriptural passage on peace that is more potent and more widely known than that found in Isaiah 2: 4. "And they shall beat their swords into plowshares, and their spears into pruning hooks: nation shall not lift up sword against nation, neither shall they learn war anymore." While this was a prophecy for the future, one can easily recognize that, 2,500 years later, this is the future. Other verses tell a similar lesson: "I call heaven and earth to witness against you this day, that I have set before thee life and death, the blessing and the curse: therefore choose life, that thou mayest live, thou and thy seed" (Deut: 30: 19). The teachings of these ancient scriptures are borne out in contemporary Judaism, as an excerpt from Rabbi David Rosen's sermon, "Judaism and Peace," indicates:

> The Hebrew word for peace — shalom — comes from the root "shalem" meaning whole, complete, and well (cf. Gen.33 v.18). Thus the word "shalom" — peace —

as it is used in the Torah in relation to society, refers to its overall social and spiritual well-being for which Torah itself aspires.

In the Midrash on Deuteronomy 20 v.10, we find a whole excursion on the virtues of Peace. These quotations, comments and homilies, conclude with the statement of Rabbi Simon ben Halafta "See how beloved is Peace: when God sought to bless Israel, he found no other vessel which could contain all the blessings He would bless them with, except for Peace, as it is written (Psalm 29 v.11) "The Lord will give strength to His People: the Lord will bless His people with peace." Indeed the Talmud in tractate Gittin declares that "the whole Torah is for the sake of peace."

Accordingly, Judaism declares it to be both our personal religious duty as well as our societal religious obligation to be compassionate and caring towards all.... The pursuit of peace and good for all is thus a supreme obligation for the covenanted Jewish people — the goal of the Messianic ideal.

Indeed, Judaism teaches that God's very Name is Peace and thus the pursuit of Peace itself is the very sanctification of His Name which our tradition declares to be the very purpose of our existence.[23]

GREG MORTENSON AT ONE OF HIS SCHOOLS IN PAKISTAN. Mortenson, a private American citizen, is the author of *Three Cups of Tea,* describing his work in building hundreds of schools for boys and girls in Afghanistan and Pakistan. The book has sold 3.2 million copies in 39 countries. The title of his second book, *Stones into Schools: Promoting Peace with Books, Not Bombs,* in Afghanistan and Pakistan provides the contrast to the war system approach to peace. He has been twice nominated for the Nobel Peace Prize. (By permission, Central Asia Institute)

The Jewish Peace Fellowship is a contemporary organization that "unites those who believe that Jewish ideals and experience provide inspiration for a nonviolent commitment to life. Drawing upon the traditional roots of Judaism and upon its meaning in the world today, the JPF maintains an active program of draft and peace education, opposition to war and believes in the reconciliation of Israel, Jews and Palestinians." The following prayer is found on their website.

> We call to You now by Your name, Shalom. In this time of war we are often confused and afraid and we need to find peace within ourselves. It is sometimes hard to know what is right and what is wrong. In this time of war help us to remember how much Your world needs Peace. As we whisper Your name Shalom with our lips, help us to hear Your name of Peace in our hearts and to make it real in the world. Spread over our soldiers Your shelter of Peace. Bring them home quickly, our soldiers who are sons and daughters, husbands and fathers, brothers and sisters; our soldiers who are aunts and uncles, nieces and nephews, cousins and friends and neighbors. They are just like us and were children not so long ago.
>
> As we pray for them, help us to pray for the Iraqis too. They too are people like us, people who love and are loved, people who laugh and cry and sing and dance and hug their children. Yes, most of all protect the children who are surrounded by war and bring home the people whose hugs make them feel happy and safe.
>
> You have taught us that You do not delight in the destruction of the wicked. That is why we pour off a drop of wine for each of the ten plagues at the Pesach Seder, and that is why we read the names of Haman's sons in one breath when we read the Megillah on Purim. Therefore, help us to find ways other than war to stop those who hurt others in the world.
>
> Help us to remember that war is not a sporting event or a video game, even though it seems like it sometimes, the way people talk about it. Real people suffer and die in war, including children, and many things that people need to live are destroyed, including Your Creation, the earth itself.
>
> As Rabbi Yudan son of Rabbi Yossi taught of You so long ago, may we also teach, Great is Peace, for the name of the Holy One is called Shalom.
>
> Blessed are You, God, Whose name is Shalom. Spread Your shelter of Peace over us, and help us to make peace in Your world. And let us say, Amen.[24]

Jewish teachings on peace abound. "Execute truth, judgment and peace within your gates" (Tractate Avot 1: 18). And the Jerusalem Talmud reads, "Rabbi Shimon ben Gamliel said: By three things is the world preserved: on judgment, truth and peace. And all three are (in effect) one. If judgment is executed and truth is vindicated, peace prevails. Rabbi Mana said: All three (are found) in one verse (Zech. 8: 16): 'Execute truth, judgment and peace within your gates'" (Jerusalem Talmud 4: 2 [68a]).

It is perhaps ironic but Shalom (Hebrew) and Salaam (Arabic) have the same Semitic roots and refer to a vision of wholeness that comes from a right relationship with God. As greetings they mean we wish to live together in harmony in peacefulness.[25] Some Muslims and Jews are living out this mutuality, having initiated the Muslim-Jewish Peace Walk:

> The Muslim-Jewish Peace Walk for Interfaith Solidarity is a religious response to the devastating impact of various forms of communal and state violence and militarism are having upon our communities and upon the memory and accomplishments of the historically positive relationship between Muslims and Jews.
>
> As an alternative to prejudice, militarism and violence, we promote the restoration of an interfaith culture of convivencia that strives to achieve Jewish, Christian and Muslim reconciliation, economic justice for women and the poor, love and concern for the well-being of one's neighbors, an embrace of non–violence and peace for all the world's children. We also believe that security for Israel is inextricably linked to a secure and viable Palestine that can realize its dream of freedom. We devote ourselves to illuminating the heart of the message revealed to the Children of Abraham to serve the One whose name is Peace by working for peace together.[26]

Current prejudices in the West, stemming from the statements and actions of Islamic extremists, have blinded us to the powerful peace tradition in Islam. Abdul Ghaffar Khan (1890–1988), the Muslim Gandhi, said, "The Holy Prophet Mohammed came into this world and taught us: 'That man is a Muslim who never hurts anyone by word or deed, but who works for the benefit and happiness of God's creatures.' Belief in God is to love one's fellow men."[27] A contemporary Islamic scholar, Imam Abdullah Khouj, who is head of the Islamic Center in Washington, D.C., sums it up this way: "You do not kill innocent people, you do not cheat, you do not lie, you do not destroy any property of other human beings," and "Human life in Islam is extremely sacred."[28] According to Muslim scholar Imam Sulayman S. Nyang of Howard University in Washington, D.C.: "The Koran is saying to humans, this is the final guidance from your Creator, for the specific purpose of worshipping him and creating a civil society where you can live in peace with one another."[29] And this does not necessarily mean an all-Muslim society. Islamic scholar Dr. Mohamed Fathi Osman writes:

> Human diversity, which can never be ignored or stopped, should not provoke hostility, nor obstruct reasonable communication among human beings; on the contrary it enriches human experience and allows a complementation of different human views and efforts. Human diversity is one of God's wonders in His creation.[30]

But for an indisputably authentic voice, we must go to the Koran itself.

> You do not believe until you want for others what you want for yourselves.[31]
> If they seek peace, then seek you peace. And trust in God for He is the One that heareth and knoweth all things [*Quran*, 8.61].

NONVIOLENT PEACEFORCE: MEL DUNCAN AND DAVID HARTSOUGH. A milestone in the historical development of nonviolence was the institutionalization of trained, civilian peacekeepers by Peace Brigades International and Christian Peacemaker Teams in the 1980s. The institution was dramatically expanded from fielding a handful of peacekeepers to fielding several hundred when Duncan (right) and Hartsough (left) founded the Nonviolent Peaceforce after meeting at the Hague Appeal for Peace conference in 1999, making Gandhi's dream of a nonviolent army a reality. NP expects eventually to field a force of 1000. (Photo supplied by the Nonviolent Peaceforce.)

> And the servants of Allah ... are those who walked on the earth in humility, and when the ignorant address them, they say "Peace" [*Quran*, 25.63].
> Allah is with those who restrain themselves [*Quran*, 16.128].
> The taking of one innocent life is like taking all of Mankind ... and the saving of one life is like saving all Mankind [*Quran*, 5:3].

Islam, like the other great religions of the world, has a strong peace tradition, nowhere more succinctly stated than by the thirteenth century Sufi mystic, Arabi:

> O marvel! a garden among the flames.... My heart has become capable of all forms. It is a meadow for gazelles and a monastery for Christian monks, A temple for idols and the pilgrim's Ka'aba, The Tables of the Law and the book of the Koran. I profess the religion of Love, and whatever direction Its steed may take, Love is my religion and my faith.[32]

Indigenous peoples may not have ancient texts but they also find sources of peace in their spiritual traditions. Chief Tecumseh of the Six Tribe Confederation, who lived from 1768 to 1813, said, "Trouble no one about their religion, respect all in their views, and demand that they respect yours."[33] A contemporary native spiritual leader and peace advocate is Arvol Looking Horse, spiritual leader of the Sioux Nation. He has made trips to Iraq and other nations to pray for peace and, with his wife, is the founder of World Peace and Prayer Day, celebrated every June 21.[34] He is the author of *White Buffalo Teaching,* wherein he offers this prayer.

> We need a great healing,
> and we need a Great Forgiving.
> But healing cannot begin without forgiveness.
> We must forgive each other,
> Forgive our loved ones,
> Forgive our friends,
> Forgive our enemies,
> Forgive ourselves.
>
> We need to pray even for a person who has done wrong!
> In our Tiyospaye — our family, when two people fight they are made brothers
>   or sisters.
> Forgiveness itself is a powerful medicine.
> We need forgiveness to create PEACE!
> Mitakuye Oyasin! (all our relations) in the Great Circle of Life,
> where there is no beginning and no end.[35]

A statement of the traditional Hopi Elders as told to Cho Qosh Auh Ho Oh, a Chumash/Yaqui/Maya Indian, reads, "These are the End times and the people must know the truth, share what we have taught you. There can be no more secrets now if we are to survive as a thinking species through these times. 'This,' they say, 'must be done because the dream of humanity can only be preserved through the combined efforts of all peoples, and the joining and merging of all cultures into a oneness.'"[36] And this, according to the famous Native American prophet, Black Elk, requires a prior transformation of the soul.

> The first peace, which is the most important, is that which comes within the souls of people when they realize their relationship, their oneness with the universe and all its powers, and when they realize that at the centre of the universe dwells the Great Spirit, and that this centre is really everywhere, it is within each of us. This is the real peace, and the others are but reflections of this. The second peace is that which is made between two individuals, and the third is that which is made between two nations. But above all you should understand that there can never be peace between nations until there is known that true peace, which, as I have often said, is within the souls of men.[37]

"Welcome to Native American Spirituality" is a website that speaks of a vision of peace, noting the well-known Native American belief that all beings are intimately related.

> This vision starts with our selves, biases must be removed for all of life is connected. A weak thread weakens the whole net. The native teachings can strengthen us in many ways. When we work together the Sacred Hoop will be strong. Such teachings, when shared with good intent and with a good heart and are dedicated to manifesting peace, will help nourish the Sacred Tree of Life.... May you transform any fear, anger, shame and hate into peace and harmony for the sake all of our relations, those above and those below.[38]

On March 12, 2003, many of the indigenous peoples of the world held a great gathering in Phoenix, Arizona, called the Indigenous Peoples Peace Initiative. Among the many calls for peace was the following by Tupac Enrique Acosta, member of the Xicano Nahuatl Nation.

> We must disarm the global regime of nationalism of the state. The psychologies of hatred and competition under which the government states of the world would have us sacrifice our humanity and our children to senseless wars will no longer be tolerated. As Indigenous Peoples of the world, we further challenge the government states of the United Nations system to criminalize the destructive impact of warfare upon the ecosystems of the Earth itself, by defining appropriate international legal protocols regarding the conduct of warfare such as the Geneva Convention.[39]

The link between indigenous spirituality and the ecology of peace is more than obvious, and even Christians are beginning to see the links between religion and care for the environment, justice, war and peace. Wendell Berry's is just one voice among a growing multitude to make these connections. In *God and Country* he has written, "The ecological teaching of the Bible is simply inescapable: God made the world because He wanted it made. He thinks the world is good, and He loves it. It is His world; He has never relinquished title to it. And He has never revoked the conditions, bearing on His gift to us of the use of it that oblige us to take excellent care of it."[40] And at a commencement address at Lindsey Wilson College in 2005 he explained, "The line that connects the bombing of civilian populations to the mountain removed by strip mining ... to the tortured prisoner seems to run pretty straight. We're living, it seems, in the culmination of a long warfare — warfare against human beings, other creatures and the Earth itself."[41]

It is well known that toxic waste dumps tend to located on or near the lands of indigenous peoples or in the neighborhoods inhabited by the poor and people of color. The ecological justice movement has grown up, often in the churches in the U.S., to publicize and combat this trend. A list of principles was drawn up in 1991 at the People of Color Environmental Leadership

Summit in Washington, D.C. and can be found online.[42] Peace without justice is no true peace, just as justice without peace is not true justice.

The central concept of ecology is the interdependence of all beings who together make up a web of life, the biosphere, where, as Barry Commoner so famously said, you "can't do just one thing."[43] When we let the grocery clerk load our purchases into a plastic bag, it very likely ends up in the enormous North Pacific Gyre, with millions of others. The Gyre, "a vast swath of the Pacific, twice the size of Texas, is full of a plastic stew that is entering the food chain. Scientists say these toxins are causing obesity, infertility ... and worse."[44] In the global ecosphere there is no "away" and everything we have and use comes from somewhere, where its creation and transport had an impact on the biosphere on which all economic activity and well-being depend. We are a single species dependent on countless other species and each other. We live by the work of others, as they do by ours, and we live at the sufferance of others, as they do of us. Living in the U.S., the tomatoes on my plate came from Mexico, the plate itself from England, the flowers on the table in the winter came from Ecuador, my shirt from Thailand, my shoes from China, and so on. And when I vote for a senator who brings military contracts to my town, the cluster bomb we make here that blows the legs off a child in Iraq is partly my doing. When I go online and send a check to Oxfam or the Heifer Project, someone in Africa or India eats; a check to the Blue Mountain Project brings health care to rural Jamaica where it had not existed before. Sitting in Chicago, I have the opportunity to cure someone's blindness in rural India. The oxygen I breathe was made by plants thousands of miles away and these plants take the carbon dioxide I breathe and process it. The truth we learn from molecular biology is that we are all made of the same basic components: adenine, thymine, guanine, cytosine — the components of DNA are the foundation of all life. The evolutionary process has worked in such a way that humans, trees, whales, every living thing is made up of the same stuff. We are all related, a single family making up the web of life.

Will we achieve a tipping point when peace overtakes and replaces the old war system? That will depend on us, individually and collectively, on the degree to which we can internalize this new philosophy that has been growing in strength over the last two centuries, this sense that we are a common humanity on a single unitary planet. It is springing up in all the spiritual traditions, as I have tried to indicate with these few sample excerpts. It is the most powerful argument for peace and was dramatically captured by astronaut Russell Schweickart as he circled the Earth repeatedly in 1969. His concept, "No Frames, No Boundaries," is worth quoting excerpts from at length as a way of ending this book.

> But up there you go around every hour and a half, time after time after time. You wake up usually in the mornings, over the Middle East and over North

Africa. As you eat breakfast you look out the window and there's the Mediterranean area, Greece and Rome and North Africa and the Sinai, that whole area. And you realize that in one glance what you're seeing is what was the whole history of humankind for years — the cradle of civilization. And you go down across North Africa and out over the Indian Ocean and you look up at that great subcontinent of India pointed down toward you as you go past it, Ceylon off to the side, then Burma, Southeast Asia, out over the Philippines and up across that monstrous Pacific Ocean, that vast body of water — you've never realized how big that is before. And you finally come up across the coast of California, and you look for those friendly things, Los Angeles and Phoenix, and on across to El Paso. And there's Houston, there's home, you know, and you look out, and you identify with it.... And you go out across the Atlantic Ocean and back across Africa, and you do it again and again and again.... And it all becomes friendly to you.

When you go around the Earth in an hour and half, you begin to recognize that your identity is with the whole thing. And that makes a change.

You look down there and you can't imagine how many borders and boundaries you cross, again and again and again, and you don't even see them. There you are — hundreds of people in the Middle East killing each other over some imaginary line that you're not even aware of, that you can't see. And from where you see it, the thing is a whole, the earth is a whole, and it's so beautiful. You wish you could take a person in each hand, one from each side in the various conflicts, and say, "Look. Look at it from this perspective. Look at that. What's important?"

And a little later on, your friend goes out to the moon. And now he looks back and he sees the Earth not as something big, where he can see the beautiful details, but now he sees the Earth as a small thing out there. And the contrast between that bright blue and white Christmas tree ornament and the black sky, that infinite universe, really comes through, and the size of it, the significance of it. It is so small and so fragile and such a precious little spot in the universe that you can block it out with your thumb. And you realize that on that small spot, that little blue and white thing, is everything that means anything to you — all love, tears, joy, games, all of it on that little spot out there that you can cover with your thumb. And you realize from that perspective that you've changed, that there's something new there, that the relationship is no longer what it was.

And toward the end he quotes essayist Archibald MacLeish.

Archibald Macleish somehow knew about this step that humanity has now taken. He writes that somehow things rather suddenly have changed, and we no longer see ourselves in the same way that we saw ourselves before. We see "the Earth now as it truly is, bright and blue and beautiful in that eternal silence where it floats," and "men and women as riders on the Earth together, on that bright loveliness in the eternal cold, brothers and sisters who know now that they are truly brothers and sisters."[45]

And so we are, "riders on the earth together," spinning toward something new, a new stage in our long cultural evolution, a new and lasting era. One people. One planet. One peace.

Appendix 1:
Twenty-Three Trends of the Last 100 Years Leading to the Evolution of a Peace System

(1) The progressive development of international institutions for adjudicating international conflict, including the International Court of Justice (World Court), the International Criminal Court, and regional courts in Europe, and Latin America.

(2) Supra-national parliamentary institutions, first the League of Nations, then the United Nations; and regional bodies such as the Parliament of the European Union, the African Union, the Organization of American States, and others.

(3) The rise of international peacekeeping: neutral forces composed of several nations, popularly known as the Blue Helmets, intervening to quell a conflict or keep it from re-igniting — even though there is no provision in the UN Charter for it — now having been deployed in dozens of conflicts around the world.

(4) The development of nonviolent struggle as a substitute for war, beginning with Gandhi, carried on by King, and perfected in the successful struggles to overthrow the dictatorial regimes of Ferdinand Marcos in the Philippines, the Soviet Empire in Eastern Europe and the Communist coup in Russia. We no longer need to resort to arms to defend ourselves.

(5) The development and spread of sophisticated new techniques of conflict resolution known as win-win negotiation or mutual gains bargaining,

(6) The rise and rapid spread of peace research institutions, and programs in peace education in the colleges, universities and schools.

(7) The rapid spread of democratic regimes in the second half of the twentieth century. Since it is historically demonstrable that democracies do not attack one another, this is cause for optimism.

(8) The emergence of regions of long-term peace: Western Europe for almost 60 years, North America for nearly 200 years, Scandinavia for over 300 years.

(9) The decline of institutionalized racism: e.g., Jim Crow in the U.S., and apartheid in South Africa.

(10) The end of political colonialism. Empire is becoming impossible due to cost and the rise of asymmetric warfare, which increases the cost.

(11) The erosion of effective national sovereignty — a nation state can't keep out missiles, immigrants, ideas, economic trends, disease organisms, and so on.

(12) The rise of women's rights and the emergence of women in positions of leadership and authority and the consequent diminishment of patriarchy in large areas of the world.

(13) The rise of the environmental sustainability movement aimed at slowing or ending the consumptive excesses that create shortages, poverty, pollution and environmental injustice in the developing world.

(14) The democratization of the arts, a further erosion of hierarchy.

(15) The spread of peace-oriented forms of religion: e.g., the Christianity of Thomas Merton, of Jim Wallace of Sojourners, and of Pax Christi; the Buddhism of the Dalai Lama; and similar movements in Judaism (the Jewish Peace Fellowship, Jewish Voice for Peace) and Islam (Muslim Peace Fellowship, Muslim Peacemaker Teams). In October 2007 138 Muslim clerics and scholars sent a letter to major Christian leaders seeking a dialogue and affirming that both religions seek peace and abhor violent extremists and that "if Muslims and Christians are not at peace then the world cannot be at peace."

(16) The successful development of a regime of international law and especially war-limiting treaties such as the ban on atmospheric testing of nuclear weapons, the ban on child soldiers, the ban on anti-personnel land mines and many others.

(17) Since 1948, the rise of the human rights movement, Human Rights Watch and Amnesty International. Human rights are now an international norm and when they are not respected it is considered an outrage in most countries.

(18) The evolution of the global conference movement. In the past 20 years there have been several seminal gatherings at the global level aimed at creating a peaceful and just world. The Earth Summit, held in Rio de Janeiro in 1992, laid the foundations for the modern global conference movement. It was convened by the United Nations, attended by 100 heads of state, 30,000 citizens from around the world and 10,000 journalists who disseminated its message with unprecedented coverage. Focused on the environment and development, it produced a dramatic shift in direction toward the elimination of toxins in production, the development of alternative energy and public transportation, deforestation, and a new realization of the scarcity of water. Five separate agreements were achieved. Major conferences have since been held on a variety of issues.

(19) The gradual evolution over several centuries of a well-established system of diplomatic relationships and norms, including diplomatic immunity.

(20) The emergence of an international development regime including large-scale international development banks (IMF, World Bank), micro-financing, and thousands of smaller, international development NGOs.

(21) The creation of the Internet, which has dramatically increased transparency of government actions (no atrocity escapes notice) and the ability of citizen peace organizations to coordinate with each other and to respond to crises, as well as making easily available crucial information about war, peace, human rights, and so on. It is a force multiplier for the peace movement.

(22) The sharp decline in old-fashioned attitudes that war is a glorious and noble enterprise. No troops now march off to war singing as they did in 1914.

(23) The gradual acceptance over the last 100 years of conscientious objection to war as a legal right.

Appendix 2: Some Common Terms to Research for Further Information and Websites

Abolish war

Accompaniment

Arms control

Civilian-based defense

Conflict resolution

Culture of peace

Disarmament

Global environmental movement

Human rights

International aid organizations

International Court of Justice

International Criminal Court

International environmental organizations

International law

International non-government
organizations

Mediation

Non-provocative defense

Nonviolence

Nonviolent communication

Nonviolent peacekeeping

Peace

Peace-building

Peace economy

Peace education

Peace history

Peacekeeping

Peacemaking

Peace organizations

Peace research

Peace studies

Peace systems

Peer mediation

Reconciliation

Religion and peace

Sustainability

Trans-armament

Treaties

United Nations

UN reform

World citizenship

World Court

World government, or governance

World Parliament

Appendix 3: A Sampling of Peace Organizations on the World Wide Web

Carnegie Endowment for International Peace, www.carnegieendowment.org
Carter Center, www.cartercenter.org/peace/index.html
Christian Peacemaker Teams, www.cpt.org/
Citizens for Global Solutions, www.globalsolutions.org
Conflict Resolution Center International, www.conflictres.org
Fellowship of Reconciliation, www.forusa.org
Greenpeace, www.greenpeace.org/
Hague Appeal For Peace, www.haguepeace.org/
Human Rights Watch, www.hrw.org/
International Peace Bureau, www.ipb.org
International Peace Research Association, http://soc.kuleuven.be/iieb/ipraweb/index.php?action=home&cat=home
Jewish Peace Fellowship, www.jewishpeacefellowship.org/index.php?p=about.prayer
Journal of Peace Education, http://www.tandf.co.uk/journals/titles/17400201.asp
Muslim Peacemaker Teams Iraq, www.mpt-iraq.org/
National Peace Foundation, www.nationalpeace.org/
Nonviolent Peaceforce, www.nonviolentpeaceforce.org
Nukewatch, www.nukewatch.com/
Oxfam International, www.oxfam.org/
Pace e Bene, www.paceebene.org.
Pax Christi, www.paxchristiusa.org
Peace Action, www.peace-action.org/
Peace Brigades International, www.peacebrigades.org
Peace and Justice Studies Association, www.peacejusticestudies.org
Ploughshares Fund, www.ploughshares.org

United For Peace and Justice, http://www.unitedforpeace.org/article.php?list=type&type=27

United Nations Association of the United States (UNA/-USA), www.unausa.org/

Veterans for Peace, www.veteransforpeace.org/

Waging Nonviolence, www.wagingnonviolence.org

WAND (Women's Action for New Directions), www.wand.org/

WILPF (Women's International League for Peace and freedom), www.wilpfinternational.org

World Federalist Movement, www.wfm-igp.org

Other lists are at http://www.webster.edu/~woolflm/peacelinks.html, http://www.arkadybooks.com/peace-organizations.php, http://www.knowledgerush.com/kr/encyclopedia/List_of_humanitarian_and_peace_organizations/, and http://www.mideastweb.org/peacelinks.htm.

Chapter Notes

Introduction

1. Kenneth Allot, ed., *The Poems of Matthew Arnold*, 2d ed. (London: Logan, 1979).

2. Paul R. Ehrlich, Carl Sagan, et al., *The Cold and the Dark: The World After a Nuclear War* (New York: Norton, 1984).

3. Paul Hawken, *Blessed Unrest: How the Largest Movement in the World Came into Being and Why No One Saw It Coming* (New York: Viking, 2007), p. 18.

4. Zbigniew Brzezinski, *Out of Control: Turmoil on the Eve of the Twenty-first Century* (New York: Scribner, 1993).

5. Experts estimate that no more than 2 percent of soldiers are aggressive psychopaths who kill without remorse. Lt. Col. Dave Grossman, *On Killing: The Psychological Cost of Learning to Kill in War and Society* (Boston: Little, Brown, 1996), p. 50.

6. Paul Hawken, *Blessed Unrest*, p. 18.

7. Quoted in Lewis Lapham, "Flies in Amber," *Harper's Magazine*, September 2007, pp. 8–13.

8. *Ibid.*, pp. 8, 10.

9. *Ibid.*, p. 11.

10. *Ibid.*

11. Kenneth Boulding, *Stable Peace* (Austin: University of Texas Press, 1978).

Chapter 1

1. The current conflicts in the Middle East go back to the English and French betrayal of the Arabs at the end of World War I and their takeover of the collapsed Ottoman Empire, inventing nations and drawing artificial boundaries, as well as encouraging European Jews to migrate in large numbers to Palestine. These were all conscious decisions taken with self-seeking advantage in mind.

2. Loretta Napoleoni, *Terrorism and the Economy: How the War on Terror Is Bankrupting the World* (New York: Seven Stories Press, 2010), p. xiv.

3. General Iberico-Saint'Jean, governor of Buenos Aires during the first junta regime, put it clearly: "First we will kill all the subversives, then we will kill their collaborators, then ... their sympathizers, then, those who remain indifferent; and finally we will kill the timid." Liam Mahony and Luis Enrique Eguren, *Unarmed Bodyguards: International Accompaniment for the Protection of Human Rights* (West Hartford, CT: Kumarian Press, 1997), p. 88.

4. *Ibid.*, p. 89.

5. Napoleoni, *Terrorism and the Economy*, pp. xiv–xv.

6. Mary Kaldor, *Global Civil Society: An Answer to War* (Cambridge, UK: Polity Press, 2003), p. 154.

7. This story is taken up in Section II, Chapter 6, "A History of Peace in Ancient and Medieval Times."

8. Percy Bysshe Shelley, in Rewey Inglois and Josephine Spear, eds., *Adventures in English Literature* (New York: Harcourt, Brace, 1958), p. 423.

9. Schmookler quoted in Lester Milbrath, *Envisioning a Sustainable Society* (Albany: State University of New York Press, 1989), p. 43.

10. Milbrath, *Envisioning a Sustainable Society*, p. 43.

11. *Ibid.*, p. 44.

12. Andrew Bard Schmookler, *The Parable of the Tribes: The Problem of Power in Social Evolution* (Albany: State University of New York Press, 1994), quoted in *In Context: A Quarterly of Humane, Sustainable Culture*, online at http://www.context.org/ICLIB/IC07/Schmookler.htm.

13. Quoted by Richard Holmes, "TV Series War Walks," and online at http://homepage.eir com.net/%257Eodyssey/Quotes/History/War_Walks.html.

14. Stephen Weir, "Trench Warfare: General

Haig and the Battle of the Somme," *Encyclopedia Idiotica: History's Worst Decisions and the People Who Made Them* (Hauppauge, NY: Baron's, 2005), p. 121.

15. *Ibid.*, p. 122.

16. Adam Gopnik, "Slaughterhouse," *New Yorker*, Feb. 12, 2007, p. 82. This is a review of David Bell's *The First Total War: Napoleon's Europe and the Birth of Warfare As We Know It* (New York: Houghton Mifflin, 2007).

17. Widely quoted, never cited. Perhaps it is apocryphal but it is certainly true.

18. http://en.wikipedia.org/wiki/Trinity_(nuclear_test).

19. Harry Truman quoted in Jonathan Schell, *The Fate of the Earth* (New York: Avon, 1982), p. 11.

20. Schell, *The Fate of the Earth*, p. 11.

21. *Ibid.*, p. 67.

22. *Ibid.*, p. 18.

23. *Ibid.*, p. 48.

24. *Ibid.*, p. 50.

25. Erhlich, Sagan, et al., *The Cold and the Dark*.

26. John LaForge, "Missile Fields Still Armed and Dangerous," *Nukewatch Quarterly* (Winter 2006-2007), p. 1.

27. Simone Weil, "The *Iliad*, the Poem of Force," in Dick Ringler, ed., *Dilemmas of War and Peace: A Sourcebook* (Madison: Board of Regents of the University of Wisconsin and the Corporation for Public Broadcasting, 1993), p. 104.

28. *Ibid.*, p. 105.

29. *Ibid.*

30. *Ibid.*, p.109.

31. http://en.wikipedia.org/wiki/Maxim_gun.

32. Winston Churchill, *The Voice of Winston Churchill*, London Records, RB100, n.d.

33. Grossman, *On Killing*, p. 100.

34. Gwynne Dyer, *War: The Lethal Custom* (New York: Carroll and Graf, 2004), p. 4.

35. Grossman, *On Killing*, p. 65.

36. Gwynne Dyer suggests of the World War I commanders that "not all of them were stupid." (The quote is from a photo caption in the book, *War* [note 34] that accompanied Dyer's PBS series of the same title.)

37. In the asymmetric warfare in Iraq and Afghanistan a variant on type two — the I.E.D., or "Improvised Explosive Devise" (in militareze) — is causing most of the U.S. casualties. They can be pressure tripped or detonated by a cell phone signal.

38. Dean Peerman, "Landmine Legacy," *Christian Century* (May 15, 2007), p. 8.

39. http://www.science.howstuffworks.com/landmine.

40. http://www.unicef.org/graca/mines.htm.

41. http://www.who.int/ionizing_radiation/env/du/en/.

42. Dan Fahey, "The Emergence of the Debate over Depleted Uranium Munitions 1991-2004," http://www.wise-uranium.org/pdf/duemdec.pdf.

43. Homer, *Iliad*, Book 4, trans. Samuel Butler, available online at http://darkwing.uoregon.edu/~joelja/iliad.html#b5.

44. *Ibid.*

45. Graphic photos of war dead can be found online by searching through Google Images.

46. Owen was killed in the last weeks of war.

47. Here Owen mocks "*Dulce et decorum est, pro patria mori*," a Roman epigram, translated as "Sweet and beautiful it is to die for one's country." Dick Ringler, ed., *Dilemmas of War and Peace*, p. 153.

48. Paul Fussell, "The Real War Will Never Get in the Books," from *Wartime: Understanding Behavior in the Second World War* (New York: Oxford University Press, 1989) and reprinted in Ringler, ed., *Dilemmas of War and Peace*, p. 168.

49. *Ibid.*, p. 169.

50. *Ibid.*

51. "Remorse," by Siegfried Sassoon, 1886–1967, http://www.poemhunter.com/poem/remorse-2/.

Chapter 2

1. Grossman, *On Killing*, p. 39.

2. The Seville Statement can be found at http://www.currentconcerns.ch/archive/2004/01/20040105.php.

3. Dick Ringler, "The Bombing of Dresden," in Ringler, ed., *Dilemmas of War and Peace*.

4. The place of religion in war and peace will be examined in a later chapter.

5. Grossman, *On Killing*, p. 118.

6. *Ibid.*, p. 3, and elsewhere.

7. *Ibid.*, p. 4.

8. *Ibid.*, p. 169.

9. Quoted in Grossman, *On Killing*, p. 170.

10. *Ibid.*, p. 149.

11. *Ibid.*, p. 35.

12. *Ibid.*, p. 250.

13. http://www.deathreference.com/Me-Nu/Metaphors-and-Euphemisms.html.

14. Grossman, *On Killing*, p. 92.

15. Most of these euphemisms come from Tom Hastings, "Doublespeak," an unpublished paper in the author's possession.

16. Richard Holmes, *Acts of War*, quoted in Grossman, *On Killing*, p. 186.

17. Grossman, *On Killing*, p. 190.

18. *Ibid.*, p. 190.

19. *Ibid.*

20. *Ibid.*, p. 251.

21. *Ibid.*, p. 252.

22. *Ibid.*, p. 253.

23. *Ibid.*, p. 254.

24. Dyer, *War*, quoted in Grossman, *On Killing*, p. 265.

25. Grossman, *On Killing*, pp. 43–44.

26. *Ibid.*, p. 71.

27. *Ibid.*, pp. 45–47.

28. *Ibid.*, pp. 270–271. This practice of drugging the soldiers is simply another illustration of the fact that they are seen merely as means to an end and not as ends in themselves. Even the language commonly used by the military reveals this — a combat unit is often referred to as a "well-trained fighting machine."

29. *Ibid.*, p. 116.

30. From the American Psychological Association, *Diagnostic and Statistical Manual of Mental Disorders*, and quoted in Grossman, *On Killing*, p. 283.

31. Shannon P. Meehan, "Distant Wars, Constant Ghosts," *Opinionator* blog, *New York Times*, Feb. 22, 2010.

32. *Ibid.*

33. *Ibid.*

34. Two articles by Richard Koenigsberg available online are "As the Soldier Dies, So Does the Nation Come Alive," http://home.earthlink.net/~libraryofsocialscience/as_the_soldier.htm, and "The Soldier as Sacrificial Victim: The Sacrificial Meaning of Warfare, Awakening from the Nightmare of History," http://www.wagingpeace.org/articles/0000/0000_koenigsberg_soldier-as-sacrificial-victim.htm.

35. Richard Koenigsberg, "As the Soldier Dies, So Does the Nation Come Alive."

36. *Ibid.*

37. Quoted in Koenigsberg, "As the Soldier Dies, So Does the Nation Come Alive."

38. *Ibid.*

39. http://en.wikipedia.org/wiki/Civil_religion.

Chapter 3

1. Robert Holmes, "The Sleep of Reason Brings Forth Monsters," in Robert Holmes, ed., *Nonviolence in Theory and Practice* (Belmont, CA: Wadsworth, 1990), pp. 132, 135.

2. Thomas Hobbes, *Leviathan*, chapter XIII, "Of the Natural Condition of Mankind Concerning Their Felicity and Misery," 1651. It was Hobbes who wrote that the natural condition of humanity before monarchial government was "solitary, nasty, brutish and short" (just the opposite of what the archeologists have discovered).

3. This is a common paraphrase of "*Igitur qui desiderat pacem, praeparet bellum*," ascribed to Publius Flavius Vegetius Renatus (c. AD 375) and probably much older. He was not a battle-hardened general but rather an apologist for the older Roman "virtues."

4. http://www.thedevilsdictionary.com/?P.

5. Daniel Leviton, *Horrendous Death and Health: Toward Action* (New York: Hemisphere, 1991).

6. http://www.accessmylibrary.com/coms2/summary_0286-9230364_ITM.

7. The largest arms dealer in the world is the United States, followed by Russia. Israel and the former Czechoslovakia have also been big players.

8. In fact, the failure has been with the original nuclear weapons states (the U.S., the Soviet Union [Russia], France and England), who have not kept their end of the bargain. The treaty called for non-nuclear states to forego the bomb and for the nuclear weapons states to phase it out, which has never happened.

9. Note that the F-22 contract was "suspended" by President Obama at a purchase level of 187 of the $140 million each planes, but the Pentagon will increase its purchases of the F-35. "Pentagon Sets New Priorities; Cancels F-22, TSAT Satellite," *Wall Street Journal*, April 6, 2009, http://www.marketwatch.com/story/pentagon-sets-new-priorities-cancels.

10. William Thomas, *Scorched Earth: The Military Assault on the Environment* (Philadelphia: New Society, 1995), pp. 8, 9.

11. *Ibid.*, p. 9.

12. http://www.fas.org/asmp/profiles/deffirm.html.

13. http://www.defense.gov/contracts/contract.aspx?contractid=4265.

14. David S. Cloud, "U.S. Set to Offer Huge Arms Deal to Saudi Arabia," *New York Times*, July 28, 2007, p. 1.

15. Thomas, *Scorched Earth*, p. 16.

16. *Ibid.*, p. 135.

17. Told to Gustave Gilbert, a psychological interrogator for the Americans. Göring committed suicide just before he was to be executed. http://www.snopes.com/quotes/goering.asp.

18. "President Barack Obama today sent to Congress a proposed defense budget of $663.8 billion for fiscal 2010. The budget request for the Department of Defense (DoD) includes $533.8 billion in discretionary budget authority to fund base defense programs and $130 billion to support overseas contingency operations, primarily in Iraq and Afghanistan," http://www.defense.gov/releases/release.aspx?releaseid=12652.

19. David E. Sanger and Thom Shanker, "U.S. Faces Choice on New Weapons for Fast Strikes," *New York Times*, April 22, 2010, p. A1.

20. Jonathan Cook, "Is Israel Using Arab Villages in Northern Israel as Human Shields?" *Washington Report*, Sept./Oct., 2006, p. 18. Of course, young Hamas and Hezbollah children frequently indulge in the hatred exercised by their parents. This phenomenon is not confined to any one culture in a war system.

21. http://www.usatoday.com/news/education/2009-12-31-jrotc_N.htm.

22. Jane Mayer, "Whatever It Takes: The Politics of the Man Behind '24,'" *New Yorker*, Feb. 19–26, 2007, pp. 66–82, p. 66.

23. *Ibid.*, p. 68.

24. Joseph J. Paczelt, "Upon St. Crispin's Day," unpublished paper in the author's possession. The title is a reference to Shakespeare's "band of brothers" speech in *Henry V.*

25. *Ibid.*, p. 2.

26. *Ibid.*, p. 11.

27. *Ibid.*

28. *Ibid.*

29. *Ibid.*, p. 12, quoting "American War Cinema," Vancouver Independent Media Centre, Jan. 2004, http://vancouver.indymedia.org.

30. *World War II History* presented by the Military Heritage Society, March 2007, Mike Haskew, ed., *World War II History* (magazine).

31. http://www.gamespot.com/pc/strategy/closecombatbattleoftb/review.html?om_act=convert&om_clk=gsbottomnav&tag=quicklinks%3B reviews.

32. http://www.gamespot.com/xbox/action/100bullets/news.html?sid=6086886&mode=previews.

33. http://www.monacome.com/2008/08/grand-theft-auto-4-video-game-violence.html.

34. Stephen A. Crockett, Jr., "For Young Fans, the Name of the Video Game Is Gore," *Washington Post*, August 24, 2002, p. A01.

35. http://www.apa.org/journals/features/psp784772.pdf.

36. www.warresisters.org/wartoys2003.pdf.

37. http://www.toydirectory.com/Awesomekids/index.htm.

38. Christa Foss, "All I Want for Christmas Is a Burned Out Dollhouse," *Globe and Mail* (Canada), Nov. 23, 2003.

39. Darlene Hammell and Joanna Santa Barbara, "War Toys/PGS Briefing Paper," http://www.criticalconcern.com/Militarization_of_Toys.pdf. (PGS is Physicians for Global Survival.)

40. The Nazi Holocaust seems to be a special case of terroristic ethnic cleansing in that it was not designed to break the morale of the Jews and others by terrible practices, nor was it an effort to cleanse a territory by driving them out, but simply to exterminate them all. As such, it is a special case of terrorism and the most extreme in history. It seems to stand by itself as obscenity unparalleled.

Chapter 4

1. Elise Boulding, *Cultures of Peace: The Hidden Side of History* (Syracuse: Syracuse University Press, 2000), p. 17.

2. J. Milburn Thompson, *Justice and Peace: A Christian Primer*, 2d ed. (Maryknoll, NY: Orbis Books, 2003), p. 121.

3. Charles Kimball, *When Religion Becomes Evil: Five Warning Signs* (San Francisco: Harper, 2002), p. 27.

4. Cited in Robert Jay Lifton, "Nuclear Culture," in *Nuclear Times* (Sept./Oct. 1986).

5. Jack Nelson-Pallmeyer, *Jesus Against Christianity* (Harrisburg, PA: Trinity Press, 2001), p. 40.

6. Quoted in Nelson-Pallmeyer, *Jesus Against Christianity*, p. 221.

7. The important Christian contribution to peace will be examined in Section II.

8. Nelson-Pallmeyer, *Jesus Against Christianity*, p. 20.

9. Leo Pfeffer, *Church, State and Freedom* (Boston: Beacon Press, 1953), p. 13.

10. *Ibid.*

11. National Conference of Catholic Bishops (USA), "The Just War Criteria," in *The Challenge of Peace: God's Promise and Our Response* (Washington, DC: United States Catholic Conference, 1983), 26–34.

12. The operative words here are "as long as there is no international authority with competence and power," the very thing I propose in later chapters.

13. National Conference of Catholic Bishops, "The Just War Criteria."

14. On February 13, 1991, two U.S. F-117 stealth bombers over Baghdad released a pair of laser guided smart bombs, the first blowing a hole in the concrete roof of the Amirihya air raid shelter and the second following all the way to the basement to explode. Some 413 people, mostly women and children, died of blasts, burns, and boiling water superheated by the explosion. It was a failure of intelligence that caused the shelter to be attacked. The U.S. blamed Iraq. Recently a U.S. drone operated from Nevada killed 23 civilians in a convoy in Afghanistan. Dexter Filkins, "Operators of Drones Are Faulted in Afghan Deaths," *New York Times*, May 30, 2010, p. A6.

15. Albert Beveridge quoted in Nelson-Pallmeyer, *Jesus Against Christianity*, p. 28. The current American war to make the Middle East into a U.S.-style democracy is not far from this sort of arrogant imperialism.

16. "The Advocate of Peace," quoted in Ray H. Abrams, *Preachers Present Arms* (New York: Round Table Press, 1933), p. 160

17. Abrams, *Preachers Present Arms*, p. 68.

18. Nelson-Pallmeyer, *Jesus Against Christianity*, p. 88.

19. http://www.inglewhite.net/pfp/sajid_islam_and_ethics_of_war_and_peace.htm.

20. *Ibid.*

21. *Ibid.*

22. *Ibid.*

23. Napoleoni, *Terrorism and the Economy*, pp. 54–55.

24. Peter Ustinov quoted in Mary-Wynne Ashford with Guy Dauncey, *Enough Blood Shed: 101 Solutions To Violence, Terror and War* (Gabriola Island, British Columbia: New Society, 2006), p. 224.

25. Nelson-Pallmeyer, *Jesus Against Christianity*, pp. 87–88.

26. Ben Cash, "The Rise of the Private Military," *Journal for the Study of Peace and Conflict*, 2006–2007, pp. 112–126.

27. "Hired Guns" (editorial), *Christian Century*, July 10, 2007, p. 5.

28. *Ibid.*

29. Cash, "Rise of the Private Military," p. 121.

30. *Ibid.*, p. 123.

31. *Ibid.*, p. 115.

32. *Ibid.*, p. 123.

33. Thomas, *Scorched Earth*, pp. 110–111.

34. *Ibid.*, p. 112.

35. Charles Southwick, *Global Ecology in Human Perspective* (Oxford: Oxford University Press, 1996), p. 316.

36. Thomas, *Scorched Earth*, pp. 112, 113, 114.

37. Southwick, *Global Ecology in Human Perspective*, p. 317.

38. Bettie Aldrich Eisendrath, "Military Ecocide: Man's Secret Assault on the Environment" (pamphlet, World Federalists, Milwaukee Chapter, 1992), p. 14.

39. Ross Mirkami with Saul Bloom, "On the Road in Iraq — The First Field Trip," in Saul Bloom et al., *Hidden Casualties: Environmental, Health and Political Consequences of the Persian Gulf War* (Berkeley, CA: North Atlantic Books, 1994), p. 151.

40. Thomas, *Scorched Earth*, p. 16.

41. *Ibid.*, p. 127.

42. *Ibid.*

43. *Ibid.*, p. 18.

44. *Ibid.*, p. xi.

45. *Ibid.*, p. 63.

46. *Ibid.*, pp. 67–68.

47. *Ibid.*, p. 56.

48. *Ibid.*, p. 80.

49. *Ibid.*, p. 156.

50. *Ibid.*, p. 136.

51. *Ibid.*, p. 183.

52. *Ibid.*, p. 135.

53. Southwick, *Global Ecology in Human Perspective*, p. 324.

54. *Ibid.*

55. John W. Birks, "Weapons Forsworn: Chemical and Biological Weapons," in Ann Ehrlich and John W. Birks, eds., *Hidden Dangers: Environmental Consequences of Preparing for War* (San Francisco: Sierra Club, 1990), p. 172.

56. Southwick, *Global Ecology in Human Perspective*, p. 325

57. *Ibid.*

58. Actually, it would take a library. For starters see Michele Stenehjem Gerber, *On the Home Front: The Cold War Legacy of the Hanford Nuclear Site* (Lincoln: University of Nebraska Press, 1997), and Russell J. Dalton, Paula Garb, Nicholas P. Lovrich, and John C. Pierce, *Critical Masses: Citizens, Nuclear Weapons Production, and Environmental Destruction in the United States and Russia* (Cambridge, MA: MIT Press, 1999).

59. Matthew L. Wald, "Disarmament Is Likely to Take Decades," *New York Times*, April 9, 2010, p. A8. It is painfully ironic that the Pentagon recently announced it was going green and would develop non-lead bullets and energy saving ways of killing people. Cf. "A Green Arms Race," *New York Times* online article, May 19, 2010, a summary of John Naish's article in the *New Statesman*.

60. Thomas, *Scorched Earth*, p. 17.

61. Don't read this as a defense of Fidel Castro's dictatorship.

62. Joseph Gerson, "From Empire to Common Security: A Prophetic Vision of Worldwide Justice," in Hugh Sanborn, ed., *The Prophetic Call* (St. Louis: Chalice Press, 2004), p. 131.

63. Kennan quoted in Gerson, "From Empire to Common Security," pp. 133–134.

64. *Ibid.*, p. 131.

65. *Ibid.*

66. *Ibid.*, p. 134.

67. *Ibid.*, p. 130.

68. Napoleoni, *Terrorism and the Economy*, p. 34. The quote is from *Rebuilding America's Defenses* and was authored by Cheney and others, including Donald Rumsfeld, Scooter Libby, Paul Wolfowitz, and Jeb Bush.

69. While a defensive missile shield sounds non-aggressive, the problem with it, as the Chinese clearly see, is that it provides a cover for a first-strike offense by rendering a counter-missile threat impotent. There is no such thing as a defensive missile.

70. Cited in Gerson, "From Empire to Common Security," p. 134. Wolfowitz later became president of the World Bank, demonstrating the close link between military and economic power.

71. Sanger and Shanker, "U.S. Faces Choice on New Weapons for Fast Strikes."

72. Mohammed Fathi Osman, "God Is the All Peace," in James L. Heft, ed., *Beyond Violence: Religious Sources of Social Transformation in Judaism, Christianity and Islam* (New York: Fordham University Press, 2004), p. 67. Osman is opposed to jihadist violence.

73. Robert Wright, "The Price of Assassination," *New York Times*, April 13, 2010.

74. Thompson, *Justice and Peace*, p. 177.

75. Thomas Merton, *Thoughts in Solitude* (New York: Farrar, Straus, Giroux, 1958), p. xii.

Chapter 5

1. The robot is a U.S. drone named "Predator." Tom Vanden Brook, "Drones' Supply, Support Lacking; Predator Demand Outpaces Fleet Size, Training of Crews," *USA Today*, March 29, 2007, p. 1.

2. http://giga-usa.com/quotes/Aristotle_aoo1.htm.

3. http://www.quotationspage.com/quote/24238.html.

4. http://www.msnbc.msn.com/id/343607 43/ns/politics-white_house//.

5. http://www.zazzle.com/we_make_war_that _we_may_live_in_peace_aristot_tshirt-23598500 1173175311.

6. http://www.democraticunderground.com/discuss/duboard.php?az=view_all&address=389 x252135.

7. *Ibid.*

8. Robert Aitkin, "The Net of Vows," in David W. Chappell, ed., *Buddhist Peacework: Creating Cultures of Peace* (Boston: Wisdom Publications, 1999), pp. 93–101, p. 97. Dependent co-arising means I exist only because you exist, and vice versa. Thich Nhat Hahn has called this phenomenon "interbeing."

9. Kaldor, *Global Civil Society*, p. 2.

10. *Ibid.*

11. Gene Sharp, "Disregarded History: The Power of Nonviolent Action," in Walter Wink, ed., *Peace Is The Way: Writings On Nonviolence from the Fellowship of Reconciliation* (Maryknoll, NY: Orbis Books, 2000), pp. 231–235, 232.

12. Arun Gandhi, foreword to Michael Nagler, *The Search for a Nonviolent Future* (San Francisco: Inner Ocean Publishing, 2004), p. x.

13. Sulak Sivaraksa, "Buddhism and a Culture of Peace," in David W. Chappell, ed., *Buddhist Peacework: Creating Cultures of Peace* (Boston: Wisdom Publications, 1999), pp. 39–46, 45.

14. Thich Nhat Hahn, "Ahimsa: The Path of Harmlessness," in David W. Chappell, ed., *Buddhist Peacework: Creating Cultures Of Peace* (Boston: Wisdom Publications, 1999), pp. 155–164, 155.

15. John Paul Lederach, *The Moral Imagination: The Art and Soul of Building Peace* (Oxford: Oxford University Press, 2005), p. 5.

16. *Ibid.*, p. ix.

17. *Ibid.*, p. 5.

18. *Ibid.*, p. 35.

19. Nagler, *The Search for a Nonviolent Future*, p. 38.

20. Lederach, *The Moral Imagination*, p. 36.

21. *Ibid.*, p. 39.

Chapter 6

1. Personal experience of the author, who was, at that time, executive director of the Wisconsin Institute for the Study of Conflict and Peace.

2. Jacket blurb for Geoffrey Perret, *A Country Made by War: From the Revolution to Vietnam — The Story of America's Rise to Power* (New York: Random House, 1989).

3. Boulding, *Cultures of Peace*, p. 15.

4. Matthew Melko, "The Delineation of Peaceful Societies," in Ringler, ed., *Dilemmas of War and Peace*, p. 246 (an excerpt from Melko's *Peaceful Societies* [Oakville, Ontario: CPRI Press, 1973]).

5. Kenneth Boulding, "Why the History of Peace Does Not Get Written," in Ringler, ed., *Dilemmas of War And Peace*, p. 239.

6. Casper Kuhlmann, *Peace — A Topic in European History Textbooks?* (Frankfurt: Verlag Peter Lang, 1985), p. 10.

7. Gwynne Dyer, "The Roots of War," in Ringler, ed., *Dilemmas of War and Peace*, p. 56.

8. *Ibid.*, pp. 55, 58.

9. Wright, quoted in Dyer, "Roots of War," p. 58.

10. Riane Eisler, *The Chalice and the Blade: Our History, Our Future* (San Francisco: Harper and Row, 1987), p. xvii.

11. *Ibid.*, p. 43.

12. *Ibid.*, p. 13.

13. Thomas Gregor, *A Natural History of Peace* (Nashville: Vanderbilt University Press, 1996), p. xxi.

14. Eisler, *The Chalice and the Blade*, p. 49.

15. Dyer, "The Roots of War," p. 60.

16. Eisler, *The Chalice and the Blade*, p. 56.

17. Ben Low, *Imagining Peace: A History of Early English Pacifist Ideas* (University Park: University of Pennsylvania Press, 1997), p. 1.

18. Charles Chatfield and Ruzannah Ilukhina, *Peace/Mir: An Anthology of Historic Alternatives to War* (Syracuse: Syracuse University Press, 1994), p. 10.

19. Pindar quoted in Chatfield and Ilukhina, *Peace/Mir*, p. 11.

20. *Ibid.*, p. 21.

21. *Ibid.*, p. 22.

22. Tacitus, in "De Vita et Moribus Iulii Agricolae," many editions; see *Agricola and Germany* (New York: Oxford University Press; reissue edition June 15, 2009).

23. Terrence, in *Heautontimoroumenos* (Société d'Edition "Les Belles Lettres"; 1st ed., 1927). Out of print.

24. Quoted in Ringler, ed., *Dilemmas of War and Peace*, p. 150. Cf. Cicero, *De Oficiis*, 1: 22: 74.

25. *Ibid.* Cf. Italicus, *Punica* 11: 592–595.

26. Vincent Kavaloski, "Pax Romana," in

Ringler, ed., *Dilemmas of War and Peace*, pp. 247–248, 248.

27. Sommer quoted in Ringler, ed., *Dilemmas of War and Peace*, p. 161.

28. For example, Kenneth Leach, *We Preach Christ Crucified* (New York: Church Publishing, 2005), and Albert Nolan, *Jesus Before Christianity* (Maryknoll, NY: Orbis Books, 1976; reprinted 2005).

29. Leach, *We Preach Christ Crucified*, p. 39.

30. *Ibid.*, p. 10.

31. Rita Nakashima Brock and Rebecca Ann Parker, *Saving Paradise: How Christianity Traded Love of This World for Crucifixion and Empire* (Boston: Beacon Press, 2008), p. 41.

32. Nolan, *Jesus Before Christianity*, p. 151.

33. This is the whole thesis of Parker and Brock's *Saving Paradise*.

34. "It took Jesus a thousand years to die. Images of his corpse did not appear in churches until the tenth century." *Ibid.*, p. ix.

35. St. Thomas Aquinas, *Summa Theologica*, quoted in Chatfield and Ilukhina, *Peace/Mir*, p. 53.

36. George Orwell, *1984* (New York: New American Library, 1961), p. 4.

37. Thomas Head and Richard Landes, eds., *The Peace of God* (Ithaca, NY: Cornell University Press, 1992), p. 3.

38. *Ibid.*, p. 1.

39. Excerpted in Chatfield and Ilukhina, *Peace/Mir*, p. 54.

40. Roscoe Balch, "The Resigning of Quarrels: Conflict Resolution in the Thirteenth Century," reprinted in Ringler, ed., *Dilemmas of War and Peace*, p. 253.

41. In Chatfield and Ilukhina, *Peace/Mir*, p. 65.

42. Peter Brock, *The Quaker Peace Testimony: 1660–1914* (York, UK: Sessions Book Trust, 1990), p. 23.

43. William Penn, "First Letter to the Delaware Indians," in Staughton and Alice Lynd, eds., *Nonviolence in America: A Documentary History* (Maryknoll, NY: Orbis Books, 1995), p. 1.

Chapter 7

1. Chatfield and Ilukhina, *Peace/Mir*, p. 81.

2. Edson L. Whitney, *The American Peace Society: A Centennial History* (Washington, DC: The American Peace Society, 1928), p. 10. This is a facsimile reprint made available by Jerome S. Ozer, Publisher, in 1972.

3. *Ibid.*, pp. 11, 12.

4. http://ipb.org/i/index.html.

5. http://womenshistory.about.com/od/howe juliaward/a/julia_ward_howe_4_mothers_day.htm.

6. http://en.wikipedia.org/wiki/Mother%27s _Day_Proclamation.

7. David Barash, *Introduction to Peace Studies* (Belmont, CA: Wadsworth, 1991), pp. 406–407.

8. Ashford with Dauncey, *Enough Blood Shed*, pp. 202, 240.

9. All of this history and a great deal more is chronicled in a work by the distinguished American peace historian Charles Chatfield, whose book, *The American Peace Movement: Ideals and Activism* (New York: Twayne Publishers, 1992), surveys the many groups and the main themes as these evolved from 1815 to the present. As Chatfield acknowledges in his introduction, such a work was made possible by the publication of many monographs and specialized studies that have appeared since the 1960s. A brief list of examples includes Patricia Neal, *Harder than War: Catholic Peacemaking in Twentieth-Century America* (New Brunswick, NJ: Rutgers University Press, 1992); J. Michael Hogan, *The Nuclear Freeze Campaign* (East Lansing: Michigan State University Press, 1994); Christian Smith, *Resisting Reagan: The U.S. Central America Peace Movement* (Chicago: University of Chicago Press, 1996); Philip Berrigan and Fred Wilcox, *Fighting the Lamb's War: Skirmishes with the American Empire: The Autobiography of Philip Berrigan* (Monroe, ME: Common Courage Press, 1996); Douglas Roche, *The Ultimate Evil: The Fight to Ban Nuclear Weapons* (Toronto: James Lorimer, 1997); and Staughton and Alice Lynd, eds., *Nonviolence in America: A Documentary History* (Maryknoll, NY: Orbis Books, 1995).

Moving away from the strictly American history of peace, there are such works as James Hinton, *Protests and Visions: Peace Politics in 20th Century Britain* (London: Hutchinson Books, 1989); and George Gill's two-volume work, *The League of Nations: International Cooperation Towards Peace in the 20th Century* (Garden City Park, NY: Avery Publishing Group, 1996). While no list this brief can even pretend to be representative, not to say complete, one cannot leave off an older but crucial work by Gene Sharp, *The Politics of Nonviolent Action* (Boston: Porter Sergeant, 1973), a three-volume set that, while mainly a manual on how to conduct nonviolent struggle, contains a wealth of historic examples from all over the world. Jill Liddington's *The Road to Greenham Common: Feminism and Anti-militarism in Britain since 1820* (Syracuse: Syracuse University Press, 1989) is an excellent example of the blending of women's' history and peace history. More books on the history of nonviolence include Susan Terkel's *People Power: A Look at Nonviolent Action and Defense* (New York: Lodestar, 1996), also containing many historical examples, and Catherine Ingram's *In the Footsteps of Gandhi: Conversations with Spiritual Social Activists* (Berkeley: Parallax Press, 1990) and

Yogesh Chadha's new biography, *Gandhi: A Life* (New York: John Wiley & Sons, 1997). Finally, the journal *Peace and Change: A Journal of Peace Research* is jointly sponsored by the Peace History Society and the Consortium on Peace Research and Education and contains many useful articles. The history of peace is being recovered, but primarily in pieces.

10. Ian Harris and Mary Lee Morrison, *Peace Education*, 2d ed. (Jefferson, NC: McFarland, 2003). Other typical works are James Page, *Peace Education: Exploring Ethical and Philosophical Foundations* (Charlotte, NC: Information Age Publishing, 2008 and Monisha Bajaj, *Encyclopedia of Peace Education (PB)* (Charlotte, NC: Information Age Publishing, 2008).

11. http://www.uwsp.edu/history/wipcs/index.aspx.

12. http://www.peacejusticestudies.org.

13. http://en.wikipedia.org/wiki/European_Peace_University.

14. http://www.brad.ac.uk/peace/.

15. http://www.upeace.org/.

16. Roger Fisher and Richard Ury, *Getting to Yes: Negotiating an Agreement Without Giving In* (New York: Random House, 1981), translated into 20 languages; and a series of follow-ups with such titles as *Getting Past No* and so on. These have been immensely influential and have helped to create a worldwide movement in alternative dispute resolution.

17. http://www.healthfinder.gov/orgs/hr3407.htm.

18. Paul Hawken, business executive and author, wrote *Blessed Unrest*, a book attempting to chronicle the growth of NGOs, and, after it was published, established "Wiser Earth: Community Tools for Establishing a Just and Sustainable World," listing contact information for thousands of NGOs (for further information, go to *Wiser Earth*, located at http://www.wiserearth.org).

19. A skeptical view of the UN can be found in a John Gray's long review essay ("The Myth and Reality of the United Nations") of Mark Mazower's book, *No Enchanted Palace: The End of Empire and the Ideological Origins of the United Nations* (Princeton, NJ: Princeton University Press, 2009), in *Harpers*, June 2010, pp. 78ff. The argument is that the UN is basically impotent.

20. It is summarized in the *Beck Index*, found online at http://www.san.Beck.org/GPJ29-Anti-NuclearProtests.html.

21. "Doomsday Clock," *Bulletin of the Atomic Scientists*, www.thebulletin.org.

22. Properly titled the "Treaty Banning Nuclear Weapon Tests in the Atmosphere, in Outer Space and Under Water." Along the way French secret agents blew up the Greenpeace ship *Rainbow Warrior*, allegedly on the orders of French President Francois Mitterrand, killing one crew member. The agents were later convicted and sent to prison.

23. http://www.state.gov/www/global/arms/treaties/spnfz.html.

24. See David Fairhall, *Common Ground: The Story of Greenham* (London: I.B. Tauris, 2006), one of several available works.

25. http://www.nukewatch.com/.

26. http://www.nukewatch.com/quarterly/index.html.

27. It is notable and regrettable that the United States under George W. Bush pulled out of the ABM Treaty and was the sole stumbling block to the Comprehensive Test Ban Treaty, as well as the major influence in enervating the Nuclear Nonproliferation Treaty.

28. http://www.sonoma.edu/users/w/wallsd/peace-movement.shtml.

29. Harry Meserve, "Meditation 496," in Unitarian Universalist Association, *Singing The Living Tradition* (Boston: Beacon Press, 1993).

Chapter 8

1. Robert Holmes, *Nonviolence in Theory and Practice* (Belmont, CA: Wadsworth, 1990), pp. 135, 137.

2. http://en.wikiquote.org/wiki/Kenneth_Boulding.

3. Robert Holmes, "The Sleep of Reason Brings Forth Monsters," in Holmes, *Nonviolence in Theory and Practice*, p. 138.

4. Henry David Thoreau in "Civil Disobedience," quoted in Holmes, *Nonviolence in Theory and Practice*, p. 39.

5. George Crowell, "The Case for Nonviolent Defense Against External Aggression," a Plowshares Working Paper, n.d., p. 5.

6. Lao Tse, *Tao Te Ching*, trans. Stephen Addiss and Stanley Lobardo (Indianapolis: Hackett Publishing, 1993), p. 30.

7. http://www.brainyquote.com/quotes/authors/l/leo_tolstoy_2.html.

8. Staughton and Alice Lynd, eds., *Nonviolence in America: A Documentary History* (Maryknoll, NY: Orbis, 1995), p. xiii. As the Lynds' valuable book documents, there is a long history of nonviolence in America.

9. Yogesh Chandha, *Gandhi: A Life* (New York: John Wiley & Sons, 1997), p. 1.

10. Holmes, *Nonviolence in Theory and Practice*, p. 2.

11. *Ibid.*, p. 3.

12. Philip Berrigan with Fred A. Wilcox, *Fighting the Lamb's War: Skirmishes with the American Empire: The Autobiography of Philip Berrigan* (Monroe, ME: Common Courage Press, 1996), p. 178.

13. Holmes, *Nonviolence in Theory and Practice*, p. 3.

14. Crowell, "The Case for Nonviolent Defense Against External Aggression," p. 2.

15. *Ibid.*, p. 9.

16. Gene Sharp, "Civilan-Based Defense: Making The Abolition of War a Realistic Goal," in in Dick Ringler, ed., *Dilemmas of War and Peace: A Sourcebook* (Madison: Board of Regents of the University of Wisconsin and the Corporation for Public Broadcasting, 1993), p. 749.

17. Crowell, "The Case for Nonviolent Defense Against External Aggression," p. 6.

18. A.J. Muste, "The Lawrence Strike of 1919," in Lynd and Lynd, *Nonviolence in America*, pp. 129–141.

19. Crowell, "The Case for Nonviolent Defense Against External Aggression," p. 6.

20. Peter Ackerman and Jack DuVall, *A Force More Powerful: A Century of Nonviolent Conflict* (New York: St. Martin's Press, 2000), chapter 1.

21. http://en.wikipedia.org/wiki/Kapp_Putsch.

22. Crowell, "The Case for Nonviolent Defense Against External Aggression," p. 3.

23. Ackerman and DuVall, *A Force More Powerful*, chapter 2.

24. This and the following quotes from http://www.worldofquotes.com/author/Mahatma-Gandhi/1/index.html.

25. http://en.wikiquote.org/wiki/Mohandas_Karamchand_Gandhi.

26. http://library.thingquest.org/CO1155/index.htm.

27. http://en.wikipedia.org/wiki/Iranian_Revolution.

28. Richard Deats, "The Philippines: The Nonviolent Revolution that Surprised the World," in Holmes, *Nonviolence in Theory and Practice*, pp. 203ff.

29. Ackerman and Duvall, *A Force More Powerful*, p. 1.

30. Lester Brown, *Plan B 4.0: Mobilizing to Save Civilization* (New York: W.W. Norton, 2009), p. 257.

31. http://www.npr.org/templates/story/story.php?storyId=120251039.

32. http://www.spiegel.de/international/germany/0,1518,654137,00.html.

33. http://travelmaven.typepad.com/the_travel_maven_blog/2009/08/exploring-berlin-and-germany-the-revolution-of-candles-and-prayers.html.

34. http://www.defense.gov/releases/release.aspx?releaseid=12652.

35. Tiananmen Square (June 3–4, 1989) is usually considered a failure of nonviolence. Actually it was a failure to properly organize it, but even so, it had far-reaching effects on the other side of the world.

36. Ackerman and DuVall, *A Force More Powerful*, p. 224.

37. *Ibid.*, p. 229.

38. Ernest Schwarcz, "Nonviolent Resistance Against the Nazis in Norway and Holland during World War II," in Holmes, *Nonviolence in Theory and Practice*, pp. 185–187.

39. http://www.theoptimists.com/theoptimists_metropolitan_bishop_Stephen_and_Kiril.htm.

40. *Ibid.*

41. http://en.wikipedia.org/wiki/history_of_the-Jews_in_Greece.

42. Ackerman and DuVall, *A Force More Powerful*, chapter 5.

43. Cf. Philip Hallie, *Lest Innocent Blood Be Shed* (New York: Harper Perennial, 1994).

44. Barbara Demming, "On Revolution and Equilibrium," in Holmes, *Nonviolence in Theory and Practice*, p. 103.

45. *Ibid.*, p. 98.

46. Reuven Kimmelman, "Nonviolence in ihe Talmud," in Holmes, *Nonviolence in Theory and Practice*, p. 21.

47. George Patterson, *An Inquiry into the Origins of Satyagraha and Its Contemporary Relevance*, crvp.org/book/Series03/IIIB-S/chapter_ii.htm.

48. Demming, "On Revolution and Equilibrium," p. 103.

49. Gene Sharp, *The Politics of Nonviolent Struggle, Part Two: The Methods of Nonviolent Action*, pp. 109–10.

50. *Ibid.*, p. 340.

51. http://www.commondreams.org/views04/0119-05.htm.

Chapter 9

1. John H. Schaar, American writer, professor emeritus of political philosophy at the University of California at Santa Cruz. This quote is widely published but never cited.

2. http://www.unac.org/peacep/intro/index.html.

3. *Ibid.*

4. http://www.unac.org/peacep/decade.

5. Robert Johansen, quoted in Timothy A. McElwee, in *Cross Currents*, excerpted online at http://www.goliath.ecnext.com/coms2/gi_3218258/Instead-of-war-the-urgency.html.

6. Lael Brainard, Derek Chollet, and Vinca LaFleur, "The Tangled Web: The Poverty-Insecurity Nexus," in Lael Brainard and Derek Chollet, eds., *Too Poor For Peace?: Global Poverty, Conflict, and Security in the 21st Century* (Washington, DC: Brookings Institution, 2007), p. 1.

7. *Ibid.*, p. 2.

8. *Ibid.*, p. 5.

9. Sharon Delgado, *Shaking the Gates of Hell: Faith-Led Resistance to Corporate Globalization* (Minneapolis, MN: Fortress Press, 2007), p. viii.

10. Ted Halstead and Clifford Cobb, "The Need for New Measurements of Progress," in Jerry

Mander and Edward Goldsmith, eds., *The Case Against the Global Economy and for a Turn Toward the Local* (San Francisco: Sierra Club, 1996), pp. 197ff.

11. WTO is a treaty arrangement of 153 nations that sets the rules for trade. It operates behind closed doors and has broad powers. Its governing philosophy is a radical "free-market" ideology. A critique of the organization can be found at http://www.globalexchange.org/campaigns/wto/. The WTO official website is at http://www.wto.org/, and also in Mander and Goldsmith, *The Case Against the Global Economy.*.

12. Cleo Paskal, *Global Warring: How Environmental, Economic and Political Crises Will Redraw the World Map* (New York: Palgrave Macmillan, 2010), p. 141. The Himalayan snow pack also provides significant water to India, Nepal, Pakistan and China. Flow reductions will be a major threat to peace if not managed cooperatively.

13. http://www.devdir.org/.

14. Tom Peterson, "End Hunger. Now!," *World Ark* (Nov./Dec. 2007). Based on a figure of $36 billion from a 2006 military budget of $540 billion. In 1970 the U.S. pledged to spend .7 percent of its GNP on ending poverty. So far the U.S. is spending only .17 percent (p. 39).

15. Brown, *Plan B. 4.0*, pp. 263–264.

16. http://www.nytimes.com/2010/05/10/world/africa/10aids.html?pagewanted=2&sq=Uganda%20aids&st=cse&scp=1.

17. Alexander Nikitin, "Analyzing the Causes of War and Peace," in Majid Tehranian and David W. Chappell, eds., *Dialogue of Civilizations: A New Peace Agenda for a New Millennium* (London and New York: I.B. Tauris, 2002), p. 171.

18. It failed through, among other things, not providing any means for enforcing the provisions that all disputes must be settled by diplomacy. Nations that signed simply changed their minds. Nevertheless, as Peter Weis asks, "Is it worth having another go at such a discredited vision? Might as well ask: was it worth trying to abolish slavery after decades of failure? To give women the suffrage after centuries of voting by men only? To establish democratic institutions after millennia of autocracies?" (http://lcnp.org/global/kosovo.htm).

19. See http://worldwithoutwar.com/.

20. http://www.caat.org.uk/.

21. Ashford with Dauncey, *Enough Blood Shed*, p. 251.

22. Nikitin, "Analyzing the Causes of War and Peace," p. 176.

23. http://www.globalpolicy.org/un-reform/un-reform-topics/un-standing-force.html.

24. A discussion of Security Council reform can be begun at http://www.globalpolicy.org/un-reform/un-reform-topics/reform-of-the-security-council-9-16.html.

25. http://www.worldparliament-gov.org/.

26. Nikitin, "Analyzing the Causes of War and Peace," p. 173.

27. A discussion of some ideas is at the Global Policy Forum website, http://www.globalpolicy.org/social-and-economic-policy/global-taxes-1-79/alternative-financing-for-the-un-1-84.html, or else one can simply google "Alternative Funding UN." Fierce opposition has come from the United States.

28. http://www.guardian.co.uk/world/2010/apr/08/barack-obama-nuclear-treaty-russia.

29. George Shultz, William Perry, Henry A. Kissinger and Sam Nunn, "Toward a Nuclear Free World," *Wall Street Journal*, January 15, 2008. The list also includes James Baker, Zbigniew Brzezinski, Frank Carlucci, Melvin Laird, Robert McNamara, Colin Powel, Madeleine Albright, Richard Allen and many other prominent names in the field of national security.

30. Jonathan Dean, "Ending Wars," in Majid Tehranian and David W. Chappell, *Dialogue of Civilizations: A New Peace Agenda for a New Millennium* (London and New York: I.B. Tauris, 2002), p. 185.

31. *Ibid.*, p. 187.

32. Nikitin, "Analyzing the Causes of War and Peace," p. 172.

33. InterPol, the International Criminal Police Organization, another treaty-based institution of international law, found online at http://www.interpol.int/.

34. Note: The cost of the current Gulf War will end up around $2 trillion or even $3 trillion, according to Nobel economist Joseph Stiglitz. (A trillion is a thousand billion and a billion is a thousand million.) Robert Hormats, vice chairman of the investment firm Goldman Sachs, pointed out in congressional testimony that the cost of one day of the war would enroll 58,000 children in Head Start or make a year of college available to 160,000 low-income students, pay the salaries of 11,000 new border patrol guards or 14,000 new police officers, raising the question of what is true security. Bob Herbert, "The $2 Trillion Nightmare," *New York Times*, March 4, 2008.

35. http://www.bicc.de/.

36. Hawken, a successful businessman and environmentalist, began to notice when he gave public talks around the world that people were coming up to him with business cards for their NGOs and he started an ongoing investigation that is revealing that the rise of NGOs is one of the revolutionary changes of the last 50 years. Cf. Hawkens, *Blessed Unrest*. See also http://www.politicalresources.net/int2.htm.

37. All of these organizations are easily available online. Simply google these names or see the list of peace organizations in the appendix. It is heartening to note that the Muslim Peacemaker

Teams were trained by the Christian Peacemaker Teams, just another example of so much peaceful cooperation that goes under the radar of the evening news.

38. Mahony and Eguren, *Unarmed Bodyguards*, p. 1.
39. http://www.peacebrigades.org/.
40. http://www.witnessforpeace.org/.
41. http://www.witnessforpeace.org/section.php?id=81.
42. http://en.wikipedia.org/wiki/Christian_Peacemaker_Teams.
43. http://www.nonviolentpeaceforce.org/about/mission.
44. http://www.amnesty.org/ and http://www.hrw.org/.
45. Full text at http://www.leftjustified.com/leftjust/lib/sc/ht/wtp/un-decla.html.
46. http://www.time.com/time/magazine/article/0,9171,962783,00.html.
47. http://www.un.org/esa/earthsummit/ga97info.htm.
48. http://www.haguepeace.org. At the website there are excellent educational materials pertaining to a variety of topics but especially the abolition of war.
49. http://www.article-9.org/en/conference/index.html. This article is part of a global campaign to abolish war.

Chapter 10

1. Brown, *Plan B 4.0*, p. xiv.
2. Of course, it borders on the ridiculous to try and open up the peace traditions in these religions in any depth in the space available here. What follows is no more than a finger pointing the way.
3. Lawrence Holben, *All the Way to Heaven: A Theological Reflection on Dorothy Day, Peter Maurin and the Catholic Worker* (Marion, SD: Rose Hill Books, 1997), pp. 25, 26.
4. Thomas Merton, *New Seeds of Contemplation* (Norfolk, CT: New Directions, 1972), pp. 73, 123.
5. *Ibid.*, p. 122.
6. Thomas Merton, *Conjectures of a Guilty Bystander* (Garden City, NY: Image Books, 1966), p. 142.
7. Thomas Merton, "Saint Maximus the Confessor on Nonviolence," in Gordon C. Zahn, ed., *The Nonviolent Alternative* (New York: Farrar, Straus, Giroux, 1980), p. 177.
8. Quoted in Thompson, *Justice and Peace*, p. 121.
9. Pax Christi, Spring Letter (2008) at http://www.paxchristiusa.org.
10. See http://www.paxchristi.net/about.
11. See http://www.ecapc.org/yourchurch.asp.

12. Ann Bragdon, quoting Walter Wink, *Engaging the Powers: Discernment and Resistance in a World of Domination* (Minneapolis, MN: Fortress Press, 1992), in "A Prophetic Vision of Building Worldwide Community," in Hugh Sanborn, ed., *The Prophetic Call* (St. Louis, MO: Chalice Press, 2004), p. 57.
13. http://www.kamat.com/mmgandhi/christian.htm. Millie Graham Polak and her husband Henry were members of Gandhi's household during the South Africa days. The passage is from her book, *Mr. Gandhi, The Man* (Mumbai, India: Vora, 1950), now out of print.
14. *Bhagavad-Gita: A Book of Hindu Scriptures in the Form of a Dialogue between Prince Arjuna and the God Krishna* (Mount Vernon, NY: Peter Pauper Press, 1959), p. 31.
15. "Katha-Upanishad," in W.B. Yeats and Shri Purohit Swami, eds., *The Ten Principal Upanishads* (New York: Macmillan, 1965), p. 25.
16. http://www.peaceprayerday.org/PeacePeople/.
17. http://www.thewildrose.net/peace_prayers.html.
18. http://www.liturgy.co.nz/reflection/peace.html.
19. Dalai Lama, *Ethics for the New Millennium* (New York: Riverhead Books, 1999), pp. 42–43.
20. http://buddhism.about.com/od/buddhismglossaryi/g/indrasnetdefine.htm.
21. Nancy Wilson Ross, *Buddhism: A Way of Life and Thought* (New York: Vintage Books, 1980), p. 91.
22. Dalai Lama, *Ethics for the New Millennium*, p. 23.
23. http://rabbidavidrosen.net/Articles/Judaism%20and%20Peace.doc.
24. http://www.jewishpeacefellowship.org/index.php?p=about.prayer.
25. Bragdon, "A Prophetic Vision of Building Worldwide Community," p. 52.
26. http://www.forusa.org/peacewalks/default.html.
27. http://www.allgreatquotes.com/peace_quotes.shtml.
28. The Islamic Center can be found at http://www.theislamiccenter.com/.
29. http://news.nationalgeographic.com/news/2001/09/0925_TVkoran.html.
30. Osman, "God Is the All Peace."
31. Qur'an, quoted in Bragdon, "A Prophetic Vision of Building Worldwide Community," p. 66.
32. http://blog.gaiam.com/quotes/authors/ibn-al-arabi?page=1.
33. The entire prayer can be found at http://quotes.liberty-tree.ca/quote/tecumseh_quote_a441.
34. http://www.pluralism.org/news/article.php?id=3844.

35. http://www.susunweed.com/Peace_Native _American_Elders.htm.

36. http://www.wovoca.com/.

37. http://www.starstuffs.com/native_spiritu ality/.

38. http://www.geocities.com/starstuffs/native /default.htm.

39. http://www.ratical.org/co-globalize/IPPI. html.

40. http://en.wikiquote.org/wiki/Wendell_ Berry.

41. *Ibid.*

42. http://www.ejrc.cau.edu/princej.html.

43. http://www.rpi.edu/dept/chem-eng/Bio tech-Environ/ECOLOGY/project.html.

44. http://www.bestlifeonline.com/cms/pub lish/health/Our_oceans_are_turning_into_plas tic_are_we_2.php.

45. http://www.context.org/ICLIB/IC03/ Schweick.htm.

Bibliography

Abrams, Ray H. *Preachers Present Arms*. New York: Round Table Press, 1933.

Ackerman, Peter, and Jack DuVall. *A Force More Powerful: A Century of Nonviolent Conflict*. New York: St. Martin's Press, 2000.

Aitkin, Robert. "The Net of Vows." In *Buddhist Peacework: Creating Cultures of Peace*, edited by David W. Chappell, 93–101. Boston: Wisdom Publications, 1999.

Allot, Kenneth, ed. *The Poems of Matthew Arnold*, 2nd ed. London: Logan, 1979.

Ashford, Mary-Wynne, with Guy Dauncey. *Enough Blood Shed: 101 Solutions to Violence, Terror and War*. Gabriola Island, British Columbia: New Society, 2006.

Balch, Roscoe. "The Resigning of Quarrels: Conflict Resolution in the Thirteenth Century." In *Dilemmas of War and Peace: A Sourcebook*, edited by Dick Ringler, 249ff. Madison: The Board of Regents of the University of Wisconsin System and the Corporation for Public Broadcasting, 1993.

Barash, David. *Introduction to Peace Studies*. Belmont, CA: Wadsworth, 1991.

Berrigan, Philip, with Fred A. Wilcox. *Fighting the Lamb's War: Skirmishes with the American Empire: The Autobiography of Philip Berrigan*. Monroe, ME: Common Courage Press, 1996.

Bhagavad-Gita: A Book of Hindu Scriptures in the Form of a Dialogue between Prince Arjuna and the God Krishna. Mount Vernon, NY: Peter Pauper Press, 1959.

Birks, John W. "Weapons Forsworn: Chemical and Biological Weapons." In *Hidden Dangers: Environmental Consequences of Preparing for War*, edited by Ann Ehrlich and John W. Birks. San Francisco: Sierra Club, 1990.

Bloom, Saul, et al. *Hidden Casualties: Environmental, Health and Political Consequences of the Persian Gulf War*. Berkeley, CA: North Atlantic Books, 1994.

Boulding, Elise. *Cultures of Peace: The Hidden Side of History*. Syracuse: Syracuse University Press, 2000.

Boulding, Kenneth. *Stable Peace*. Austin: University of Texas Press, 1978.

_____. "Why The History Of Peace Does Not Get Written." In *Dilemmas of War and Peace: A Sourcebook*, edited by Dick Ringler, 239–41. Madison: The Board of Regents of the University of Wisconsin System and the Corporation for Public Broadcasting, 1993.

Bragdon, Ann. "A Prophetic Vision of Building Worldwide Community." In *The Prophetic Call*, edited by Hugh Sanborn, 51ff. St. Louis, MO: Chalice Press, 2004.

Brainard, Lael, Derek Chollet, and Vinca LaFleur. "The Tangled Web: The Poverty-Insecurity Nexus." In *Too Poor For Peace?: Global Poverty, Conflict, and Security in the 21st Century*, edited by Lael Brainard and Derek Chollet, 1ff. Washington, DC: Brookings Institution, 2007.

Brock, Peter. *The Quaker Peace Testimony: 1660–1914.* York, UK: Sessions Book Trust, 1990.

Brock, Rita Nakashima, and Rebecca Ann Parker. *Saving Paradise: How Christianity Traded Love of This World for Crucifixion and Empire.* Boston: Beacon Press, 2008.

Brook, Tom Vanden. "Drones' Supply, Support Lacking; Predator Demand Outpaces Fleet Size, Training of Crews." *USA Today*, March 29, 2007: 1.

Brown, Lester R. *Plan B 4.0: Mobilizing to Save Civilization.* New York: W.W. Norton, 2009.

Brzezinski, Zbigniew. *Out of Control: Global Turmoil on the Eve of the Twenty-first Century.* New York: Scribner, 1993.

Cash, Ben. "The Rise of the Private Military." *Journal for the Study of Peace and Conflict* (2006–2007): 112–126.

Chandha, Yogesh. *Gandhi: A Life.* New York: John Wiley & Sons, 1997.

Chatfield, Charles. *The American Peace Movement: Ideals and Activism.* New York: Twayne Publishers, 1992.

_____, and Ruzannah Ilukhina. *Peace/Mir: An Anthology of Historic Alternatives to War.* Syracuse: Syracuse University Press, 1994.

Churchill, Winston. *The Voice of Winston Churchill.* London Records, RB100, n.d.

Cloud, David S. "U.S. Set to Offer Huge Arms Deal to Saudi Arabia." *New York Times*, July 28, 2007.

Cook, Jonathan. "Is Israel Using Arab Villages in Northern Israel as Human Shields?" *Washington Report* (September/October 2006).

Crockett, Stephen A., Jr. "For Young Fans, the Name of the Video Game is Gore." *Washington Post*, August 24, 2002: A01.

Crowell, George. "The Case for Nonviolent Defense Against External Aggression." A Plowshares Working Paper, n.d.

Dalai Lama. *Ethics for the New Millennium.* New York: Riverhead Books, 1999.

Dalton, Russell J., Paula Garb, Nicholas P. Lovrich, and John C. Pierce, *Critical Masses: Citizens, Nuclear Weapons Production, and Environmental Destruction in the United States and Russia.* Cambridge, MA: MIT Press, 1999.

Dean, Jonathan. "Ending Wars." In *Dialogue of Civilizations: A New Peace Agenda for a New Millennium*, edited by Majid Tehranian and David W. Chappell, 179ff. London and New York: I.B. Tauris, 2002.

Deats, Richard. "The Philippines: The Nonviolent Revolution that Surprised the World." In *Nonviolence in Theory and Practice*, edited by Robert Holmes, 203ff. Belmont, CA: Wadsworth, 1990.

Delgado, Sharon. *Shaking the Gates of Hell: Faith-Led Resistance to Corporate Globalization.* Minneapolis, MN: Fortress Press, 2007.

Demming, Barbara. "On Revolution and Equilibrium." In *Nonviolence in Theory and Practice*, edited by Robert Holmes, 95ff. Belmont, CA: Wadsworth, 1990.

Dyer, Gwynne. "The Roots of War." In *Dilemmas of War and Peace*, edited by Dick Ringler, 53ff. Madison: The Board of Regents of the University of Wisconsin System and the Corporation for Public Broadcasting, 1993.

_____. *War: The Lethal Custom.* New York: Carroll and Graf, 2004.

Ehrlich, Paul R., Carl Sagan, et al. *The Cold and the Dark: The World After a Nuclear War.* New York: W.W. Norton, 1984.

Eisendrath, Bettie Aldrich. "Military Ecocide: Man's Secret Assault on the Environment." Pamphlet published by the World Federalists, Milwaukee Chapter, 1992.

Eisler, Riane. *The Chalice and the Blade: Our History, Our Future.* San Francisco: Harper and Row, 1987.

Fairhall, David. *Common Ground: The Story of Greenham.* London: I.B. Tauris, 2006.

Filkins, Dexter. "Operators of Drones Are Faulted in Afghan Deaths." *New York Times,* May 30, 2010: A6

Fisher, Roger, and Richard Ury. *Getting to Yes: Negotiating an Agreement Without Giving In.* New York: Random House, 1981.

Foss, Christa. "All I Want for Christmas Is a Burned Out Dollhouse." *Globe and Mail* (Canada), Nov. 23, 2003.

Fussell, Paul. "The Real War Will Never Get In the Books." In *Wartime: Understanding Behavior in the Second World War.* New York: Oxford University Press, 1989. Reprinted in *Dilemmas of War and Peace: A Sourcebook,* edited by Dick Ringler, 167ff. Madison: The Board of Regents of the University of Wisconsin System and the Corporation for Public Broadcasting, 1993.

Gerber, Michele Stenehjem. *On the Home Front: The Cold War Legacy of the Hanford Nuclear Site.* Lincoln: University of Nebraska Press, 1997.

Gerson, Joseph. "From Empire to Common Security: A Prophetic Vision of Worldwide Justice." In *The Prophetic Call,* edited by Hugh Sanborn, 129ff. St. Louis: Chalice Press, 2004.

Gopnik, Adam. "Slaughterhouse." *New Yorker,* Feb. 12, 2007.

Gray, John. "The Myth and Reality of the United Nations." *Harpers* (June 2010): 78ff.

"A Green Arms Race." *New York Times* online article, May 19, 2010.

Gregor, Thomas. *A Natural History of Peace.* Nashville: Vanderbilt University Press, 1996.

Grossman, Lt. Col. Dave. *On Killing: The Psychological Cost of Learning to Kill in War and Society.* Boston: Little, Brown, 1996.

Hallie, Philip. *Lest Innocent Blood Be Shed.* New York: Harper Perennial, 1994.

Halstead, Ted, and Clifford Cobb. "The Need for New Measurements of Progress." In *The Case Against the Global Economy and for a Turn Toward the Local,* edited by Jerry Mander and Edward Goldsmith. San Francisco: Sierra Club, 1996.

Harris, Ian, and Mary Lee Morrison. *Peace Education,* 2nd ed. Jefferson, NC: McFarland, 2003.

Haskew, Mike, ed. *World War II History* (magazine).

Hastings, Tom. "Doublespeak" (an unpublished paper in the author's possession).

Hawken, Paul. *Blessed Unrest: How the Largest Movement in the World Came into Being and Why No One Saw It Coming.* New York: Viking, 2007.

Head, Thomas, and Richard Landes, eds. *The Peace of God.* Ithaca, NY: Cornell University Press, 1992.

Herbert, Bob. "The $2 Trillion Nightmare." *New York Times,* March 4, 2008.

"Hired Guns" (editorial). *Christian Century,* July 10, 2007: 5.

Hobbes, Thomas. *Leviathan,* chapter XIII, "Of the Natural Condition of Mankind Concerning Their Felicity and Misery," 1651. In *Thomas Hobbes Leviathan,* edited by J.C.A. Gaskin. Oxford: Oxford University Press, 2009.

Holben, Lawrence. *All the Way to Heaven: A Theological Reflection on Dorothy Day, Peter Maurin and the Catholic Worker.* Marion, SD: Rose Hill Books, 1997.

Holmes, Robert. *Nonviolence in Theory and Practice.* Belmont, CA: Wadsworth, 1990.

_____. "The Sleep of Reason Brings Forth Monsters." In *Nonviolence in Theory and Practice,* edited by Robert Holmes, 132ff. Belmont, CA: Wadsworth, 1990.

Inglois, Rewey, and Josephine Spear, eds. *Adventures in English Literature.* New York: Harcourt, Brace, 1958.

Kaldor, Mary. *Global Civil Society: An Answer to War.* Cambridge, UK: Polity Press, 2003.

Kavaloski, Vincent. "Pax Romana." In *Dilemmas of War and Peace: A Sourcebook,* edited by Dick Ringler, 247–48. Madison: The Board of Regents of the University of Wisconsin System and the Corporation for Public Broadcasting, 1993.

Kimball, Charles. *When Religion Becomes Evil: Five Warning Signs.* San Francisco: Harper, 2002.

Kimmelman, Reuven. "Nonviolence in the Talmud." In *Nonviolence in Theory and Practice,* edited by Robert Holmes, 20–27. Belmont, CA: Wadsworth, 1990.

Kuhlmann, Casper. *Peace — A Topic in European History Textbooks?* Frankfurt: Verlag Peter Lang, 1985.

LaForge, John. "Missile Fields Still Armed and Dangerous." *Nukewatch Quarterly* (Winter 2006-2007): 1.

Lao Tse. *Tao Te Ching.* Translated by Stephen Addiss and Stanley Lobardo. Indianapolis: Hackett Publishing, 1993.

Lapham, Lewis. "Flies in Amber." *Harper's Magazine* (September 2007): 8–13.

Leach, Kenneth. *We Preach Christ Crucified.* New York: Church Publishing, 2005.

Lederach, John Paul. *The Moral Imagination: The Art and Soul of Building Peace.* Oxford: Oxford University Press, 2005.

Leviton, Daniel. *Horrendous Death and Health: Toward Action.* New York: Hemisphere, 1991.

Lifton, Robert Jay. "Nuclear Culture." In *Nuclear Times* (September/October 1986).

Low, Ben. *Imagining Peace: A History of Early English Pacifist Ideas.* University Park: University of Pennsylvania Press, 1997.

Lynd, Staughton, and Alice Lynd, eds. *Nonviolence in America: A Documentary History.* Maryknoll, NY: Orbis, 1995.

Mahony, Liam, and Luis Enrique Eguren. *Unarmed Bodyguards: International Accompaniment for the Protection of Human Rights.* West Hartford, CT: Kumarian Press, 1997.

Mander, Jerry, and Edward Goldsmith, eds. *The Case Against the Global Economy and for a Turn Toward the Local.* San Francisco: Sierra Club, 1996.

Mayer, Jane. "Whatever It Takes: The Politics of the Man Behind ''24.'''" *New Yorker,* February 19–26, 2007: 66–82.

Meehan, Shannon P. "Distant Wars, Constant Ghosts." *Opinionator* blog. *New York Times,* February 22, 2010.

Melko, Matthew. "The Delineation of Peaceful Societies." In *Dilemmas of War and Peace: A Sourcebook,* edited by Dick Ringler, 242–46. Madison: The Board of Regents of the University of Wisconsin System and the Corporation for Public Broadcasting, 1993.

Merton, Thomas. *Conjectures of a Guilty Bystander.* Garden City, NY: Image Books, 1966.

_____. *New Seeds of Contemplation.* Norfolk, CT: New Directions, 1972.

_____. "Saint Maximus the Confessor on Nonviolence." In *The Nonviolent Alternative,* edited by Gordon C. Zahn, 172ff. New York: Farrar, Straus, Giroux, 1987.

_____. *Thoughts in Solitude.* New York: Farrar, Straus, Giroux, 1958.

Milbrath, Lester. *Envisioning a Sustainable Society.* Albany: State University of New York Press, 1989.

Mirkami, Ross, with Saul Bloom. "On the Road in Iraq — The First Field Trip." In *Hidden Casualties: Environmental, Health and Political Consequences of the Persian Gulf War,* edited by Saul Bloom et al., 149ff. Berkeley, CA: North Atlantic Books, 1994.

Nagler, Michael. *The Search for a Nonviolent Future.* San Francisco: Inner Ocean Publishing, 2004.

Napoleoni, Loretta. *Terrorism and the Economy: How the War on Terror is Bankrupting the World.* New York: Seven Stories Press, 2010.

National Conference of Catholic Bishops (USA). "The Just War Criteria." In *The Challenge of Peace: God's Promise and Our Response.* Washington, DC: United States Catholic Conference, 1983.

Nelson-Pallmeyer, Jack. *Jesus Against Christianity.* Harrisburg, PA: Trinity Press, 2001.

Nikitin, Alexander. "Analyzing the Causes of War and Peace." In *Dialogue of Civilizations:*

A New Peace Agenda for a New Millennium, edited by Majid Tehranian and David W. Chappell, 171ff. London and New York: I.B. Tauris, 2002.

Nolan, Albert. *Jesus Before Christianity*. Maryknoll, NY: Orbis Books, 1976; reprint 2005.

Orwell, George. *1984*. New York: New American Library, 1961.

Osman, Mohammed Fathi. "God Is the All Peace." In *Beyond Violence: Religious Sources of Social Transformation in Judaism, Christianity and Islam*, edited by James L. Heft, 57–73. New York: Fordham University Press, 2004.

Owen, Wilfred. "Dulce Et Decorum Est." In *Dilemmas of War and Peace: A Sourcebook*, edited by Dick Ringler, 153. Madison: The Board of Regents of the University of Wisconsin System and the Corporation for Public Broadcasting, 1993.

Paczelt, Joseph J. "Upon St. Crispin's Day" (unpublished paper in the author's possession).

Paskal, Cleo. *Global Warring: How Environmental, Economic and Political Crises will Redraw the World Map*. New York: Palgrave Macmillan, 2010.

Patterson, George. *An Inquiry into the Origins of Satyagraha and Its Contemporary Relevance*, crvp.org/book/Series03/IIIB-S/chapter_ii.htm.

Peerman, Dean. "Landmine Legacy." *Christian Century*, May 15, 2007.

Penn, William. "First Letter To The Delaware Indians." In *Nonviolence in America, A Documentary History*, edited by Staughton and Alice Lynd, 1. Maryknoll, NY: Orbis Books, 1995.

Perret, Geoffrey. *A Country Made by War: From the Revolution to Vietnam—The Story of America's Rise to Power*. New York: Random House, 1989.

Peterson, Tom "End Hunger. Now!" *World Ark* (November/December 2007).

Pfeffer, Leo. *Church, State and Freedom*. Boston: Beacon Press, 1953.

Ringler, Dick. "The Bombing of Dresden." In *Dilemmas of War and Peace: A Sourcebook*. Madison: The Board of Regents of the University of Wisconsin System and the Corporation for Public Broadcasting, 1993.

Ross, Nancy Wilson. *Buddhism: A Way of Life and Thought*. New York: Vintage Books, 1980.

Sanger, David E., and Thom Shanker. "U.S. Faces Choice On New Weapons for Fast Strikes." *New York Times*, April 22, 2010: A1.

Schell, Jonathan. *The Fate of the Earth*. New York: Avon, 1982.

Schmookler, Andrew Bard. *The Parable of the Tribes: The Problem of Power in Social Evolution*. Albany: State University of New York Press, 1994.

Schwarcz, Ernest. "Nonviolent Resistance Against the Nazis in Norway and Holland during World War II." In *Nonviolence in Theory and Practice*, edited by Robert Holmes, 185ff. Belmont, CA: Wadsworth, 1990.

Sharp, Gene. "Civilian-Based Dense: Making the Abolition of War a Realistic Goal." In *Dilemmas of War and Peace: A Sourcebook*, edited by Dick Ringler, 749. Madison: The Regents of the University of Wisconsin System & Corporation for Public Broadcasting, 1992.

_____. "Disregarded History: The Power of Nonviolent Action." In *Peace Is the Way: Writings on Nonviolence from the Fellowship of Reconciliation*, edited by Walter Wink, 231–235. Maryknoll, NY: Orbis Books, 2000.

_____. "Nonmilitary Means of Defense." *Politics of Nonviolent Action, and The Politics of Nonviolent Action, Part Two: The Methods of Nonviolent Action*. Boston: Porter Sargent, 1973.

Shultz, George, William Perry, Henry A. Kissinger, and Sam Nunn. "Toward A Nuclear Free World." *Wall Street Journal*, January 15, 2008.

Sivaraksa, Sulak. "Buddhism and a Culture of Peace." In *Buddhist Peacework: Creating Cultures of Peace*, edited by David W. Chappell, 39–46. Boston: Wisdom Publications, 1999.

Southwick, Charles. *Global Ecology in Human Perspective.* Oxford: Oxford University Press, 1996.

Stringer, Chris, and Peter Andrews. *The Complete World of Human Evolution.* New York: Thames and Hudson, 2005.

Tacitus. "De Vita et Moribus Iulii Agricolae." In *Agricola and Germany.* New York: Oxford University Press; reissue edition June 15, 2009.

Terrence. *Heautontimoroumenos.* Société d'Edition "Les Belles Lettres"; 1st edition, 1927.

Thich Nhat Hahn. "Ahimsa: The Path of Harmlessness." In *Buddhist Peacework: Creating Cultures of Peace,* edited by David W. Chappell, 155–164. Boston: Wisdom Publications, 1999.

Thomas, Claude Anshin. *At Hell's Gate: A Soldier's Journey from War to Peace.* Boston: Shambhala Books, 2004.

Thomas, William. *Scorched Earth: The Military Assault on the Environment.* Philadelphia: New Society Publishers, 1995.

Thompson, J. Milburn. *Justice and Peace: A Christian Primer.* Maryknoll, NY: Orbis Books, 2003.

Wald, Matthew L. "Disarmament Is Likely to Take Decades." *New York Times,* April 9, 2010: A8.

Weil, Simone, "The *Iliad,* the Poem of Force." In *Dilemmas of War and Peace: A Sourcebook,* edited by Dick Ringler, 104ff. Madison: The Board of Regents of the University of Wisconsin System and the Corporation for Public Broadcasting, 1993.

Weintraub, Stanley. *Silent Night: The Story of the World War I Christmas Truce.* New York: The Free Press, 2001.

Weir, Stephen. "Trench Warfare: General Haig and the Battle of the Somme." In *Encyclopedia Idiotica: History's Worst Decisions and the People Who Made Them,* 120–125. Hauppauge, NY: Baron's, 2005.

Whitney, Edson L. *The American Peace Society: A Centennial History.* Washington, DC: The American Peace Society, 1928. (Reprint made available by Jerome S. Ozer, Publisher, in 1972.)

Wright, Robert, "The Price of Assassination." *Opinionator* blog, *New York Times,* April 13, 2010.

Yeats, W. B., and Shri Purohit Swami, eds. "Katha-Upanishad." *The Ten Principal Upanishads.* New York: Macmillan, 1965.

Index

Numbers in *bold italics* indicate pages with photographs.